The Triumph of Grace

The Triumph of Grace

Augustine's writings on Salvation

N. R. Needham

GRACE PUBLICATIONS TRUST
175 Tower Bridge Road
LONDON SE1 2AH
England

Joint Managing Editors
J.P.Arthur MA
H.J.Appleby

First published 2000
© N.R.Needham 2000

ISBN 0 946462 58 5

Distributed by:-
EVANGELICAL PRESS
Faverdale North Industrial Estate
DARLINGTON
DL3 OPH
England

Printed by:-
Creative Print and Design, Ebbw Vale, Wales

Cover design:-
Colin Fairchild

Dedication

To my academic colleagues at the Highland Theological College, Dr Andrew McGowan, Hector Morrison, Noel Due and Alistair Wilson. They have all tasted of the same grace that saved Augustine and are committed to the same theology

Contents

Comments between square brackets [ ] are the translator's

Foreword

The Protestant Reformation was a *re-formation* of Christian theology and of the Church, not a *revolution*. In restating the Christian gospel of God's sovereign grace, and rediscovering its sources in Scripture, the Reformers did not repudiate the Catholic Christianity which they inherited. At the same time as they denounced the medieval theology of merit and the corruptions of the Church, they reaffirmed the Trinitarian and Christological dogmas formulated from Scripture by the Church fathers. But their minds and hearts were particularly captivated by theological outlook of Augustine of Hippo, especially his anti-Pelagian writings, with their emphasis on God's free grace in Christ. Martin Luther was an Augustinian monk, familiar with this tradition even when his eyes were closed to its significance. And John Calvin once said that he would be happy to confess his faith entirely in the words of Augustine.

To have the thought of Augustine brought to our attention once again must be a good thing. Nick Needham has done a great job in judiciously selecting and bringing together representative statements on divine grace from Augustine's many writings. His introductions to each chapter are skilful and knowledgeable. I hope that the book will lead to a deeper understanding of the saving grace of God which Augustine exemplified in his own experience and championed in his writings, and to a renewed appreciation of the abiding legacy which shaped and gave substance to the theology of the Reformation.

Paul Helm
Professor of History and Philosophy of Religion
King's College, London, WC2R 2LS

Introduction

People must not be ungracious with God's grace, or miserly with great things.

Augustine, **On the Merits and Forgiveness of Sins, 1:54**

Why should an Evangelical learn theology from a 5th century African bishop who believed in baptismal regeneration? It is an interesting question. The answer is probably that this bishop knew more about God's grace, both theologically and in his spiritual experience, than almost any other Christian who has ever lived. The bishop is of course Augustine of Hippo, the early Church father whose conversion is the most famous in history, next after Saul of Tarsus. Down through the centuries, a huge and mighty host of Western Europe's most godly people and most influential Church leaders have sat at Augustine's feet, and found rich food for their minds and hearts in the African's masterly expositions of God's way of salvation in Jesus Christ. Many of the most spiritually minded believers of the Middle Ages were disciples of Augustine — men like the Venerable Bede, Anselm of Canterbury, Bernard of Clairvaux, John Wyclif and John Huss. Even Thomas Aquinas, usually regarded as a bit of a villain by Protestants, was a devout "Augustinian" in his convictions about the sovereignty of divine grace in the salvation of sinners. Certainly the Protestant Reformers were devoted to Augustine's vision of grace. Theologically speaking, Martin Luther and John Calvin saw themselves as doing little more than trying to restore true Augustinian doctrine and spiritual practice to the Church.

Encountering Augustine

I well remember my own first encounter with Augustine. It was almost exactly a year after my conversion. We were on holiday in Westgate on the coast of Kent, England, in the summer of 1977; I was a 17 year old who had loved books before becoming a Christian, became a Christian largely through reading books, and now loved reading Christian books best of all. For some reason now lost in the mists of memory, I decided over that holiday to read Augustine's Confessions, his spiritual autobiography. It would not be too extravagant to say that I had no idea what was going to hit me. My mental and spiritual universe was transformed.

It wasn't Augustine's theology of grace that changed me — it does not figure very prominently in the **Confessions**, at least in any overt way. Maybe that was just as well; I might have reacted against it, since at that point my own theology of grace was far from being Augustinian. I had no belief in the helpless slavery of the unredeemed human will to the power of indwelling sin, still less any belief in God's unconditional predestination of those who were to be saved by His sovereign grace alone. In fact, if I had starred in a horror film, it would have had to be called **I Was A Teenage Pelagian**, since in many ways, through lack of teaching, that was the confused atmosphere of my own very shallow thinking about sin and grace. (If you don't know what a Pelagian is, read on.) No, it was the sheer richness and intimacy of Augustine's relationship with God that bowled me over. Here was clearly a man who loved and revered God, more totally than anyone I had ever known, either in person or in their writings. And here was a man who suffered from no unnatural divorce between "mind" and "heart", thought and emotion. Augustine loved God with his mind, not just with his feelings. He was determined to think about his God, to bring the whole universe of his thinking into harmony with the truth of God. In the days of ancient Athens, before the coming of Christ, they used to say that meeting Socrates was like gripping an electric eel. In Augustine, I had met my Christian Socrates.

Not long after that memorable encounter, I was led to embrace the doctrines about sin and grace that Augustine had championed. Ironically but fittingly, this was not through reading Augustine, but through studying what the Bible said about the perseverance of the saints, which then branched out into a study of election and predestination. But by then I knew enough to know that in seeing these doctrines in the Bible, I was not some isolated eccentric. The noble Augustine had seen them there before me. And so had multitudes of others in the "Augustinian" family — such as the Puritans, for whom I was beginning to feel a growing admiration. After what almost amounted to a second conversion as these doctrines dawned on me, I immediately read a book by one of the greatest fans Augustine ever had — Martin Luther. The book was Luther's **Bondage of the Will**. It was heady stuff. Why had I never heard theology like this being preached from pulpits? (Probably because preachers were too busy telling people to have experiences and be nice to each other.)

Augustine's life and outlook

This is not the place to tell once again in any detail the story of Augustine's life. It has been done often enough. Briefly, though, by way of the barest thumbnail sketch, Augustine was born in Thagaste in Roman North Africa in 354, led a sexually immoral youth, joined the cult-like sect of the Manichees, and was finally converted to Christ in 386. His description of his conversion is worth hearing, even if we have heard it before. Augustine is in a garden in Milan, overwhelmed by his sinfulness, especially his slavery to sexual desire:

"I flung myself down, I do not know how, under a fig-tree, where I gave free course to my tears. The streams of my eyes gushed forth, an acceptable sacrifice to You. And, not in these very words, yet to this effect, I spoke much to You: 'But You, O Lord, how long? How long, Lord? Will You be angry for ever? O do not remember against us our former iniquities' — for I felt that I was enslaved by them. I sent up these sorrowful cries: 'How long, how long? Tomorrow, tomorrow? Why not now? Why is there not this hour an end to my uncleanness?'

"I was saying these things, and weeping in the most bitter contrition of my heart, when I heard the voice of a boy or girl, I do not know which, coming from a neighbouring house, chanting and repeating the words, 'Pick up and read! Pick up and read!' Immediately my attitude changed, and I began most earnestly to consider whether it was usual for children in any kind of game to sing these words. I could not remember ever hearing it before. So, restraining the torrent of my tears, I rose up, interpreting the child's voice as a command to me from heaven to open the Scripture, and to read the first chapter my gaze fell on. For I had heard about Antony [the great desert father of Egypt], that he accidentally entered church while the gospel was being read, and received the exhortation as if the reading were addressed to him: 'Go and sell what you have, and give it to the poor, and you shall have treasure in heaven; and come, follow Me.' And by this oracle he was immediately converted to You.

"So I quickly returned to the place where Alypius [Augustine's friend and companion in the search for truth] was sitting; for that is where I had put down the volume of the apostles when I had risen from that spot. I grasped it, opened it, and in silence read the first paragraph on which my eyes first fell. It said: 'not indulging in revelry and drunkenness, nor in lust and debauchery, nor in quarrelling and jealousy. On the contrary, clothe yourselves with the Lord Jesus Christ, and make no provision for gratifying your fleshly cravings' (Rom.13:13-14). I would read no further. I did not need to. Instantly, as the sentence ended, a light of assurance was instilled into my heart, and all the darkness of doubt vanished away" (**Confessions, 8:28-29**).

Augustine was baptised in 387 by the great early Church father, Ambrose of Milan, along with Augustine's 15 year old illegitimate son, Adeodatus, who was converted soon after his father (Adeodatus died three years later). After founding a sort of monastic community back in Thagaste, in 391 Augustine was ordained (against his will) as the "assistant pastor" to bishop Valerius of Hippo Regius — pastors were called "bishops" in those days. When Valerius died in 396, Augustine himself became bishop of Hippo, a position he filled till his death in 430.

There is one crucial point that is vital for understanding Augustine: he was a *Catholic* Christian. He was the bishop of the *Catholic* church in Hippo. We will sometimes come upon the word "Catholic" in the quotations from Augustine's writings which I have collected in this book. The term does *not* mean "Roman Catholic". "Catholic" simply means "universal" (so "I'm a Catholic" means "I'm a Universal.") In those days, Christians called themselves "Catholics" ("Universals") to distinguish themselves from various deviant groups who also claimed to be Christians, much as Jehovah's Witnesses, Mormons and Moonies claim to be Christians today. There were quite a few deviant groups in Augustine's time — the Manichees, the Marcionites, the Montanists, the Novatianists, the Donatists, the Arians. True Christians "throughout the world" (the root meaning of the Greek *katholikos*) rejected the errors of these groups. Whatever cults and sects might say, the one true gospel was everywhere confessed by the faithful. "Catholic" thus very easily slid over into meaning "orthodox". In one way or another, non-Catholics had strayed from the orthodox gospel: either by adding to the faith pet ideas of their own which they then imposed on everyone else as a test of real Christianity, or by subtracting essential truths from the faith. The Montanists, for example, *added* to the faith by insisting that they alone had the Holy Spirit dwelling among them, manifest in prophecy, so that all who opposed them were "prophet-killers"; the Arians *subtracted* from the faith by denying the deity of Christ.

Augustine lived and died a Catholic. The Christianity he believed in was Catholicism: the universal faith of all orthodox Christians, not the passwords of any local sect. This has always been part of Augustine's bequest to the Church. That is why, when Augustine's spiritual children, the Protestant Reformers, criticised the Roman papacy of their day, they did so not as innovators, but as Catholics. The Reformation was carried out against Rome in the name of Catholicism. Luther and Calvin were accusing Rome of having added to the universal faith of true believers; they intended to restore authentic Catholicism by purging away the false innovations of the popes. As the eminent Puritan William Perkins put it in the title of one of his greatest books, a Protestant is not a Roman Catholic but "A Reformed Catholic". In making this claim, Perkins spoke as a true Augustinian.

Origins of the Pelagian controversy

Augustine took part in a number of theological controversies in defence of the Catholic faith, but the most important was the Pelagian controversy. Pelagius (pronounced "Pell-ay-jee-us"), after whom the controversy was named, is an elusive figure; we know almost nothing about him as a man. It is not certain when he was born, or when and where he died. What we do know comes from hostile pens or merely incidental evidence in his own writings (or what little has survived of them — quotations in Augustine and Jerome, mostly). What we *can* say is that Pelagius was British, which seems appropriate since Pelagianism has been called the "natural heresy" of the British people — the belief that deep down inside, we're all good and decent, all on the same side really. But it was not in Britain that Pelagius became a star. He blossomed as a leading Christian personality in Rome between about 383 and 409.

In the great capital city of the Western half of Rome's Empire, Pelagius stood at the forefront of a sort of moral and spiritual reform movement, aimed at getting Roman Christians to live up to their professions of faith rather more credibly. An important part of this movement was "asceticism" — bodily self-denial as an aid to spiritual growth — at that time very popular among all serious minded Christians. Pelagius's theology was very much a secondary issue, at least for Pelagius himself. His main concern was to promote the

ascetic movement in Rome, to discuss the life of holiness in practical
terms, not to conduct a doctrinal investigation into original sin, free
will, grace or predestination. He comes across to us today as much
more of a self-appointed prophet of "how to lead the victorious
Christian life" than a professional theologian.

Still, Pelagius did have a serious interest in at least some aspects
of theology, such as the doctrine of the Trinity, on which he was
perfectly orthodox, and he dabbled in biblical exposition (Pelagius
wrote a commentary on the thirteen letters of Paul, which has
survived in a worked-over version by Jerome). And Pelagius's moral
and spiritual teaching was certainly weighted with a rather optimistic
theology of human nature. He seems to have thought that the most
effective way of getting people to obey his exhortations to Christian
living was to insist that everyone was perfectly capable of obeying
them. In fact, people could be sinlessly perfect, if only they tried
hard enough. If God has given us commands to be holy and perfect,
obviously we can fulfil them. Here is Pelagius in full flow:

"Instead of seeing the commands of our glorious King as a
privilege, we cry out against God. In the scoffing laziness of our
hearts, we say, 'This is too hard, too difficult. We can't do it. We
are only human. We are hampered by the weakness of the flesh.'
What blind folly! What presumptuous blasphemy! We make out
that the all-knowing God is guilty of a double ignorance — ignorant
of His own creation, ignorant of His own commands. As if He had
forgotten the human weakness of His own creatures, and laid upon
us commands we cannot bear! And at the same time (God forgive
us!), we ascribe unrighteousness to the Righteous One, cruelty to
the Holy One: unrighteousness, by complaining that He has
commanded the impossible; cruelty, by imagining that a person will
be condemned for what he could not help. The result (O the
blasphemy of it!) is that we think of God as seeking our punishment,
not our salvation. No-one knows the extent of our strength better
than the God Who gave it. He has not willed to command anything
impossible, for He is righteous. He will not condemn people for
what they could not help, for He is holy" (**Letter to Demetrias, 16**).

We need to be clear that Pelagius was not just saying that
Christians can obey God and be perfect. *Anyone* can. Pelagius
had enough common sense to realise that God's commands are not
just addressed to Christians. God, the Creator of all human beings,
has commanded all to be virtuous and good. Therefore everyone

can be virtuous and good, otherwise God has commanded the impossible. The secret of obedience lies in God's most precious gift — free will. One can almost imagine Pelagius saying in his worst moments, "God so loved the world that He gave us free will, so that whoever tries hard enough can become holy and make it to heaven." Christians have a mighty advantage over others in the incentives of the gospel, but in a tell-tale slip of the tongue, Pelagius said that these made it "easier" for us to resist Satan. Christians have it "easier"; but in principle, anyone and everyone can get right with God through obedience, if only they listen to their conscience and exert their free will strongly enough. Pelagius did not think it out with the same clarity as some of his disciples, but there was obviously no real place in his system for original sin, the bondage of the fallen will, the grace of God in regeneration, or ultimately even Christ as a genuine Saviour — only Christ as the great Teacher and inspiring Example.

Granted his exalted view of free will, it is not surprising that Pelagius was shocked and offended when he heard a preacher in Rome quote favourably a prayer from Augustine's **Confessions**, "Give what You command, and command what You will." This is found a number of times in the **Confessions**. For example, when Augustine is discussing his temptation to seek human praise:

"By these temptations, O Lord, we are daily tried. Indeed, we are unceasingly tried. Our daily furnace is the human tongue. And in this respect also You command us to be restrained. Give what You command, and command what You will. Regarding this matter, You know the groans of my heart, and the rivers of my eyes. For I am not able to ascertain how far I am clean of this plague [love of praise], and I stand in great fear of my 'secret faults', which Your eyes perceive, though mine do not" (**Confessions, 10:60**).

Here in Augustine was a vision of sin — deep, complicated, subtle, ruinous, not always conscious, all-pervasive, enslaving — which did not fit in with Pelagius's more straightforward and superficial view of sin as basically a deliberate act. Augustine's radical, dark perception of sin moved him to cast himself on God in tears of self-despair, and pray that the God Who had *commanded* him to be holy and obedient would *grant* to him the holiness and the obedience as blood-bought gifts of redemption in Christ. Yes, even the very faith that called upon God for these gifts was itself a gracious gift of God. Salvation was *all* of grace, from its first beginnings to its final completion. "Not to us, O Lord, not to us, but to Your name be glory, because of Your grace and truth" (Ps.115:1). To Pelagius, however, this all seemed thoroughly irresponsible. It was just a lazy excuse for a person to absolve himself from using his glorious God-given free will, and doing what God had told him to do. If Augustine's salvation-motto was "Cast yourself on God!", Pelagius's was "Get on with it!" Two utterly conflicting visions faced each other. There was a war in the making.

Augustine against the Pelagians

However, Augustine need not have come in contact with Pelagius and his teachings at all, if it had not been for the essentially non-theological factor of the Visigothic army under its leader Alaric, which in 408 and 409 besieged Rome, and in 410 sacked it. The exodus of refugees brought Pelagius and his disciple Celestius to Carthage, capital city of Roman North Africa. Pelagius, however, left for Palestine in 411, and never met Augustine. Celestius hung around in Carthage; and that is how the trouble started. Celestius, a lawyer of aristocratic birth, had thought out his theology more consistently than Pelagius, and was a far more aggressive personality than his master. Augustine gave an outline of Celestius's teaching thus:

"(i) Adam was created mortal, and he would have died whether he sinned or not. (ii) Adam's sin injured himself alone, not the human race. (iii) The law as well as the gospel leads to the kingdom [of heaven]. (iv) There were people without sin before Christ's coming. (v) New-born infants are in the same condition as Adam before the Fall. (vi) It is not through the death or the fall of Adam that the whole human race dies, nor through the resurrection of Christ that the whole human race rises again" (**On the Proceedings of Pelagius, 23**).

These became the classic doctrinal positions summed up in the word "Pelagianism". Fortunately or otherwise, North African Christians knew their Bibles better than Celestius did, and when he tried to get himself ordained as a presbyter of the African Catholic Church, he was condemned and excommunicated for heresy at the synod of Carthage in 411. Henceforth, African Catholic opposition to Pelagianism was assured. And once Augustine had been convinced by Pelagius's book **On Nature** that the British ascetic was dangerously unsound in faith (it took a long time for Augustine to be convinced — he respected Pelagius's high reputation as a holy man), the bishop of Hippo stepped forward as the leader of North Africa's anti-Pelagian crusade.

While Celestius was busy getting himself excommunicated in Carthage, his master Pelagius was enjoying the hospitality of bishop John of Jerusalem. Alas for Pelagius, another of the great 5th century Church fathers was also in the area — Jerome, the most brilliant Hebrew and Greek scholar the early Church ever produced. Jerome was not so clear-thinking a theologian as Augustine, but he knew there was something suspiciously odd about Pelagius's teaching. Also Jerome enjoyed a good theological fight. We are not quite sure what ignited the blaze (not that Jerome ever needed much ignition), but soon Pelagius and Jerome were jousting furiously. Because bishop John had fallen out personally with Jerome, he sided with Pelagius. This was the situation when Orosius, a Spanish presbyter from Catalonia, sailed into Palestine, carrying two letters from Augustine to Jerome about the Pelagian dispute. Henceforth Orosius became the most fervent foe of the Pelagians, the Celestius of the Augustinian camp. The result was the famous synod of Jerusalem, summoned by bishop John on 30th July 415.

The synod invited Orosius to clarify the background to the controversy between Pelagius and Jerome. Orosius mishandled his case badly; with rather inflammatory arrogance, the Spaniard told the synod that the African condemnation of Celestius at the synod of Carthage was a quite sufficient indictment of the Pelagian heresy, and that all he required of them was their assent to this decision. This did not go down well with the Eastern fathers and brethren. Charged by Orosius with fathering the falsehoods of Celestius, Pelagius proved himself orthodox by condemning all who denied the need for divine grace (it wasn't genuine proof, because as Augustine tirelessly pointed out, Pelagius had his own peculiar definition of "grace"). Orosius realised he had ruined his case, and hastily suggested that since the whole controversy was a Western affair, it should be referred to pope Innocent 1 — bishops of Rome could be quite orthodox theologians in those days. The synod agreed, and dissolved.

Bishop John of Jerusalem, however, to whom Orosius had been very rude, turned the tables completely in September by suddenly denouncing the Spaniard — to his face, in public — as a heretic who believed that not even grace could overcome sin. To make matters worse, bishop Eulogius of Caesarea convened a council of thirteen bishops (including John of Jerusalem) in December at Diospolis to deal with fresh accusations against Pelagius. Once again Pelagius convinced everyone of his orthodoxy. He also disowned his disciple Celestius as a radical who had gone too far, which was perhaps not entirely honest on Pelagius's part. Anyway, the council vindicated him entirely. To cap it all, far-out radical Celestius was ordained a presbyter of the Catholic Church in Ephesus. It seemed like a total repudiation of the North Africans by the Christian East. The North Africans responded with a vigorous condemnation of Pelagius and Celestius at two councils in Carthage and Milevis.

For Augustine and the Africans, everything now depended on pope Innocent. He was the bishop of the West's most important church, which is what the popes basically were at that point — not yet "vicars of Christ", although Innocent was the first bishop of Rome to insist theologically that his authority flowed from the apostle Peter.[1] If Innocent also upheld Pelagius, the Africans were on their own. The North African bishops set in motion all their diplomatic machinery to convince Innocent that Pelagius was a heretic, bombarding Rome with signed petitions and other incriminating documents, including Pelagius's now notorious **On Nature**. It was **On Nature**, the book that had opened Augustine's eyes to Pelagius's heresies, that also seems to have clinched the case with pope Innocent in favour of Augustine and his African brother bishops; Innocent could see that Pelagius had gone several light years over the top in exalting the powers of human nature and free will, to the detriment of God's saving grace in Christ. In January 417, Innocent excommunicated both Pelagius and Celestius until they should prove themselves to be true Catholics to Rome's satisfaction. The Africans were jubilant; "the cause is finished," pronounced Augustine.

Unfortunately, a month later Innocent himself was finished, and his successor, pope Zosimus, quickly succumbed to the charm and argumentative brilliance of Celestius, who had hurried back to Rome on hearing of Innocent's death. Celestius also managed to win over

---

[1] A different pope Innocent, Innocent III, was the first to give official sanction to the title "vicar of Christ". Innocent III was pope from 1198 to 1216 – in other words, 750 years after Augustine.

a Roman synod. Meanwhile, a letter of commendation from the new bishop of Jerusalem, Praylius, persuaded the Romans that Pelagius too was fundamentally Catholic. In September, pope Zosimus cancelled the excommunication of Pelagius and Celestius. Everything seemed back to square one.

However, at this juncture the Pelagians in Rome snatched defeat from the jaws of victory. Party passions were running dangerously high. They spilled out into violence when a group of Pelagians assaulted a Catholic named Constantius, who unluckily turned out to be a retired government official. (One would have thought that this kind of thing might have shown the Pelagians there was just as much original sin in them as in anyone!) Such civil unrest under the banner of religion would not be tolerated by the government in Italy. In April 418, from the imperial palace at Ravenna, emperor Honorius issued his famous "rescripts" (decrees) condemning Pelagianism, and banishing Pelagius and Celestius from Rome (in fact Pelagius may still have been in Palestine). "This pestilent poison," thundered Honorius, "has so strongly infected the minds of certain persons that the path of orthodox belief has been smashed, schools of opinion torn into parties, and occasion for violent sedition introduced.... This subtle heresy even considers it a mark of lower class pettiness to agree with other people, and the height of good sense to overturn what is accepted by the whole community."

The next day, on May 1st 418, a general council of the African Catholic Church assembled. The 200 bishops present sanctioned nine anti-Pelagian canons, which formulated the Augustinian doctrine of sin and grace in uncompromising language.[2] Celestius packed his bags and beat a hasty retreat from Rome. Pope Zosimus, already wavering, gave in, excommunicated Pelagius and Celestius again, and confirmed a more moderately worded version of the African canons. All Western bishops were required by Zosimus to subscribe to the anti-Pelagian canons; eighteen who refused were deposed from office. Bishop Praylius of Jerusalem withdrew his support from Pelagius, who went perhaps to Egypt, and is heard of no more. His doctrines were officially condemned at the Council of Ephesus in 431, the third of the great "ecumenical" or general Councils of the early Church. The mantle of Pelagius's cause fell to the new rising star of the movement, Julian of Eclanum, a young Italian bishop

---

[2] For the text of the anti-Pelagian canons, see Appendix 1.

who had been deposed for refusing to sign the anti-Pelagian canons. Augustine spent much of the last ten years of his life duelling with Julian.

And not only with Julian. The deposed Italian ex-bishop was an ardent Pelagian; but another challenge to Augustine had arisen in southern France. Some of the bishops and monks there were strongly opposed to Pelagius, but had not been convinced by some of Augustine's positions. They agreed with Augustine that the whole human race had fallen in Adam, and that all were stained with original sin. But surely, they said, this has not left us in a state of complete bondage to sin. We may not be able to save ourselves or merit heaven; thus far, Augustine is right, and Pelagius wrong. However, surely we can at least take the first step towards salvation by crying out to God for His undeserved mercy? A sick man may not be able to heal himself, but he can at least call in the doctor.

Those who held such views — distinguished men like John Cassian, Faustus of Riez, and Vincent of Lerins — were later christened "Semi-Pelagians". I suppose today we would call them "Arminians". Augustine treated them more gently than he treated Pelagius, Celestius and Julian. A stubborn Pelagian could not be a Christian at all; but Cassian, Faustus and Vincent were erring brothers in Christ. (Why Augustine was not satisfied with their theological halfway house, we will see in a moment.) It was more with the "Semi-Pelagians" in mind that the bishop of Hippo wrote some of his greatest books on the doctrine of grace — **On Grace and Free Will, On Rebuke and Grace, On the Gift of Perseverance**.

The aftermath of the controversy

The controversy continued after Augustine died in 430 as his city of Hippo was under siege from an invading Vandal army. His disciples, notably Prosper of Aquitaine, Fulgentius of Ruspe, Avitus of Vienne and Caesarius of Arles, defended the bondage of the will, the sovereignty of grace, predestination and the perseverance of the saints against "Semi-Pelagian" criticisms. An important document known as the **Indiculus** ("catalogue") appeared some time between 435 and 442; probably edited by Prosper of Aquitaine, it summarised the Augustinian doctrine of sin and grace on the basis of papal decrees, the decisions of the North African councils, and statements in the Church's liturgy. The **Indiculus** attained a status of high authority in the West. Still, the controversy rumbled on in various ways, until Augustinianism triumphed at the French synod of Orange in 529. The canons of Orange were given the seal of approval by pope Boniface II in 531. Unfortunately the documents that enshrined the canons of Orange became lost in the mists of medieval history, and played no enduring part in shaping the Augustinian tradition until their rediscovery in the 16th century.[3]

Despite the mysterious vanishing act performed by the canons of Orange, most of the great Western theologians throughout the Middle Ages were to be Augustinians in their fundamental outlook on sin and grace. I can remember the surprise and pleasure I felt when I took up the weighty tomes of Thomas Aquinas, the ultimate medieval theologian, the architect of the foul doctrine of transubstantiation, and saw the shining clarity with which Aquinas taught the doctrine of election and the absolute sovereignty of God's grace in regeneration. Who said the Middle Ages were all dark? If we are Reformed believers, good old Aquinas is closer to us than John Wesley is on the doctrine of grace. We also find surprising brothers and sisters in the Roman Catholic "Jansenists" of 17th century France. They were a group who ardently maintained the Augustinian doctrine of grace, and brought down the wrath of the Jesuits and the papacy on their heads for so doing. The Jansenists' greatest figure was the noble Blaise Pascal.[4]

Augustine's reputation today often hinges simply on whether or not people agree with his views on original sin, the bondage of the will and predestination. On whichever side of that debate we fall, the fact remains that we still find in Augustine some of the deepest, clearest and most eloquent presentations of these doctrines and others linked with them. And if we are indeed Reformed by conviction, then the apostle Paul is our father and Augustine is our elder brother. Family affection demands that we acquaint ourselves with the bishop-monk of Hippo. That is why I have put this book

---

[3] For the text of the Indiculus and the canons of Orange, see Appendix 1.

[4] On the other hand, it is hard to find any present-day Roman Catholics who agree with Augustine, Aquinas and the Jansenists on the sovereignty of grace in election. I have only ever met one, and he bemoaned his comparative isolation in his own Church. The Augustinian legacy lives on in the Reformed wing of Protestantism.

together. It is an introduction to Augustine's own writings on "the doctrine of grace", as he and his fellow-workers and disciples called it. If what Augustine says here drives us back to Paul, and to Scripture as a whole, so that we not only grasp the doctrine of grace but taste the reality, I'm sure that Augustine, now in heaven by grace alone, will be satisfied.

One last word: let's remember that Augustine was a Catholic. Not a *Roman* Catholic, but a defender of universal Christian truth. He founded no sect. The doctrines set forth in this volume are the inner substance and legacy of all Christians everywhere. And yet, we might ask, how could Augustine be defending the universal faith of Christians, when there were and still are Christians who disagree with him? It is a question worth pondering. Augustine would have said it had two answers. First, not everyone who takes the name of Christian is in fact a Christian. Pelagius, Celestius and Julian claimed to be Christians, but they were eventually expelled from the Church as counterfeits. Augustine's Catholicism was the Catholicism of God's true children, not of everyone who happens to take shelter under the mere name "Christian".

The second answer is more profound. Augustine appealed to a crucial principle. In Latin it reads *lex orandi lex credendi*. That is, "the law of praying is the law of believing." How do true Christians pray? Do they come before God and say, "Thank you for sending Your Son to die for me, O Lord; but as for the rest — my faith, repentance, conversion, good works, growth in holiness — well, Lord, You owe me some hearty congratulations. Thanks be to me!" Of course not. No true Christian ever prays such prayers. All the redeemed children of God give thanks to God, not just for the Saviour's atoning death, but for their conversion too, their spiritual gifts and graces, and their preservation in the faith. Even the Semi-Pelagian position, that it is only the first step of faith that we owe to ourselves, is untenable; for without that first step, none of the others would follow — and therefore our actual salvation would hinge ultimately on ourselves. But we cannot say of our salvation what a foolish poet once said about a revival:

That God from aye to aye may carry on
The amazing work that Harris hath begun!

It is God, not Harris, Who begins revivals, whether in communities or in the individual human soul. "Thanks be to God that though you used to be slaves to sin, you wholeheartedly obeyed the form of teaching to which you were entrusted" (Rom.6:17). Thanks be to God: the keynote of all Christian praise and confession. When they pray and praise, all true Christians are Augustinians. They give thanks to God for their own salvation, and they pray to God for the salvation of others. In his head, Charles Wesley was doctrinally an Arminian (Semi-Pelagian). But how did he sing to his God?

> Long my imprisoned spirit lay,
> Fast bound in sin and nature's night.
> Thine eye diffused a quickening ray;
> I woke, the dungeon flamed with light;
> My chains fell off, my heart was free,
> I rose, went forth, and followed Thee.

As the great Scottish Augustinian, Rabbi John Duncan, said: "Where's your Arminianism now, friend?" *Lex orandi lex credendi.* If all Christians theologised as they prayed, there would be no more arguments over the sovereignty of grace in salvation. In that profound sense, Augustine was defending Catholic truth — the universal faith of all Christians everywhere — when he defended grace. In their hearts, in their prayers, God's redeemed people are at one in confessing that their salvation is by grace alone. Augustine wanted to confess it in his theology too. By the gracious blessing of God, may he help us to do so as well.

THE LIFE AND TIMES OF AUGUSTINE

YEAR	AUGUSTINE'S LIFE, THE PELAGIAN CONTROVERSY	THE OTHER EVENTS
354	Augustine born.	
368		Death of Hilary of Poitiers.
370		Basil becomes bishop of Caesarea. Jerome baptised.
372	Death of Augustine's father. Augustine starts living with a girl outside of marriage.	
373	Birth of Adeodatus (probable date). Augustine appointed professor of rhetoric in Carthage. Becomes a Manichee.	Death of Athanasius.
374		Ambrose becomes bishop of Milan. Jerome becomes hermit in Syrian desert.
379		Death of Basil of Caesarea. Gregory of Nazianzus becomes bishop of Constantinople. Theodosius the Great becomes Eastern emperor.
381		Theodosius summons second ecumenical Council of Constantinople, which promulgates the "Nicene Creed".
382		Jerome settles in Rome. Begins translating Bible into Latin — the "Vulgate".

383	Augustine moves to Rome	Pelagius settles in Rome (probable date).
384	Becomes professor of rhetoric in Milan. Comes under influence of Neoplatonism and Ambrose.	Jerome goes back to the East.
386	Augustine's conversion.	John Chrysostom becomes presbyter in Antioch.
387	Augustine baptised with Adeodatus by Ambrose.	
388	Returns to Thagaste; founds pioneer African monastery.	
390	Death of Adeodatus (probable date).	Death of Gregory of Nazianzus.
391	Augustine ordained presbyter in Hippo.	
394		Death of Gregory of Nyssa.
396	Augustine becomes bishop of Hippo.	
397	Augustine's *Confessions*.	Death of Ambrose. Council of Carthage – first official Western list of the canonical books of the New Testament.
398		Chrysostom becomes patriarch of Constantinople. Death of Didymus the Blind.
399	Augustine begins writing *On the Trinity*.	
403		Chrysostom's first banishment.

404		Chrysostom's second banishment.
407		Death of Chrysostom
410		Sack of Rome. Pelagius and Celestius flee to Carthage.
411	Pelagius goes to Palestine. Celestius excommunicated in Carthage. Augustine begins writing against the Pelagians.	
412	Jerome begins writing against the Pelagians.	Cyril becomes patriarch of Alexandria.
415	Synods of Jerusalem and Diospolis: Pelagius cleared of heresy.	
416	Pelagian mob burns down Jerome's Bethlehem monastery. Two North African Councils condemn Pelagius and Celestius.	
417	January: pope Innocent excommunicates Pelagius and Celestius. September: new Pope Zosimus restores Pelagius and Celestius to fellowship.	
418	April: Western emperor Honorius condemns Pelagius and Celestius, banishing them from Rome. Pope Zosimus excommunicates them again.	
419	Julian of Eclanum begins writing against Augustine.	
420		Death of Jerome

426	Augustine begins writing against the 'Semi-Pelagians'.	
428		Nestorius becomes patriarch of Constantinople
430	Death of Augustine	
431		Third ecumenical Council of Ephesus: Nestorius deposed, the Virgin Mary declared to be *theotokos* ("birth-giver of God", *i.e.* of God incarnate). The Council also condemns Pelagianism.

Chapter 1

Creation, the Fall and Original Sin

The Lord Jesus knew by what the human soul, that is, the rational mind, made in the image of God, could be satisfied: only, that is, by Himself. This He knew, and knew that it was as yet without that fullness.

*Augustine, **Sermons on the Gospels, 95:2***

The medicine for all the wounds of the soul, and the one propitiation for human sins, is to believe in Christ. Nor can anyone be cleansed at all, whether from original sin which he derived from Adam, in whom all have sinned and become by nature children of wrath, or from the sins which they have themselves added, by not resisting the lust of the flesh, but by following and serving it in unclean and ruinous deeds, unless by faith they are united and cemented into Christ's Body...

*Augustine, **Sermons on John, 93:1***

Malcolm Muggeridge once told an American audience that he believed in original sin, not original virtue. They seemed to understand what he meant, even if they didn't agree with him. "Original sin" is one of the few theological phrases that has passed into common currency. Perhaps this is because it earths itself in universal human experience in a way that something like "justification by faith" doesn't. Parents realise soon enough that they don't have to teach their children to misbehave. There seems to be some selfish, mischief-making impulse built into them from the word go. And no matter how adult and educated and civilised we may become, we can never work that impulse out of our systems. The lesson is writ large in human history and our own lives. We are all too obviously, as the Bible and Augustine tell us, Adam and Eve's children. Like father, like son. Like mother, like daughter.

Original sin is a cosmic tragedy, a violation of nature. It would be a terrible misunderstanding of Augustine if we think he means that we are evil "by nature", in the sense that water is wet by nature, or light is bright by nature. Water is wet because God created it wet; light is bright because God created it bright. But of course, God did not create human nature evil. He created Adam and Eve good. If we say we are evil "by nature", we need to understand that this refers to a secondary "acquired" nature, by which our originally good nature has been distorted and disfigured. This perverting of our true nature as God first created it in Adam is the tragedy of original sin.

For Augustine, we can't understand original sin unless we understand creation. Sin perverts human nature; so we have to see human nature in its original beauty and goodness, in unfallen Adam and Eve, if we would truly appreciate the reality and ugliness of the Fall. The glory of Adam is that he was created "in the image of God". Augustine taught that this image rested not in Adam's body, but in his soul. He was created with a "rational soul", a soul blessed with the knowledge of his Creator. (For a human soul not to know God is a sort of irrationality, a madness.) Augustine also argued that each human soul bears the image of the Trinity. Our souls are a mysterious combination of understanding, memory and will: three distinct faculties and activities which blend as one. Further, Augustine — often accused, like the apostle Paul, of being anti-woman — was very clear that God's image rested equally in man and in woman. Indeed, Augustine was so impressed by the distinctive glory of manhood and womanhood, he argued that the distinction would endure in the resurrection and for all eternity.

The basic problem Augustine had with Pelagius was that Pelagius simply did not take the Fall seriously. Pelagius's descriptions of how exalted and powerful and free human nature is would all be very well, if we were still in the Garden of Eden. The Pelagians "praise the work of the Creator so much, they destroy the mercy of the Redeemer" (**Against Two Letters of the Pelagians, 1:11**). But we are not in Eden. We are born into a world that lies under the dark shadow of sin and death. We all sin; we all die. Why? How is it that Adam's sin has affected us all so deeply? Why are infants not (as Pelagius fantasised) innocent, but inwardly corrupted with the seed of original sin? Adam brought his corruption upon himself, but we are conceived in sin. Is this just and fair?

Augustine argued that Adam's sin was in fact not merely his own; it was not just a personal private sin of a personal private individual. In some ultimately mysterious way, the whole human race was present in Adam when he sinned. Adam was Humanity. In his sin, we sinned. On that basis, Augustine taught that Adam's sin was "imputed" to each and all of his children. The original transgression committed by Adam in paradise is reckoned and accounted to me — not as someone else's sin, but as truly mine; for though I cannot fathom how, I and all humanity participated in the sin of the first man. Adam's fall was the fall of the race. That is why everyone is sinful, rather than 50% of us being sinful and the other 50% sinless. The fault is not in our environment. It is within us. That is why everyone dies, including infants. If sinless infants died, God would be punishing them unjustly. Their very death proves they are caught up in the web of Adam's disobedience.

One argument that Augustine often used to support the doctrine of original sin was the practice of infant baptism, which by the late 4th century was fast becoming the universal norm in the Church. Here, Augustine's legacy will not commend itself to that large branch of the Augustinian family that practises *believer's* baptism. Even so, we must surely appreciate Augustine's motives. His Pelagian foes accepted infant baptism too; and Augustine saw that he could impale them on the horns of a fatal dilemma. Was baptism not the sacramental sign of being united with Christ in His death (Rom.6:3-4) for the forgiveness of sins and spiritual regeneration? Well then, if Pelagians baptised infants, their practice contradicted their theory that new-born babes were innocent and sinless! They must either stop baptising infants, or else (the option they actually took) wriggle about pathetically trying to deny that infant baptism had anything to do with union with Christ in His death, the forgiveness of sins, or regeneration. On this harsh anvil, Augustine pulverised the Pelagians into sub-atomic particles.[1]

The biblical and Augustinian doctrine of original sin is being ever more widely rejected today, among those who call themselves Evangelical Christians. It is timely that we should listen to what Augustine has to say on this subject. If we misunderstand the Fall, we will misunderstand redemption. It is the universal guilt and death of the whole race in the first Adam that reveals humanity's universal need of the second Adam for forgiveness and life.

****

Creation, the Fall and Original Sin

Why God brought the human race into existence from one man

It is easy to see how much better it was that God chose to produce the human race out of the one individual man He created, rather than starting with many humans. He created some living creatures that love solitude, naturally seeking lonely places, such as eagles, kites, lions, wolves, and suchlike. But He made others gregarious, herding together and preferring to live in company, such as doves, starlings, stags, fallow deer, and so forth. Yet God produced neither of these types by starting with an individual; He called many into existence at once.

---

[1] When we hear Augustine talking about "the washing of regeneration" and pleading with Pelagians to let infants come to Christ for salvation, he is referring to the spiritual rebirth of infants in baptism. In many passages, he clearly makes baptism the instrument Christ uses to convey His risen life to dead souls. Yet in other passages, Augustine equally clearly makes *faith* the instrument of union with Christ. It seems to me that we are faced with an unresolved paradox in Augustine's thinking at this point. (We find it in Luther too.) But again, if we prefer the Augustine who speaks of faith as the channel of salvation, we should

On the other hand, humanity was created as a kind of midway point between the angels and the animals. If man submitted to his Creator as his true sovereign Lord, and dutifully kept His commands, he would pass into the fellowship of the angels, and obtain a blessed and endless immortality without having to go through death. But if man offended the Lord his God by a proud and disobedient use of his free will, he would live like the animals, subject to death, the slave of his own desires, and destined after death to eternal punishment.

Therefore God created only one single man. This was not because God intended man to be solitary and deprived of human society. Rather, God's purpose was to bring home more powerfully to us the unity of human society and the bonds of human sympathy. For the human race would be bound together not just by similarity of nature, but also by family affection. [We all have one father.] Indeed, God did not even create man's wife, the woman, in the same way that He created the man. He created her out of the man, so that from the one original man the whole human race might be derived.

City of God, 12:22

The unity of the human race

With good cause, therefore, does the true religion recognise and proclaim that the same God who created the universal cosmos, also created all living creatures, souls as well as bodies. Among the earthly creatures, humanity was made by Him in His own image, and, for

---

still try to appreciate our African brother's noble motives in expounding infant baptismal regeneration. Infants do not choose to be baptised. It happens to them without anyone consulting them on the matter. And so it becomes a brilliant illustration of the sovereign initiative of God's grace in salvation! Augustinian Baptists need to learn a severe lesson or two at this point, and stop speaking about baptism as if its essence lay in the baptised person's obedience and testimony. Baptism is first and foremost something *Christ* does to *us*, using the sign of water to declare that we are His forgiven people through our God-given faith in Him. What we do is submit to what He does. In this way, the sovereign initiative of grace *and* the grace-inspired human response of faithful obedience are both present in the act of baptism.

the reason I have given, was made as one individual, though he was not left solitary. For there is nothing so social by nature (and so unsocial by its corruption) as the human race. And human nature has nothing more appropriate for preventing discord, or for healing discord where it exists, than to remember the first parent of us all. We should remember that God was pleased to create Adam alone, so that all human beings might be derived from one man, and that they might thus be exhorted to preserve unity among their whole multitude. And from the fact that the woman was made for Adam from his side, it was clearly meant that we should learn how intimate the bond between man and wife should be.

These works of God do certainly seem extraordinary, because they are the first works. Those who do not believe them ought not to believe in any marvels; for they would not be called marvels if they did not happen out of the ordinary course of nature. But is it possible that anything should happen in vain, however hidden its cause, in this majestic dominion of divine providence? One of the holy psalmists says, "Come, behold the works of the Lord, what marvels He has performed in the earth" (Ps.46:8). Why God made woman out of man's side, and what this first marvel prefigured, I shall (with God's help) tell in another place. But for now, since this chapter must be concluded, let us simply say that in this first man, who was created in the beginning, there was laid the foundation — not in evident deed, but in God's foreknowledge — of the two cities or societies into which the human race would be divided. For from Adam all human beings were to be derived — some of them to be associated with the good angels in their reward, others with the wicked in punishment, and all being arranged by the secret yet righteous judgment of God. For since it is written, "All the paths of the Lord are mercy and truth" (Ps.25:10), His grace can never be unjust, nor can His justice ever be cruel.

City of God, 12:28

The image of God is in our minds, not our bodies

"The life was the light of men" (Jn.1:4). Was it the light of cattle? For this light is the light of human beings and of cattle. Yet there is a distinctive light of human beings. So let us see how far humans differ from the cattle, and then we shall understand what is the "light of men". You do not differ from the cattle except in your intellect. Do not glory in anything else! Do you presume upon your strength? You are surpassed by the wild beasts. Do you presume upon your swiftness? You are surpassed by the flies. Do you presume upon your beauty? What great beauty is there in the feathers of a peacock! In what, then, are you better? In the image of God. Where is the image of God? In the mind, in the intellect. You are in this respect, then, better than the cattle, that you have a mind by which you may understand what the cattle cannot understand; and this is what makes you human, better than the cattle. So the "light of men" is the light of *minds*. But the *light* of minds is above minds and surpasses all minds. This was that life by which all things were created.

Sermons on John, 3:4

The image of God is in both man and woman

True reason and also the authority of the apostle himself declare that man was not made in the image of God according to the shape of his body, but according to his rational mind. If we think that God is imprisioned within physical limits by the contours of bodily members, the thought is a debased and empty one. Further, does not the same blessed apostle say, "Be renewed in the spirit of your mind, and put on the new man, which is created after God" (Eph.4:23-4)? And in another place more clearly, "Putting off the old man," he says, "with his deeds, put on the new man, which is renewed to the knowledge of God after the image of Him that created him" (Col.3:9-10). So then, we are renewed "in the spirit of our mind", and "the new man" is renewed "in the knowledge of God after the image of Him that created him".

No-one can doubt, then, that man was made after the image of Him that created him, not according to the body, nor according to just any part of the mind, but according to the *rational* mind, in which the knowledge of God can exist. And it is according to this renewal, too, that we are made sons of God by the baptism of Christ; and putting on the new man, we certainly put on Christ through faith. Who is there, then, who will hold that women are strangers to this fellowship? No, they are fellow-heirs of grace with us. In another place the same apostle says, "For you are all the children of God by faith in Christ Jesus; for as many as have been baptised into Christ have put on Christ: there is neither Jew nor Greek, there is neither bond nor free, there is neither male nor female; for you are all one in Christ Jesus" (Gal.3:26-8). Now, believing women have not lost their bodily sex. But they are renewed according the image of God in that part of themselves where there is no sex, just as man is made according to the image of God in that part of him where there is no sex — that is, in the spirit of the mind.

On the Trinity, 12:12

The image of God is completely in each individual person, not parcelled out among man, woman and child

They do not seem to me to put forward a probable opinion, who lay it down that a trinity of the image of God in three persons can be discovered in human nature as being completed in the marriage of male and female and in their offspring. They say that the man symbolises the person of the Father, while the child he begets symbolises the Son; and so the third person of the Spirit is symbolised (they say) by the woman, who has proceeded from the man in such a way as to be neither his son nor daughter, although it was by the woman's act of conception that sons and daughters were born. For the Lord has said of the Holy Spirit that He proceeds from the Father, and yet the Spirit is not a son of the Father.

In this erroneous opinion, there is only one point with any probable truth, which can be sufficiently shown according to the faith of the Holy Scripture. It is this: in the account of the original creation of the woman, what comes into existence from one person to make another person, cannot in every case be called a child. For the person of the woman came into existence from the person of the man, and yet she is not called his daughter. All the rest of this opinion is in reality so absurd, indeed so false, that it is most easy to refute it. For I cannot even take the time to think that the Holy Spirit is the mother of the Son of God, and the wife of the Father ...

God said, "Let us make man in our image, after our likeness." A little later it is said, "So God created man in the image of God." Certainly, since it is in the plural, the word "our" would not be rightly used if a human being were made in the image of only one person, whether of the Father, or of the Son, or of the Holy Spirit. No, Adam was made in the image of the Trinity; and on that account it is said, "After our image."

On the Trinity, 12:5-6

The image of the Trinity in each human mind: understanding, memory, will

These three — memory, understanding, will — are not three [human] lives, but one life; not three minds, but one mind. It follows certainly that they are not three essences, but one essence.... [2] For I *remember* that I have memory and understanding and will. And I *understand* that I understand, and will, and remember. And I *will* to will, and to remember, and to understand.

I remember together my whole memory, and understanding, and will. For if there were something in my memory which I did not remember, it would not be in my memory! But nothing is so much in the memory as memory itself. Therefore I remember the whole memory. Also, whatever I understand, I know that I understand it. And I know that I will whatever I will. But if I know something, I remember it. Therefore I remember the whole of my understanding, and the whole of my will. Likewise, when I understand these three things, I understand them together as a whole. For the only understandable things which I do not understand are the things I do not know. But if I do not know something, I do not remember it

---

[2] By "essence" Augustine means the fundamental reality of a thing. If we take a human being as our example, the essence or fundamental reality of a human being is his human nature — he is human. He possesses understanding, memory and will, but these do not split him up into three separate essences or realities. Human understanding, memory and will are therefore aspects and dimensions of the one reality of the human mind or human life. They are "one life, one mind, one essence". Augustine sees here an image of the Trinity in the human mind. God is three distinct persons in one divine essence; the human mind is three distinct faculties and activities (understanding, memory, will) in the essence of one human soul. And just as Father, Son and Spirit dwell inseparably in each other, so do understanding, memory and will mysteriously blend in the unity of the human mind.

either, nor do I will it. Therefore, if there are things that could be understood, but I do not understand them, it follows that as well as not understanding them, I do not remember them or will them either. Again, if there are understandable things that I remember and will, it follows that I must understand them. My will too embraces the whole of my understanding and the whole of my memory, as I make use of all that that I understand and remember.

Thus understanding, memory and will each fully embrace the other two….. These three are one — one life, one mind, one essence.

On the Trinity, 10:18

Male and female: the distinction is so good it will endure for eternity, and even symbolises Christ and the Church

From the words, "Till we all come to a perfect *man*, to the measure of the full stature of Christ" (Eph.4:13), and from the words, "Conformed to the image of the Son of God" (Rom.8:29), some conclude that women will not be resurrected as women, but that in the resurrection all will be men. For God created man alone out of the earth, but woman out of the man [and so all resurrected bodies will be *recreated* out of the earth as male bodies]. In my judgment, however, they seem to be wiser who make no doubt that both sexes will be present in the resurrection. For there will then be no lust, which is now the cause of confusion. Before they sinned, the man and the woman were naked, and were not ashamed. From those bodies, then, vice will be removed, while nature will be preserved; and the sex of woman is not a vice, but her nature. Woman's resurrected nature will indeed be superior to carnal intercourse and child-bearing. Nevertheless, the endowments of woman's body will remain — adapted no longer to the old uses, but to a new beauty. This beauty, so far from provoking a now extinct lust, will inspire praise to the wisdom and mercy of God; for He both created what did not exist, and then rescued from corruption what He had created.

At the beginning of the human race, the woman was created from a rib taken from the side of the man while he slept. For it seemed fitting that even then, Christ and His Church should be foreshadowed in this event. That sleep of the man prefigured the death of Christ, Whose side, as He hung lifeless upon the cross, was pierced with a spear. Blood and water flowed from His side (Jn.19:34); and these we know to be the sacraments [baptism and Lord's supper] by which the Church is "built up." For Scripture used this very word, not saying that God "formed" or "framed" Eve, but "built her up into a woman" (Gen.2:22). So also the apostle speaks of the upbuilding of the body of Christ, which is the Church (Eph.4:16). The woman, therefore, is a creature of God even as the man; but by creating woman from man, God commends unity to us. And the manner of woman's creation prefigured, as I have said, Christ and the Church. He, then, who created both sexes will restore both [in the resurrection].

City of God, 22:17

Why was the human race created when it was?

As to those who are always asking why humanity was not created during the countless ages of the infinitely extended past [God's eternity], and came into being so recently that, according to Scripture, less than 6,000 years have elapsed since we began to exist — I would reply to them regarding the creation of humanity, just as I replied regarding the origin of the world to those who insist that the world is eternal and had no beginning. (Even Plato himself most plainly declares that the world is not eternal, though some think his statement was not consistent with his real opinion.) If it offends them that the time that has elapsed since the creation of humanity is so short, and his years so few according to our Scriptures, let them take this into consideration: nothing that has a limit is long. Because all the ages of time are finite, they are very little, or indeed nothing at all, when compared to unending eternity. Consequently, if there had elapsed since the creation of humanity, I do not say five or six, but even sixty or six hundred thousand years, or sixty times as many, or six hundred or six hundred thousand times as many, or this sum multiplied until it could no longer be expressed in numbers, the same question could still be put, "Why was humanity not created before?"

The past and boundless eternity during which God abstained from creating humanity is very great. Compare it with what vast and untold number of ages you please, so long as there is a definite end to this unit of time, it is not even as if you compared the tiniest drop of water with the ocean that everywhere flows around the globe! For of these two, one indeed is very small, and the other incomparably vast, yet both are finite. But that length of time which starts from some beginning, and is limited by some ending, let it be of what extent it may, if you compare it with what has no beginning [eternity], I do not know whether to say we would reckon it the very tiniest thing, or nothing at all....

Therefore, what we now demand after five thousand odd years, our descendants might with equal curiosity demand after six hundred thousand years, supposing these dying generations of humanity continue so long to decay and be renewed, and supposing our offspring continue as weak and ignorant as ourselves. The same question might have been asked by those who lived before us and while humanity was even more recent upon the earth. The first man himself, in short, might the day after his creation, or on the very day of his creation, have asked why he was created no sooner. And no matter at what earlier or later period he had been created, this controversy about the beginning of this world's history would have had precisely the same difficulties as it has now.[3]

City of God, 12:12

Why did God forbid Adam to eat from the tree of knowledge?

God had made this prohibition, in order to show that the nature of the rational soul ought not to be in its own power, but in subjection to God, and that the soul guards the order of its salvation through obedience, but corrupts it through disobedience. That is also why He called the forbidden tree "the tree of the knowledge of good and evil". For when man touched it in defiance of the prohibition, he would experience the penalty of sin, and so would know the difference between the good of obedience, and the evil of disobedience.

On the Nature of Good, 35

---

[3] Augustine's argument here is based on the view that the human race was created "less than 6,000 years" before Augustine's day. In **City of God, 12:11**, he specifically argues against those who believed in the great antiquity of the human race.

Why did Adam sin?

We cannot believe that Adam was deceived, and supposed the devil's word to be truth, and therefore transgressed God's law. Rather, he yielded to the woman, the husband to the wife, the one human being to the only other human being, by the attractions of kinship. For the apostle said with great significance, "And Adam was not deceived, but the woman being deceived fell into transgression" (1 Tim.2:14). He speaks thus, because the woman accepted as true what the serpent told her, whereas the man could not bear to be separated from his only companion, even though this involved a partnership in sin. He was not on this account less blameworthy, but he sinned with his eyes open.

And so the apostle does not say, "He did not sin," but, "He was not deceived." For Paul shows that Adam sinned when he says, "By one man sin entered into the world" (Rom.5:12), and immediately after more distinctly, "In the likeness of Adam's transgression" (Rom.5:14). Paul meant that deception reigns over those who do not judge that what they do is sin; but Adam knew. Otherwise how were it true "Adam was not deceived"? But having as yet no experience of the divine severity, he was possibly deceived to the extent that he thought his sin excusable. And consequently he was not deceived as the woman was deceived, but he was deceived about the judgment which God would pass on his plea of self-justification: "The woman whom You gave to be with me, she gave me, and I did eat" (Gen.3:12). What need of saying more? Although they were not both deceived by credulity, yet both were entangled in the snares of the devil, and taken captive by sin.

City of God, 14:11

Adam fell freely

God created man with free will. Man was happy, because he was ignorant of his future fall, and thought he had it in his grasp to remain free from both death and misery. And if he had willed by his own free will to continue in this state of uprightness and freedom from sin, he would have received for his worthy conduct the fullness of blessing that the holy angels enjoy, without any experience of death or misery. That blessing would have involved the removal of any further possibility of falling, and the absolutely certain knowledge of this. For even Adam himself could not be blessed in paradise — indeed, he would not have been there at all, since misery was impossible there — if the foreknowledge if his fall had made him miserable with the dread of that disaster. But because he forsook God by his own free will, he experienced the righteous judgment of God — condemnation for himself, and for his whole race which sinned in him, because it then had its existence in him. For those of the human race who are rescued by God's grace are certainly rescued from a condemnation in which they were already held captive. So even if none were rescued, no-one could rightly argue against God's justice.

On Rebuke and Grace, 28

How God's wise providence operated in the fall of Adam

The sins of humans and angels do nothing to hinder the "great works of the Lord which accomplish His will" (Ps.111:2). For He Who by His providence and omnipotence distributes to every one his own portion, is able to make good use not only of the good, but also of the wicked. He made a good use of the wicked angel, who, in punishment of his first wicked choice, was doomed to a hardheartedness that prevents him now from willing any good. Why should not God have permitted him to tempt the first man, who had been created upright, that is to say, with a good will? For man had been so constituted, that if he looked to God for help, man's goodness would defeat the angel's wickedness. But if by proud self-pleasing man abandoned God, his Creator and Sustainer, he would be conquered. If his will remained upright, through leaning on God's help, he would be rewarded; if his will became wicked, by forsaking God, he would be punished.

Yet even this trusting in God's help could not itself be accomplished without God's help, although man had it in his own power to renounce the benefits of divine grace by pleasing himself. It is not in our power to live in this world without sustaining ourselves by food; but it is in our power to refuse this nourishment and cease to live, as those do who kill themselves. Likewise, it was not in man's power, even in paradise, to live as he ought without God's help; but it was in his power to live wickedly, though by so doing he would cut short his happiness, and incur very just punishment.

Since, then, God was not ignorant that man would fall, why should He not have allowed him to be tempted by an angel who hated and envied him? It was not, indeed, that God was unaware that man would be conquered. But He foresaw that by the man's seed, aided by divine grace, this same devil himself would be conquered, to the greater glory of the saints. All was brought about in such a way that no future event escaped God's foreknowledge; and yet His foreknowledge did not *compel* anyone to sin. He arranged things to demonstrate in the experience of the intelligent creation, human and angelic, how great a difference there is between the private conceit of the creature and the Creator's protection. For who will dare to believe or say that it was not in God's power to prevent both angels and humans from sinning? But God preferred to leave this in their own power, and thus to show both what evil could be accomplished by their pride, and what good accomplished by His grace.

City of God, 14:27

God foresaw the fall

God was not ignorant that man would sin, and that, being himself made subject now to death, he would propagate mortals doomed to die. God knew that these mortals would run to such enormities in sin, that even the beasts devoid of rational will, who were created in such numbers from the waters and the earth, would live more securely and peaceably with their own kind than humans, who had been propagated from one individual for the very purpose of commending harmony. For not even lions or dragons have ever waged with their kind such wars as humans have waged with one another. But God foresaw also that by His grace a people would be called to adoption, and that they, being justified by the forgiveness of their sins, would be united by the Holy Spirit to the holy angels in eternal peace, when the last enemy, death, was destroyed. And He knew that this people would derive profit from considering that God had caused all human beings to be derived from one, for the sake of showing how highly God prizes unity in a multitude.

City of God, 12:22

Many sins were contained in the one sin of Adam

However, even in that one sin, which "by one man entered into the world, and so passed upon all men" (Rom.5:12), and on account of which infants are baptised, a number of distinct sins may be observed, if we analyse it (so to speak) into its separate elements. For in Adam's sin there is *pride*, because man chose to be under his own dominion, rather than under the dominion of God; and *blasphemy*, because he did not believe God; and *murder*, for he brought death upon himself; and *spiritual fornication*, for the purity of the human soul was corrupted by the seducing flatteries of the serpent; and *theft*, for man perverted to his own use the food he had been forbidden to touch; and *avarice*, for he had a craving for more than should have been adequate for him; and whatever other sin can be discovered on careful reflection to be involved in this one admitted sin.

Enchiridion, 45

The greatness of Adam's sin

Nevertheless, that one sin of Adam, admitted into a place where such perfect happiness reigned, was of so monstrous a character, that in one man the whole human race was originally condemned – condemned in the root, as one may say. And it cannot be pardoned and blotted out except through "the one Mediator between God and men, the man Christ Jesus" (1 Tim.2:5), Who alone has had the power to be born so as not to need a second birth.

Enchiridion, 48

The consequences of Adam's sin

God had threatened Adam with this punishment of death if he sinned, leaving him indeed to the freedom of his own will, but yet commanding his obedience under pain of death; and He placed him amid the happiness of Eden, in a sort of protected haven of life, with the intention that, if he preserved his righteousness, he should ascend from there to a better place.

So then, after Adam's sin, he was driven into exile, and by his sin the whole race of which he was the root was corrupted in him, and thereby subjected to the penalty of death. And so it happens that all descended from him, and from the woman who had led him into sin and was condemned at the same time with him, are the offspring of carnal lust on which the same punishment of disobedience was visited. So those descendants were tainted with the original sin, and were by it drawn through various errors and sufferings into that last and endless punishment which they suffer in common with the fallen angels, their corrupters and masters, and the partakers of their doom. And thus "by one man sin entered into the world, and death by sin; and so death passed upon all men, because all have sinned" (Rom.5:12). By "the world" the apostle, of course, means in this place the whole human race.

Thus, then, matters stood. The whole mass of the human race was under condemnation, was lying steeped and wallowing in misery, and was being tossed from one form of evil to another, and, having joined the faction of the fallen angels, was paying the well-merited penalty of that ungodly rebellion. For whatever the wicked freely do through blind and unbridled lust, and whatever they suffer against their will in the way of open punishment, this all evidently pertains to the just wrath of God. But the goodness of the Creator never fails either to supply life and vital power to the wicked angels (without which their existence would soon come to an end); or, in the case of humanity, which springs from a condemned and corrupt stock, to impart form and life to their seed, to fashion their members, and through the various seasons of their life, and in the different parts of the earth, to quicken their senses, and bestow upon them the nourishment they need. For God judged it better to bring good out of evil, than not to permit any evil to exist.

Enchiridion, 25-27

The coming of death

It is asked what was the death with which God threatened our first parents if they transgressed the command they had received from Him, and failed to preserve their obedience. Was it the death of the soul, or of the body, or of the whole person? Or was it what is called the second death? We must answer, It is all of these. For the first consists of two elements; the second is the complete death, which consists of all. As the whole earth consists of many lands, and the Church universal consists of many churches, so death universal consists of all deaths. The first consists of two elements, one of the body, the other of the soul. So the first death is a death of the whole human person, since the soul without God and without the body suffers punishment for a time. But the second death is when the soul, without God but with the body, suffers everlasting punishment. When, therefore, God said to that first man whom he had placed in paradise, referring to the forbidden fruit, "In the day that you eat it, you shall surely die" (Gen.2:17), that threat included not only the first part of the first death, by which the soul is deprived of God; nor only the subsequent part of the first death, by which the body is deprived of the soul; nor only the whole first death itself, by which the soul is punished in separation from God and from the body. No, it includes whatever of death there is, even up to that final death which is called the second death, and to which no other death is subsequent.

City of God, 13:12

The nature of death: body, soul and God

I see I must speak a little more carefully about the nature of death. For we rightly affirm that the human soul is immortal, yet the soul also has a certain death of its own. It is called immortal, because (in a sense) the soul does not cease to live and to feel; while the body is called mortal, because it can be forsaken by all life, and cannot by itself live at all. The death of the soul takes place when God forsakes it, just as the death of the body occurs when the soul forsakes it. Therefore the death of both — that is, of the whole human person — occurs when the soul, forsaken by God, forsakes the body. For in this case, God is no longer the life of the soul, and the soul is no longer the life of the body. And this death of the whole human person is followed by that which, on the authority of the divine revelation, we call "the second death" (Rev.20:14).

The Saviour referred to this when He said, "Fear Him Who is able to destroy both soul and body in hell" (Matt.10:28). Now this happens only after the soul is joined to its body so that they cannot be separated at all [in the resurrection]. So we may wonder how the body can be said to be killed by that death in which it is not forsaken by the soul, but feels torment because it is animated and rendered sensitive by the soul. For in that penal and everlasting punishment, which we will speak about more fully in its own place, the soul is rightly said to die, because it does not live in communion with God. But how can we say that the body is then dead, seeing that it lives by the soul? For it could not otherwise feel the bodily torments which are to follow the resurrection. Perhaps it is because life of every kind is good, while pain is an evil, that we decline to say that the [resurrection] body [of the condemned] "lives". For in that body, the soul is the cause, not of life, but of pain.

The soul, then, lives by God when it lives virtuously, for it cannot live virtuously except by God producing in it what is good. And the body lives by the soul when the soul lives in the body, whether the soul is living by God or not. For the wicked person's life in the body is a life not of the soul, but of the body. And even dead souls — that is, souls forsaken by God — can confer bodily life upon bodies, however little of their own proper immortal life they retain. Now, in the last condemnation, a person does not cease to feel. Yet because his feeling is neither sweet with delight nor wholesome with tranquillity, but painfully penal, it is not without reason called death rather than life. And it is called the "second" death, because it follows the first that separates the two essences that had dwelt in each other, whether these are God and the soul, or the soul and the body. Of the first and bodily death, then, we may say that to the good it is good, and to the evil it is evil. But doubtless, the second death, which happens to none of the good, can be good for none.

City of God, 13:2

We all sinned in Adam

God created man upright, for God is the author of natures, not of their defects. But man was corrupted through his own will, and righteously condemned, and so he begot corrupted and condemned offspring. For we were all *in* that one man, since we all were that one man, who fell into sin through the woman who was made from him before the sin. We did not yet each have an individual form, created and assigned for us to live in as individuals; but the human nature from which, as from a seed, we were to be begotten, already existed in Adam. Since this nature was depraved through sin, and bound by the chains of death, and righteously condemned, human could not be born from human in any other condition. And so from the misuse of free will began a sequence of disasters, carrying humanity from its depraved origin as from a corrupted root, right up to the destruction of the second death which has no end. The only ones who escape are those who are set free by God's grace.

City of God, 13:14

Original sin is more than just following Adam's example

No doubt we *do* imitate Adam if we break any of God's commands by disobedience. But it is one thing for us to sin by our own choice, influenced by Adam's bad example. It is quite another thing for us to be born with a sinful nature, inherited from Adam! Consider that all Christ's people imitate Him by pursuing righteousness. In Paul's words, "Imitate me, just as I also imitate Christ" (1 Cor.11:1). But as well as this imitation of Christ, Christ's grace works *within* us to enlighten and justify us. Paul speaks of this when he says, "Neither he who plants is anything, nor he who waters, but God Who gives the increase" (1 Cor.3:7) ... So Christ, "in Whom all are made alive" (1 Cor.15:22), does offer Himself as an example to those who imitate Him. But more than this, He gives to His believing people the inward grace of His Spirit, which He secretly imparts even to infants.

In the same way, Adam "in whom all die" (1 Cor.15:22) is not merely an example imitated by those who wilfully disobey the Lord's command; he also corrupted his own nature, and thereby corrupted everyone who is descended from him, by the inward corruption of his own sinful desire. This sin of Adam, corrupting all human nature from birth, is what Paul means when he says, "through one man sin entered the world, and death through sin, and thus death spread to all men, because in his sin all sinned" (Rom.5:12).[4]

On the Merits and Forgiveness of Sins, 1:10.

---

[4] Augustine's Latin Bible, in the last part of Rom.5:12, said, "death came to all

If we were sinners by imitation, Paul would have pointed to Satan, not to Adam

"For if by the one man's offence, death reigned through the one, much more will those who receive abundance of grace and the gift of righteousness reign in life through the one, Jesus Christ" (Rom.5:17). Why did death reign on account of the sin of one man? Surely because humanity is held captive in Adam by the chains of death. We all sinned in Adam, even supposing we added no personal sins of our own. If that is not true, then it was not on account of Adam's sin that death reigned through Adam. Rather, it was on account of the many sins of individual sinners.

But let us suppose that the reason why we die through Adam's sin is that we have imitated Adam by following his footsteps into sin. If this "imitation" view is correct, then even Adam himself died through the sin of another – namely, the devil, who sinned before Adam, and persuaded Adam to sin. Adam, however, did not persuade his descendants to sin. The many who (according to Pelagius) have "imitated" Adam, have in fact not even heard of Adam's existence, or of his sin in paradise, or else utterly disbelieve it! If the apostle Paul had wanted to teach us in Romans 5 that we are sinful by *imitating* Adam, rather than by *inheriting depravity* from Adam, then he would have done better to point to the devil as the author of sin, and as the one from whom sin and death have spread to all.

On the Merits and Forgiveness of Sins, 1:17

([4] cont.) men, in whom [or in which] all sinned." Augustine took "in whom" or "in which" to mean "in Adam" or "in Adam's sin". Almost all modern translations (correctly) read the verse as saying, "death came to all men *because* all sinned." Even so, this does not break the link between Adam's sin and ours. Some classic modern commentators, such as C.E.B.Cranfield, argue that "because all sinned" means "because all human beings have unavoidably sinned as a result of the inborn corruption we have inherited from Adam's sin". Others, such as John Murray, argue that "because all sinned" means "because all sinned in the sin of Adam". Murray's view is virtually the same as Augustine's, despite the different translation; Cranfield's view still accepts the Augustinian doctrine of original sin as lying beneath Paul's words.

If we derive sin from imitating Adam, we must derive righteousness from imitating Abel!

If people become sinners through Adam simply by imitating him,
why doesn't simple imitation make people righteous through Christ?
Paul says, "As through one man's offence, judgment came to all
men, resulting in condemnation, even so through one man's righteous
act the free gift came to all men, resulting in justification of life"
(Rom.5:18). If the "imitation" theory were correct, then "the one
man" and "the one man" both mentioned here cannot be Adam and
Christ. They must be Adam and Abel! For many people have sinned
before we did in this life, and have been imitated in their sin by those
who sinned afterwards; yet Paul mentions Adam alone, as the one in
whom all have sinned — by imitation, as the Pelagians will have it.
They say Paul mentions Adam alone, because Adam was the first
man ever to sin. But on the same principle, Paul ought to have
mentioned Abel as "the one man" in whom all are justified by
imitation, because Abel was the first man ever to live righteously.

On the Merits and Forgiveness of Sins, 1:19

Sin is not just evil deeds, but a corruption of our nature

"We have," says Pelagius, "first of all to discuss the position
maintained by some, that our nature has been weakened and changed
by sin. I think that before anything else, we must inquire what sin is.
Is it a substance? Or is it a word that does not describe a substance?
Does 'sin' express not a thing, not a being, not some sort of body,
but the doing of an evil deed? I think this is the case. If so, how can
sin, which lacks all substance, possibly have weakened or changed
human nature?"

Please notice how in his ignorance Pelagius struggles to overthrow
the most healthy words of the health-giving Scriptures: "I said, 'Lord,
be merciful to me; heal my soul, for I have sinned against You'"
(Ps.41:4). Now how can a thing be healed, unless it is wounded, or
hurt, or weakened, or corrupted? But since there is something here
that requires healing, from where did it receive its injury? You hear
David confessing the fact; what need is there of discussion? He says,
"Heal my soul." Ask him how the soul whose healing he desires

became sinful, and then listen to his following words: "For I have sinned against you."

Let Pelagius, however, put his question to David and ask him what Pelagius thinks is a proper inquiry: "O you who exclaim, 'Heal my soul, for I have sinned against You' — tell me, what is sin? Is it a substance? Or is it a word that does not describe a substance? Does 'sin' express not a thing, not a being, not some sort of body, but the doing of an evil deed?" To this, David replies: "It is just as you say. Sin is not a substance. It is a name that expresses the doing of an evil deed." But Pelagius responds: "Then why cry out, 'Heal my soul, for I have sinned against You'? How could sin possibly have corrupted your soul, if it lacks all substance?" To this, David, worn out with the agony of his wound, desiring to avoid being distracted from prayer by this discussion, briefly answers: "Please, leave me alone. Discuss this point, if you can, with Him Who said, 'Those who are well have no need of a physician, but those who are sick. For I did not come to call the righteous, but sinners to repentance'" (Matt.9:12-13). In these words, of course, Christ described the righteous as those who are well, and sinners as those who are sick.

On Nature and Grace, 21

Sin is the corruption of a nature that is good

Scripture calls "God's enemies" those who oppose His rule, which they do, not by nature, but by sin. They have no power to hurt God, but only themselves. For they are His enemies, not through their power to hurt Him, but by their will to oppose Him. God is unchangeable, and completely immune to injury. Therefore the sin that makes those who are called God's enemies resist Him, is an evil not to God, but to themselves. And to them it is an evil, purely because it corrupts the goodness of their nature. It is not our nature, therefore, but our sin, which is contrary to God. For evil is contrary to the good. And who will deny that God is the Supreme Good?

Sin, therefore, is contrary to God, as evil to good. Further, the nature it corrupts is a good thing, and therefore sin is also contrary to our nature. But while sin is contrary to God only as evil to good, it is contrary to the nature it corrupts, both as something evil and as something hurtful. To God, no evils are hurtful. Evils are hurtful only to natures that are changeable and corruptible, even though those natures were originally good, as the sins themselves testify. For if our natures were not good, sins could not hurt them. And how do sins hurt our natures except by depriving them of integrity, beauty, welfare, virtue, and, in short, every natural good that sin is accustomed to diminish or destroy? But if there is no good to take away, then no injury can be done, and consequently there can be no sin. For it is impossible that there should be a harmless sin.

From this we gather that though sin cannot injure the Unchangeable Good [God], the only thing sin can injure is good; for wherever sin exists, it injures. This, then, may formulated as follows: sin cannot exist in the Highest Good, but must exist in some [lesser] good. Things purely good, therefore, can in some circumstances exist; but things purely evil can never exist. For even those natures which are corrupted by an evil will, to the extent that they are indeed corrupted, are evil; but to the extent that they are natures, they are good. And when a corrupted nature is punished, in addition to the good it enjoys in being a nature, it has another good — the good of being punished. For punishment is just, and certainly everything just is good. No-one is punished for natural evils, but for voluntary evils. Some sins, by force of habit and long continuance, have become a second nature; but even they had their origin in the will.[5]

City of God, 12:3

---

[5] Augustine's point in this important quotation is that sin is basically unnatural. God created human nature good. It is good to have such gifts as understanding, memory, will, creativity, conscience, and so forth. The problem is not these natural powers; the problem is the sin that has corrupted them. To the extent that our natures have been corrupted by sin, we have acquired an unnatural "second nature" which distorts the original good nature created by God. Rabbi John Duncan put it like this: "A lady once said to me, 'The more I see of myself, I see nothing so properly mine as my sin.' I said to her, 'Well, you do not see deep enough. There is something far more properly yours than your sin; and your sin is *improperly* yours. It is a blot in your being, which, if you do not get quit of it, will never cease to be unnatural to you. No; the *image of God* is more properly yours, though you had no share in the production of it.'" The great Scottish Calvinist here spoke as a true Augustinian.

Sin is not a substance, but a wound in our being

Now can you see the drift and direction of this controversy? It is to make null and void the Scripture which says, "You shall call His name Jesus, for He will save His people from their sins" (Matt.1:21). How can Jesus save where there is no sickness? For the sins that Matthew's Gospel says Christ will save His people from, are not substances; and therefore, according to Pelagius, they are incapable of corrupting human nature. O my brother, how good it is to remember that you are a Christian! To believe might perhaps be enough; but still, since you want to persevere in discussion, there is no harm in this. Indeed, there is benefit, if a firm faith undergirds the discussion. So then, let us not suppose that human nature cannot be corrupted by sin. Rather, let us believe from the inspired Scriptures that human nature is corrupted by sin, and then inquire how this could possibly have happened.

We have already learned that sin is not a substance. Well, not to mention any other example, we would also agree that "not to eat" is not a substance. Food is a substance; but to abstain from eating food is to abandon a substance. So then, the act of "abstaining from food" is not a substance. And yet if we do abstain totally from food, the substance of our body grows weak, and is impaired by broken health, and exhausted of its strength, and weakened and broken by utter weariness. Even if the starved body stays alive, it is scarcely able to go back to eating food, the very food whose absence has so corrupted and injured the body. In the same way, sin is not a substance; but God is a substance — He is the supreme substance, and the only true life-source of the rational creature. If we depart from God by disobedience, we become unable through weakness to receive what we should really rejoice in. The consequence you see in the psalmist: "My heart is stricken and withered like grass, so that I forget to eat my bread" (Ps.102:4).

On Nature and Grace, 22

Humanity is corrupt by its own fault

"The next question we have to ask," says Celestius, "is this: if humanity cannot be sinless, whose fault is it — humanity's, or someone else's? If it is humanity's own fault, then I ask: in what way is it our fault, if we are sinful when we cannot be otherwise?" We reply that it is humanity's fault that humanity is sinful. By the human will alone [i.e. Adam's will], humanity has fallen into a necessity of sinning which cannot be overcome by the human will alone.

On Human Perfection, 2:13

The Pelagians teach the innocence of new-born babies

Celestius maintained this false doctrine with greater enthusiasm. When he was on trial before the bishops of Carthage, he actually refused to condemn those who say, "Adam's sin injured Adam alone, not the human race; infants at their birth are in the same state Adam was in before his transgression." In the written statement, too, which he presented to the most blessed pope Zosimus at Rome, he declared with particular clarity: "Original sin binds no infant whatever."

On the Grace of Christ and Original Sin, 2:2

Scripture teaches the guilt and corruption of infants through Adam

Let Julian persist in asking his question, "By what means can sin be discovered in an infant?" He may find an answer in the inspired pages: "Through one man sin entered the world, and death through sin, and thus death spread to all men, for in him all sinned." "By the one man's offence, the many died." "The judgment came from one offence and resulted in condemnation." "By one man's offence, judgment came to all men, resulting in condemnation." "By one man's disobedience, the many were made sinners" (Rom.5:12-19). See, then, by what means sin can be discovered in an infant. Let Julian now believe in original sin, and let him permit infants to come to Christ that they may be saved.

On Marriage and Concupiscence, 2:47

Infants must have original sin if Christ is to be their Saviour

Let Julian spare infants! Let him not uselessly praise their condition, and defend them cruelly. Let him not declare them to be safe. Let him permit infants to come — not to Pelagius for praise, but to Christ for salvation. For, that this book may be now brought to a close, since the dissertation of Julian is ended, which was written on the short paper you sent me, I will close with Julian's own last words: "Really believe that all things were created by Jesus Christ, and that without Him nothing was created." Well, let him grant that Jesus is Jesus even to infants. Just as Julian confesses that all things were created by Christ, since He is God the Word, so let him acknowledge that infants too are saved by Him, since He is Jesus. Let Julian admit this, if he wants to be a Catholic Christian. For thus it is written in the Gospel: "You shall call His name Jesus, for He will save His people from their sins" (Matt.1:21) — "Jesus" because Jesus means "Saviour". He shall indeed save His people; and among His people, surely there are infants. "From their sins" He will save them; so in infants too there is original sin, because of which He can be Jesus, Saviour, even to them.

On Marriage and Concupiscence, 2:60

If Christ died for infants, they must be sinful

"You assert," says Julian to me, "that those who have never been born might possibly have been good; those, however, who have peopled the world, and for whom Christ died, you decide to be the work of the devil, born in a disordered state, and guilty from the very beginning." I wish that he only solved the entire controversy as he unties the knot of this question! For will he pretend to say that he merely spoke of adults in this passage? Why, the topic under discussion is infants, human beings at their birth; and it is about these that he raises resentment against us, because we define them as guilty from the very first, and declare them to be guilty, since Christ died for them. And why did Christ die for them if they are not guilty? It is entirely from them, yes, from them, we shall find the reason why he thought resentment should be raised against me. He asks: "How are infants guilty, for whom Christ died?" We answer: No, but how are infants not guilty, since Christ died for them?

This dispute needs a judge to settle it. Let Christ be the Judge, and let Him tell us the profitable object of His death. "This is my blood," He says, "which is shed for many *for the forgiveness of sins*" (Matt.26:28). Let the apostle, too, be His assessor in the judgment; since even in the apostle it is Christ Himself that speaks. Speaking of God the Father, Paul exclaims: "He who spared not His own Son, but delivered Him up for us all!" I suppose that he describes Christ as "delivered up for us all", intending that infants in this matter are not separated from ourselves. But what need is there to dwell on this point, since even Julian no longer raises a contest over it? The truth is, he not only confesses that Christ died even for infants, but on this basis he also reproves us, because we say that these same infants for whom Christ died are guilty. Now, then, let the apostle, who says that Christ was delivered up for us all, also tell us why Christ was delivered up for us. "He was delivered," says he, "for our offences, and rose again for our justification" (Rom.4:25).

If, therefore, even Julian both confesses and professes, both admits and objects, that infants too are included among those for whom Christ was delivered up; and if it was for our sins that Christ was delivered up, then it follows that even infants must have original sin, since Christ was delivered up for them. Christ must have something in them to heal, for He (as He Himself affirms) is not needed as a Physician by the healthy, but by the sick. He must have a reason for saving infants, seeing that He came into the world, as the apostle Paul says, "to save sinners" (1 Tim.1:15). He must have something in them to forgive, since He testifies that He shed His blood "for the forgiveness of sins." He must have good reason for seeking them out, if He came, as He says, "to seek and to save that which was lost" (Lk.19:10). The Son of man must find in infants something to destroy, seeing that He came for the express purpose, as the apostle John says, "that He might destroy the works of the devil" (1 Jn.3:8). Now to this salvation of infants Julian must be an enemy, since he asserts their innocence in such a way that he denies them the medicine which is required by the hurt and wounded.

On Marriage and Concupiscence, 2:56

The death of infants shows that they have sin

How can the Pelagians say it was only death that passed upon us by means of Adam? For if we die because Adam *died,* but Adam died because he *sinned,* they are saying that the punishment is passed on to us without the guilt! That means that innocent infants are punished with an unjust penalty by deriving death without deserving death.

Against Two Letters of the Pelagians, 4:6

The mysterious nature of sin's transmission to the newly conceived human

A man had fallen into a well where the amount of water was enough to break his fall and save him from death, but not deep enough to cover his mouth and deprive him of speech. Another man approaches, and on seeing him cries out in surprise: "How did you fall in here?" He answers: "I beseech you to plan how you can get me out of this, rather than ask how I fell in." So, since we admit and hold as an article of the Catholic faith, that the soul of even a little infant requires to be delivered by the grace of Christ out of the guilt of sin, as out of a pit, it is enough for the soul of such a one that we know the way in which it is saved, even though we should never know the way in which it came into that wretched condition. But I thought it our duty to inquire into this subject, in case we should incautiously hold any one of those opinions concerning the manner of the soul's becoming united with the body which might contradict the doctrine that the souls of little children require to be delivered, by denying that they are subject to the chain of guilt.

This, then, being very firmly held by us, that the soul of every infant needs to be freed from the guilt of sin, and can be freed in no other way except by the grace of God through Jesus Christ our Lord, if we can determine the cause and origin of the evil itself, we are better prepared and equipped for resisting adversaries whose empty talk I call not reasoning but quibbling. If, however, we cannot determine the cause, the fact that the origin of this misery is hidden from us is no reason for our being slothful in the work which compassion demands from us.

Letter 167:2

Being born of Christian parents does not make someone a Christian

The guilt of that corruption about which we are speaking will remain in the fleshly children of the regenerate, until the washing of regeneration washes away that corruption in them too. A regenerate man does not give *new* birth to his children, but only birth according to the flesh. So he transmits to his offspring the condition of the physically born, not of the spiritually reborn. So then, whether a man is guilty of unbelief or a perfect believer, he does not beget believing children, but sinful ones, just as the seeds both of a wild olive and a cultivated olive produce not cultivated olives but wild ones. Likewise, the first birth holds us in that bondage from which nothing but the second birth delivers us. The devil holds us, Christ liberates us. Eve's deceiver binds us, Mary's Son sets us free. Satan, who approached the man through the woman, enslaves us; Christ, Who was born of a woman who never approached a man, emancipates us. The devil, who produced in the woman the cause of lust, imprisons us; Jesus, Who was conceived in the woman without any lust, gives us liberty....

The sin that changed humanity for the worse in paradise is far greater than we can ever comprehend. It defiles everyone at birth, and is forgiven only in those who are born again. This disordered state of human nature is passed on even from parents who *have* been born again, in whom sin is forgiven and covered. The result is that their children are born into a state of condemnation, unless these children — bound by their first and fleshly birth — are absolved by a second and spiritual birth. The Creator has given us an amazing example of this amazing fact in the case of the olive tree and the wild olive tree; for both from a wild olive tree and a cultivated olive tree, only a wild olive ever springs.

Now even in people whose natural birth is followed by new birth through grace, there still exists this fleshly lust that wages war against the law of the mind (Rom.7:23). However, this is forgiven in the forgiveness of sins, and is no longer counted against them as sin. Nor is it in any way harmful unless they surrender themselves to its impulses and commit unlawful deeds. But their children are not begotten from spiritual desire, but fleshly desire, like a wild olive from the good olive. So children derive guilt from their natural birth, and cannot be liberated from this sickness unless they are born again.

On the Grace of Christ and Original Sin, 2:45, 58.

Everyone is born spiritually blind

If we reflect on what is meant by the deed which the Lord did here [giving sight to the man born blind, Jn.9], that blind man stands for the human race. For this blindness fell upon the first man through sin, and he is the origin from which we all spring, not only in respect of death, but also of unrighteousness. For if unbelief is blindness, and faith is enlightenment, whom did Christ find a believer when He came? The apostle Paul, himself belonging to the nation of the prophets, says: "We also were by nature children of wrath" (Eph.2:3). If we were "children of wrath", then we were children of vengeance, children of punishment, children of hell. And how is this "by nature", except that through the first man's sin, moral evil took root in our human nature itself? If evil has so taken root within us, everyone is born mentally blind. For if a person sees, he has no need of a guide. But if he needs a Guide to enlighten him, then he is blind from birth.

Sermons on John, 44:1.

Chapter 2

Free Will

I am, moreover, fully persuaded that the soul has fallen into sin, not through the fault of God, nor through any necessity either in the divine nature or in its own, but by its own free will; and that it can be delivered from the body of this death neither by the strength of its own will, as if that were in itself sufficient to achieve this, nor by the death of the body itself, but only by the grace of God through our Lord Jesus Christ, and that there is not one soul in the human family to whose salvation the one Mediator between God and men, the man Christ Jesus, is not absolutely necessary.

Augustine, *Letter 166:5*

Free will is a controversial subject. It always has been. You may well have had arguments yourself with other Christians about "free will". You may have heard someone assert, "Well, I believe in free will!" as if that were enough to disprove the doctrine of predestination. In fact, it isn't as simple as that — for either side in the debate.

It is comforting to realise that this is indeed no new debate. Human free will was one of the central issues in the Pelagian controversy. To see why, we need to appreciate something of the background. Up until the 5th century, the context in which Christians had discussed human freedom was their controversy with paganism and the Gnostics. Pagan religion included astrology within its multi-coloured texture, and astrology taught "fate" — that the destiny of individuals is determined by the stars. In order to counter this pagan belief in a "determinism of the stars", Christians had emphasised the dignity and freedom of the individual. We are responsible for our own characters, our own actions, and our own destinies; these things are not thrust upon us by the tyranny of fate or astral influence. To that extent, the Church was guarding a crucial truth of Scripture.

As for the Gnostics, many of them — especially the Manichees, the last and most successful flowering of Gnosticism in the Roman Empire, to whom Augustine had once belonged — taught that only some people, the "pneumatics" ("spiritual ones"), are capable of salvation. The rest, and even the pneumatics prior to their enlightenment, are coerced into sinning by their fleshly, bodily natures, even against their rational wills. Gnostics regarded physical matter as the source of all evil; liberation of the will from the tyranny of flesh was essential to the Gnostic vision of salvation. Against this, Christians had insisted that salvation is available to all, not just to a "spiritual" class, and that no-one is ever coerced or compelled into sinning by anything — sin is always voluntary and willing sin, the self-moving action of the will that sins. Again, to that extent the Church was preserving vital biblical truths.

However, with the benefit of hindsight, it is easy for us to see how the whole debate with astrology and Gnosticism did not exactly produce an atmosphere in which Christians could think very clearly about the Scriptural doctrine of the *bondage* of the human will. Any such talk might have sounded too much like astrological fate or Gnostic determinism. Not that Christians prior to Augustine had absolutely no doctrine of "the bondage of the will", but we find it only in scattered utterances, without any consistency. Statements about the freedom and bondage of the will jostle alongside each other, set forth in contradictory ways. But the emphasis is usually on the "freedom" side of the equation. No controversy had yet arisen to force Christians to think out the "bondage" side of the equation clearly and systematically. With the coming of Pelagius, that controversy had at last arrived.

Pelagius took the accepted Christian views of human dignity, freedom and responsibility, and fashioned them into a system which in reality (despite his protests) denied the need for God's grace in the conversion and sanctification of sinners. For Pelagius, the freedom of the will meant that our wills are, so to speak, hanging in the air, suspended between good and evil, and capable of choosing between them by the will's own in-built power. In other words, Pelagius interpreted freedom to mean that the human will is always the final cause of all its own choices and actions. He acknowledged (sometimes very eloquently) the power of environment and habit to tempt and pervert the will; but in the last analysis, the will always retained an ultimate power of self-caused choice in both good and evil.

Augustine had once held similar views as a young Christian, but a deeper study of Scripture, and the harsh lessons of experience, had taught him a different view long before the Pelagian controversy broke out. Augustine realised that the Pelagian view of free will cut human beings loose both from the reality of sin and the grace of God. Apart from God's liberating grace in Jesus Christ, unredeemed sinners are in fact the slaves of sin, not the wonderfully free and autonomous beings that Pelagius seemed to make them. Such is the testimony both of Scripture and sad experience.

However, it would at this point be fatally easy for us to misunderstand Augustine's doctrine of the will, whether we consider ourselves "Augustinians" or not. For in his own way, Augustine no less than Pelagius inherited the early Christian view of human dignity, freedom and responsibility. This is especially clear in Augustine's insistence that we can still speak of free will in the unredeemed sinner. The argument between Augustine and Pelagius was not whether this free will existed, but what was the *nature* of its freedom. Augustine held that the essence of the will's freedom in the unredeemed sinner lay in its *freedom from outward compulsion or coercion.* No external power compels our wills to sin — neither the stars, nor fate, nor environment, nor the flesh, nor Satan. We always sin from the depths of our own wills — willingly, voluntarily, personally — and in that sense, freely. In this way, Augustine conserved the early Church view of humanity's dignity, freedom and responsibility in the face of various tyrannies that threatened to swallow up the individual, making us into mere pawns or puppets of a greater power.

Even so, Augustine insisted that in the very midst of this freedom of the will from outward compulsion, our wills exist in a state of deep bondage. When we sin, we sin willingly — true enough, said Augustine. But the problem is that the unredeemed sinner never does anything else. He keeps on sinning willingly. He is never willing to obey God. Further, his sin is as inward as his will. It is not so much bad deeds, but the false love that lies behind them. The unredeemed sinner wills to love created things rather than the Creator. And this false love is a permanent condition. Bad deeds may erupt only now and then, but all the time, in the depths of his will, the sinner is loving the creature, not the ever-blessed Creator. The will, for Augustine, meant this fundamental inclination of the heart, this deep inward preference or "penchant" of the self, either for God or for created things, which lies behind and ultimately determines our conscious choices. So while human sin is certainly "willing" in nature, it is a willing sinfulness to which, paradoxically, we are hopelessly enslaved. Unless the unconditional grace of God converts us, we will never do anything other than sin — unforced, uncoerced, willingly and readily, from the central depths of our self-loving will — until we sin ourselves into hell.

So then, the tragedy of the fallen human will, said Augustine, is not that it is tyrannised over by external powers, as the pagan astrologers and Gnostics think. Rather the fallen will is in bondage to itself, to its own self-moving spontaneous sinfulness. If Augustine had known the modern language of drug addiction, he might have said that the problem is the will's addiction to sin. We are so profoundly addicted that, even though we might want to be rid of the painful consequences of sin, we cannot bear to give up sin itself. Who can heal the fallen will of this addiction? Not its own choices or exertions, which are all conditioned by the addiction: no, only the sovereign grace of God in Jesus Christ. So while it is true that the unredeemed will is the final cause of its own sinful choices (here Pelagius was right), it is not true that the redeemed will is the final cause of its own holy choices. God's grace is the final cause of these, because God is the *Redeemer* and we are the *redeemed*. But of course, not even here is there any compulsion, any divine tyranny forcing us to be good. In a mysterious way, Augustine argued, God works in the depths of the fallen will by His transforming grace, and changes the will's direction; the unredeemed sinner who was unwilling to obey God or come to Christ becomes, by grace, the redeemed sinner who is willing to obey and to come. In redemption, then, we are still free in the sense of being free from outward compulsion. Grace does not externally compel: it inwardly transforms.

Here Augustine brought another and higher view of freedom into the picture. The best kind of freedom for the will, he said, is not that it should simply enjoy the liberty of being voluntary and free from coercion. Far better is freedom from *sin* — the state of spiritual liberation in which the very idea of choosing the "pleasures" of sin is unthinkable. It is the freedom of loving God so perfectly that our love can do nothing other than love Him, and go on loving Him, and be utterly dead to any thought of loving anything He does not love. This kind of freedom, Augustine said, is enjoyed by the holy angels and the souls of glorified saints in heaven. The Christian on earth does not yet enjoy it (alas, choosing the pleasures of sin is still all too thinkable for us), but the redeemed sinner is at least now on his way to this perfect freedom through the healing grace of Christ. We are no longer in bondage to sin; we have not yet arrived in the fullness of true freedom.

****

Free Will

The importance of the will

The character of the human will is of great significance. For if the will is wrong, these emotions of the soul will be wrong; but if the will is right, these emotions of the soul will be not merely blameless, but even praiseworthy. For the will is in all emotions; indeed, emotions are nothing else than movements of the will! For what are desire and joy, but a will to consent to the things we wish? And what are fear and sadness, but a will to turn away from the things which we do not wish? But when the will's consent takes the form of seeking to possess the things we wish, this is called desire; and when the will's consent takes the form of enjoying the things we wish, this is called joy. Likewise, when we turn with aversion from what we do not wish to happen, this act of will is termed fear; and when we turn away from what has happened against our will, this act of will is called sorrow. And so it is generally, in respect of all that we seek or shun. As a person's will is either attracted or repelled, so it is changed and turned into these different affections.

Therefore the person who lives according to God, and not according to a human outlook, ought to be a lover of good, and therefore a hater of evil. Now, no-one is evil by nature, but whoever is evil is evil by sin. So he who lives according to God ought to cherish towards evil people a perfect kind of hatred; he neither hates the person because of his sin, nor loves the sin because of the person, but hates the sin and loves the person. For the sin being cured, all that ought to be loved, and nothing that ought to be hated, will remain.

City of God, 14:6

We are always free, but not always good

There is always within us a *free* will, but it is not always *good*. For it is either free from the control of righteousness when it serves sin — and then it is an evil will; or else it is free from the control of sin when it serves righteousness — and then it is a good will. But the grace of God is always good; and it is by grace that a human being comes to have a good will, though previously he had an evil one.

On Grace and Free Will, 31

Our wills are not subject to any outward necessity

We sometimes give the name "necessity" to something that is not in our power — something that achieves its effect even though we are unwilling. An example is the necessity of death. But it is manifest that our wills, by which we live uprightly or wickedly, are not under such a necessity; for we do many things which, if we were not willing, we would certainly not do. This is primarily true of the act of willing itself. For if we will, the act of willing *is*; if we do not will, the act of willing is *not*— for we would not *will,* if we were *unwilling!*

However, if we define necessity differently, as when we say, "It is necessary that something be of such or such a nature, or be done in such and such a manner," I cannot see why we should fear that *this* necessity will take away the freedom of our will. For we do not put the life of God or the foreknowledge of God under the rule of necessity if we say, "It is necessary that God must live forever, and foreknow all things." God's power is not diminished, either, when we say that He is "not able" to die or fall into error. For this is impossible to God in such a way that, if it *were* possible for Him to die or fall into error, He would be less powerful than He is. But assuredly He is rightly called all-powerful, though He is not able either die or fall into error. For God is called all-powerful on account of doing what He wills to do, not on account of suffering what He wills not to do (for if that happened to Him, He would by no means be all-powerful). Therefore, there are some things God cannot do for the very reason that He is all-powerful.

So also, when we say, "It is necessary that, when we will, we will by free choice," we affirm what is true beyond doubt, and we do not subject our wills to a necessity that destroys liberty. Our wills, therefore, exist as wills, and themselves do whatever we do by willing, and which would not be done if we were unwilling[1] ...

---

[1] Here is Augustine's understanding of free will. Our wills are free, even as unredeemed sinners, in the sense that our wills are not manipulated or coerced by any external force of necessity. The only "necessity" that binds the human will is the will itself – the internal law of its own being. It is *necessary* that the will should be a will! Therefore, by its very nature, the will is a willing and voluntary thing, acting not out of external compulsion, but out of its own inner spontaneity. This kind of freedom – the freedom of "willingness" – is quite compatible with the will being ceaselessly, unchangingly and spontaneously sinful, and in need of redemption by God's sovereign grace in Christ.

It is not the case, then, that because God *foreknew* what would be in the power of our wills, there is therefore *nothing* in the power of our wills. For He who foreknew this did not foreknow nothing! Moreover, if He who foreknew what would be in the power of our wills did not foreknow nothing, but something, then certainly there is something in the power of our wills, even though He did foreknow it. So our belief in the foreknowledge of God does not take away the freedom of the will, nor does our belief in the freedom of the will deny that God foreknows future things (an ungodly thing to deny!). No, we embrace both free will and God's foreknowledge. We faithfully and sincerely confess both. We confess God's foreknowledge, in order that we may believe rightly; we confess the freedom of the will, in order that we may live rightly. For he lives wrongly who does not believe rightly concerning God. Far be it from us, then, in order to maintain our free will, that we should deny the foreknowledge of God, by Whose help we are or shall be free.

Consequently, it is not in vain that laws are enacted, and that we make use of reproaches, exhortations, praises, and criticisms. For God also foreknew these, and they are of great benefit, even as great as He foreknew that they would be. Prayers, also, are of benefit to obtain those things which God foreknew He would give to those who prayed. Rewards have been appointed for good deeds, and punishments for sins, and justly so. For the reason why a person sins is not because God foreknew he would sin. Indeed, it cannot be doubted that when a person sins, it is the person himself who sins. For God, Whose foreknowledge is infallible, foreknew that not fate, not fortune, nor anything else would sin, but that the person himself would sin. And unless a person *wills* to sin, he does not *sin.* But if a person does *not* will to sin, God foreknew this too.

City of God, 5:10

The Pelagian view of free will

We must resist the Pelagians with the strongest ardour and vigour when they teach that without God's help, the mere power of the human will by itself can achieve perfect righteousness, or advance steadily towards it. If we press them hard for their arrogance in asserting that this can be achieved without God's help, they change their tune, because they realise what an ungodly and intolerable thing they have said. They then argue that God does help us in our striving after righteousness, in this sense: God created us with the choice of free will, and He teaches us how to live by giving us commandments. God assists us (they say) by taking away our ignorance, instructing us in the knowledge of what we should avoid and what we should desire in our actions. In this way, they say, by means of our natural free will which God has given us, we enter on the pathway that is pointed out to us; and by persevering in a righteous and godly life, we deserve to arrive at the blessedness of eternal life.

On the Spirit and the Letter, 4

The Pelagians teach that we can avoid sin by free will, without grace

"First of all," says Celestius, "if someone denies human ability to live a sinless life, we must ask him what sin is in all its forms. Can this sin be avoided? Or is it unavoidable? If it is unavoidable, then it is not sin. If it can be avoided, then a person can live without the sin that can be avoided. Reason and justice prevent us from calling something 'sin' if it cannot in any way be avoided."

Our answer to this is as follows: sin *can* be avoided *if* our corrupted nature is healed by God's grace through our Lord Jesus Christ. For to the degree that our nature is not sound, to that degree it fails to see on account of blindness, or fails to accomplish on account of weakness, what it ought to do. "For the flesh lusts against the Spirit, and the Spirit against the flesh," so that a person does not do the things he wishes (Gal.5:17).

On Human Perfection, 2

Pelagius thinks more highly of free will than he thinks of God!

Pelagius speaks about "being worthy of divine grace by doing the will of God". Perhaps he will explain this as meaning that grace is added to those who believe and lead godly lives, so that they can boldly withstand the tempter. But he will admit, perhaps, that their first reception of grace was to *enable* them to do the will of God. Well, if he explains it like this, let us consider some other words of Pelagius on this subject: "The person who hastens to the Lord, and desires to be governed by Him, who makes his own will depend on God's, who unites himself so closely to the Lord as to become one spirit with him (in the apostle's words, 1 Cor.6:17), does all this by nothing else except the freedom of his will." Behold what a great result he states here to have been accomplished merely by free will! Indeed, he supposes that we can unite ourselves to God *without the help of God!* That is the force of his words, "by nothing else except the freedom of his will".

According to Pelagius, then, we unite ourselves to the Lord without His help, and then on account of this we become worthy of receiving His assistance. For he goes on to say: "Whoever makes a right use of his free will entirely surrenders himself to God, and completely puts to death his own will, so that he can say with Paul, 'It is no longer I that live, but Christ lives in me' (Gal.2:20). Yes, he places his heart in the hand of God, so that God turns it wherever He pleases."

Well, the help of God's grace is indeed great, so that He turns our heart in whatever direction He pleases. But according to the foolish opinion of Pelagius, no matter how great God's help may be, we become worthy of it all at the point when — without any assistance beyond the freedom of our own will — we hasten to the Lord, desire His guidance and direction, make our will depend entirely on His, and become one spirit with Him by close union with Him. And according to Pelagius, all these vast endeavours of goodness we accomplish (believe it or not) simply by the liberty of our own free will! Then, because we have already achieved these worthy efforts, we thereby secure God's grace, so that He turns our hearts wherever He pleases.

Well now, how can this be "grace" when it is not given freely? How can it be "grace" if it is given in payment of a debt? How does this fit in with Paul's teaching? "It is not of yourselves, it is the gift of God: not of works, in case anyone should boast" (Eph.2:8-9). Again, "If it is by grace, then it is no longer by works, otherwise grace is no longer grace" (Rom.11:6). How can this be true, if we do such good works before we receive grace, and those works secure grace for us? Under these circumstances, there is no free gift from God, only the paying of a well-deserved reward! Is it really the case that in order to receive God's help, people run to God *without* God's help? Do we unite ourselves to God without God's help, in order that we may then receive His help after we have entered into union with Him? What greater gift, what equal gift, could grace itself give a person, if he has — already, without grace — been able to make himself one spirit with the Lord, by no other power than his own free will?

On the Grace of Christ and Original Sin, 1:24

The grace given to Adam's will in paradise

The first man did not possess that grace by which he would never will to be evil. But certainly Adam had grace, in which — if only he willed to abide in it — he would never be evil. And he also had the grace without which he could not be good by free will alone, and yet which by free will he could forsake. God, therefore, did not choose that even Adam should be without His grace, which He left in Adam's free will; for free will is sufficient for evil, but is too little for good, unless it is aided by Almighty Goodness. And if Adam had not forsaken that gracious assistance of his free will, he would always have been good; but he forsook it, and so he was forsaken. For such was the nature of the help, that Adam could forsake it when he would, and could continue in it if he would. But Adam did not have such help that would effectively bring it about that he actually would continue in grace.

This is the grace which was given to the first Adam; but more powerful than this is the grace of the second Adam. For the first grace is that by which it is accomplished that a person *may* have righteousness *if he wills to have it.* But the second grace can do more than this, since by this grace it is even accomplished that a person *actually* wills, and wills so much, and loves with such ardour, that by the will of the Spirit he overcomes the will of the flesh that lusts in opposition to it.

Still, it was no small grace in Adam by which the power of free will was demonstrated. For Adam was so assisted that without this assistance he could not continue in good; but he could forsake this assistance if he would.

On Rebuke and Grace, 31

Free will in unfallen Adam and the angels

At that time [before the fall], God had given to man a good will. God had created him in that state of will, since God created man upright. God had also given help, without which man could not continue in goodness even if he would; but God left it in the power of man's free will to choose to continue in goodness. Man could therefore continue if he would, because the help was present by which man could (and without which he could not) perseveringly hold fast the good *if he would.*

But it is absolutely man's fault that he willed not to continue in good. It would have been Adam's merit if he had willed to continue, as indeed the holy angels did. For the holy angels, when others fell by free will, themselves stood firm by the same free will, and thus deserved to receive the due reward of this continuance. The reward was such a fullness of blessing that would give them the fullest certainty of always abiding in it. If, however, this help [of grace] had been lacking, either to angel or to man when they were first created, it would not have been their fault that they fell, because the help would have been lacking without which they could not continue in good. For their nature was created such that, without the divine help, it could not abide in good even if it would.

On Rebuke and Grace, 32

The human will in innocence and in redemption

God would have been willing to preserve even the first man in that state of salvation in which he was created. After Adam had begotten sons, God would have removed him at a suitable time, without the intervention of death, to a better place, where he would have been not only free from sin, but free even from the desire of sinning. God would have been willing to do this, if He had foreseen that Adam would have the constant will to persevere in the state of innocence in which he was created. But since God foresaw that Adam would make a bad use of his free will, that is, would sin, God arranged His own designs with a view to do good to man even in his sinfulness. Thus the good will of the Almighty would not be cancelled out by the evil will of man, but be fulfilled in spite of it.

Now it was expedient that man should at first be created, in such a way that it was in man's power both to will what was right, and to will what was wrong. He would be rewarded if he willed the former, and punished if he willed the latter. But in the future life, it will not be in our power to will evil; and yet this will constitute no restriction on the freedom of our will. On the contrary, the human will shall be much *more* free when it is completely impossible for it to be the slave of sin! We would never think of blaming the will, or saying that it wasn't a genuine will, or that it was not really free, when we desire happiness so strongly that we shrink from misery, and indeed find it utterly impossible to do otherwise. As, then, the soul even now finds it impossible to desire misery, so in the future life it will be utterly impossible for it to desire sin.

However, God's arrangement was not to be broken, according to which He willed to show how good is a rational being who can refrain from sin, and yet how much better is one who cannot sin at all. Likewise, that was an inferior sort of immortality, and yet it was immortality, when it was possible for human beings to avoid death; but there is reserved for the future a more perfect immortality, when it will be impossible for human beings to die. The first kind of immortality, humanity lost through the exercise of free will; the second kind we will obtain through grace, whereas, if we had not sinned, we would have obtained it by deserving it. Even in that case, however, there could have been no merit without grace! For even though the mere exercise of human free will was enough to bring in sin, free will would not have been enough for maintaining human nature in righteousness, unless God had assisted Adam's will by imparting to it a portion of His own unchangeable goodness.

It is within a human being's power to die whenever he will (for, not to speak of other means, anyone can put an end to himself by simply abstaining from food). But the human will by itself cannot preserve life in the absence of food and the other means of life. Likewise, Adam in paradise was able by his own mere will, simply by abandoning righteousness, to destroy himself. But to maintain a life of righteousness would have been too much for Adam's will, unless it had been sustained by the Creator's power. After the fall, however, a more abundant exercise of God's mercy was needed, because the human will itself had to be set free from the bondage in which it was held by sin and death. And the will does not owe its freedom in any degree to itself, but solely to the grace of God which comes by faith in Jesus Christ. Thus our will, through which we accept all the other gifts of God that lead us on to His eternal gift, is itself prepared by the Lord, as the Scripture says (Proverbs 8:35, Septuagint).

Enchiridion, 104-106

Some crucial distinctions

We must consider with diligence and attention in what respect these pairs differ from each other: (i) to be able not to sin, and not to be able to sin; (ii) to be able not to die, and not to be able to die; (iii) to be able not to forsake good, and not to be able to forsake good. For the first man was able not to sin, was able not to die, was able not to forsake good. But are we to say that he who had such a free will could not sin? Or that he to whom it was said, "If you sin you shall die the death," could not die? Or that he could not forsake good, when he would indeed forsake good by sinning, and so die? Therefore the first liberty of the will was to be able not to sin; but the last will be much greater, not to be able to sin. The first immortality was to be able not to die; but the last will be much greater, not to be able to die. The first was the power of perseverance, to be able not to forsake good; but the last will be the blessedness of perseverance, not to be able to forsake good. The last blessings will be preferable and better! But were those first ones, therefore, no blessings at all, or trifling ones?

On Rebuke and Grace, 33

The bondage of the fallen will

But this part of the human race to which God has promised pardon and a share in His eternal kingdom — can they be restored through the virtue of their own works? God forbid. For what good work can a lost human being perform, except to the extent that he has been delivered from destruction? Can sinners do anything good by the free determination of their own will? Again I say, God forbid. For it was by the evil use of his free will that man destroyed both it and himself. For, as a man who kills himself must, of course, be alive when he kills himself, but after he has killed himself ceases to live, and cannot restore himself to life; so, when man by his own free will sinned, then sin being victorious over him, the freedom of his will was lost. "For whatever overcomes a man, by this he is brought into bondage" (2 Pet.2:19). This is the judgment of the apostle Peter, which is certainly true.

So what kind of liberty, I ask, can the bond-slave possess, except when it pleases him to sin? For a slave is *freely* in bondage if he does the will of his master with pleasure. Accordingly, he who is the servant of sin is free to sin. But he will not be free to do right, until he is set free from sin, and begins to be the servant of righteousness. And this is true liberty, for he now has pleasure in the righteous deed; and it is at the same time a holy bondage, for he is obedient to the will of God. But what is the origin of this liberty to do right for the person who is in bondage and sold under sin? He must be redeemed by Him who has said, "If the Son sets you free, you shall be free indeed" (Jn.8:36). Before this redemption is accomplished in a person, when he is not yet free to do what is right, how can he talk of the freedom of his will and his good works? He can do so only if he is inflated by that foolish pride of boasting which the apostle restrains when he says, "By grace you are saved, through faith" (Eph.2:8).

Enchiridion, 30

Sin has robbed us of our freedom to be good

"The next question that requires a solution," says Celestius, "is this: by what means does it come about that humanity is sinful? Is it by necessity of nature, or by freedom of choice? If it is by necessity of nature, humanity cannot be blamed for it; if it is by freedom of choice, then who gave us this freedom of choice? God, of course. Well, God's gifts are certainly good. No-one disputes this. But how can human freedom be good, if it is more prone to evil than to good? And it is more prone to evil than to good, if by means of this freedom a human being can sin, but cannot be without sin."

The answer is this: humanity sinned through its freedom of choice. But this sin was followed by the punishment of corruption, so that human freedom gave birth to necessity. That is why faith cries out to God, "Bring me out of my necessities" (Ps.25:17, Vulgate — psalm 24, according to the Vulgate's numbering). With these necessities laid upon us, we are unable to understand what we desire; or else we are not strong enough to accomplish what we have come to desire and understand. Now it is precisely liberty that the Liberator promises to believers. He says, "If the Son sets you free, you shall be free indeed" (Jn.8:36). Human nature has been conquered by the sin into which it fell by its own will, and has lost its liberty. As another Scripture says, "For whatever overcomes a man, by this he is brought into bondage" (2 Pet.2:19).

Therefore, just as "those who are well have no need of a physician, but those who are sick" (Matt.9:12), so likewise it is not the free who need the Deliverer, but only the enslaved. That is why believers cry with joy to Him over their deliverance: "You have saved my soul from the straits of necessity!" (Ps.31:7, Vulgate — or in the Vulgate's reckoning, Ps.30:8). For true liberty is also real health, and this would never have been lost if the will had remained good. But because the will has sinned, a harsh necessity of sinning will pursue the sinner, until his sickness is completely healed. When his freedom is fully regained, he will enjoy a permanent will to live happily, and a voluntary and happy necessity of living virtuously and never sinning.

On Human Perfection, 9

Grace doesn't just make it "easier" for free will to obey

The grace of God, by which "His love is poured out in our hearts by the Holy Spirit Who was given to us" (Rom.5:5) – this grace must be truly confessed. The person confessing it must show his firm belief that no goodness at all, no godliness or real holiness, can be accomplished without grace. The grace I mean is what Paul refers to when he says, "The love of God has been poured into our hearts by the Holy Spirit Who was given to us" (Rom.5:5). Pelagius does not confess grace in this way. He shows clearly enough what he thinks of it when he says, "Grace is bestowed so that what God commands may be more easily fulfilled." Of course, that means that even without grace, God's commands can be fulfilled, although less "easily"!

In a book he addressed to a certain godly virgin, there is a passage where Pelagius plainly shows what he believes on this subject. He speaks of "our deserving the grace of God, and by the Holy Spirit's help resisting the evil spirit more easily". Why did he insert that phrase, "more easily"? Wasn't it true enough to say, "and by the Holy Spirit's help resisting the evil spirit"? Who can fail to see what harm he has done by inserting "more easily"? Of course, he wants people to think that the powers of our nature are so great (he is always in a hurry to exalt the powers of human nature), that even without the help of the Holy Spirit the evil spirit can be resisted — less easily, maybe, but still resisted to some degree.

Again, in the first part of his **Defence of the Freedom of the Will**, Pelagius says: "It is true, we have within us a free will, strong and steadfast against sinning, which the Creator has implanted in human nature universally. But even so, by God's indescribable goodness, we are further defended by His daily help." Who needs God's help, if free will is so strong and so steadfast against sinning?

On the Grace of Christ and Original Sin, 1:27-29

God's commands do not prove that we can obey them by our natural free will

"But," they say, "when it is said, 'If you believe, you shall be saved,' one of these things is required — the other is offered. What is required is in *our* power; what is offered is in *God's*." Why are not *both* in God's power — what He commands *and* what He offers? After all, we ask Him to *give* what He *commands*! Believers ask that their faith may be increased; they ask on behalf of those who do not believe, that faith may be given to them. Therefore, both in its increase and in its beginnings, faith is the gift of God. As for "If you believe, you shall be saved," this is meant in the same way that it is said, "If by the Spirit you mortify the deeds of the flesh, you shall live" (Rom.8:13). For in this case too, one thing is required, the other is offered. It is said, "If by the Spirit you shall mortify the deeds of the flesh, you shall live." Therefore, it is *required* that we mortify the deeds of the flesh, but it is *offered* that we may live.

Is it, then, fitting for us to say that to mortify the deeds of the flesh is *not* a gift of God? Shall we fail to confess it to be a gift of God, merely because we hear that it is *required* of us, with the offer of life as a reward if we do it? How shocking that those who claim to be the partakers and champions of grace should approve of this! This is the damnable error of the Pelagians, whose mouths the apostle immediately stopped when he added, "For as many as are led by the Spirit of God, they are the sons of God" (Rom.8:14) — in case we should believe that we mortify the deeds of the flesh by our own spirit, rather than by God's Spirit. And moreover, he was speaking of this Spirit of God in that verse where he says, "But one and the self-same Spirit works all these gifts, distributing to everyone what is His own, as He wills" (1 Cor.12:11). Among all these gifts, as you know, he also named faith. Therefore, although it is the *gift of God* to mortify the deeds of the flesh, yet mortification is still *required of us*, and life is set before us as a reward. So likewise faith is the gift of God; yet faith is still required of us, when it is said, "If you believe, you shall be saved," and salvation proposed to us as a reward.

On the Predestination of the Saints, 22

No-one is forced to sin

What your correspondent and others say is not true. We do not teach that "everyone is forced into sin," as if they were unwilling, "by the necessity of the flesh." If someone is mature enough to exercise the choice of his own mind, he is held captive in sin *by his own will*. By his own will he is rushed along from one sin to another. For even Satan, who persuades and deceives sinners, does not act in them except by getting them to sin by their own wills, either through ignorance of the truth, or through a positive relish for evil, or through both at once, both blindness and weakness.

So the human will is free — to do evil, because it takes pleasure in evil. But it is not free to do good, because it has not been set free. No-one wills anything good unless he is helped by Him Who cannot will anything evil — that is, by the grace of God through Jesus Christ our Lord. For "whatever is not from faith is sin" (Rom.14:23).

And so the good will which withdraws itself from sin is the believing will; for, "The just shall live by faith" (Rom.1:17). And the function of faith is to believe in Christ. And no-one can believe in Christ — that is, come to Him — unless this is given to him (Jn.6:65). No-one, therefore can have a righteous will, unless he has received the true gratuitous grace from above, without any virtue of his own going beforehand.

Against Two Letters of the Pelagians, 1:17

Free to do evil — set free to do good

In defending free will, the Pelagians are quick to put their confidence in it for achieving righteousness, rather than trusting in God's help. They glory in themselves, not in the Lord. Besides, which of us will say that by the sin of the first man, free will perished out of the human race? Freedom perished through sin, true enough. But it was the kind of freedom Adam had in paradise, that is, the freedom to attain to perfect righteousness with immortality. The loss of this kind of freedom is why human nature needs divine grace, for the Lord said, "If the Son sets you free, you shall be free indeed" (Jn.8:36) — that is, free to live a good and righteous life.

Now, free will in the sinner survives to this extent: by means of free will, everyone sins, especially those who sin with relish and with a love of sin. What they are pleased to do gives them pleasure. So Paul says, "When you were slaves of sin, you were free in regard to righteousness" (Rom.6:20). See, Paul shows that sinners cannot be slaves to sin, except by another kind of freedom. They are free *from righteousness* by the choice of their wills; but they do not become free *from sin* except by the grace of the Saviour.

For this reason, the admirable teacher made this distinction: "For when you were slaves of sin, you were free in regard to righteousness. What fruit did you then have in the things of which you are now ashamed? For the end of those things is death. But now, having been set free from sin, and having become slaves of God, you have your fruit to holiness, and the end, everlasting life" (Rom.6:20-23). He says that they are "free" from righteousness, not "set free" from it. Yet he does not say they were "free" from sin, but "set free" from sin. If he had merely said "free", they might have attributed this to themselves; so he quite deliberately says "set free", thus referring their freedom to what the Lord said: "If the Son sets you free, you shall be free indeed" (Jn.8:36). The children of men do not live good lives unless they are made into the children of God. So why does Julian want to say that the power of living a good life belongs to free will, when this power is given only by God's grace? As the Gospel says, "As many as received Him, to them He gave the power to become children of God" (Jn.1:12).

Perhaps the Pelagians will respond thus: believers may indeed have "the power to become the children of God", but they deserve to receive this power because they first "received Him" by free will without the help of grace. (This is the purpose of their efforts to destroy grace — so that they can argue it is given according to what we deserve.) They want to split up the statement of the Gospel, so as to refer to human goodness the part that says, "as many as received Him". As for what follows, "to them He gave the power to become the children of God" — here, they say this grace is not given freely, but as a reward to this prior goodness.

Yet if we ask them what "received Him" means, will they say anything else but "believed in Him"? Well, in order that they may know that faith too comes from grace, let them read what Paul says: "Not in any way terrified by your adversaries, which is to them a proof of destruction, but to you of salvation, and that from God. For to you it has been granted on Christ's behalf, not only to believe in Him, but also to suffer for His sake" (Phil.1:28-29). Clearly Paul says that both things were "granted". Let them read what Paul also said: "Peace be to the brothers, and love with faith, from God the Father and the Lord Jesus Christ" (Eph.6:23). Let them also read what the Lord Himself said: "No-one can come to Me unless the Father Who sent Me draws him" (Jn.6:44).

Against Two Letters of the Pelagians, 1:5-6.

The practice of prayer is inconsistent with relying on free will

Our heavenly Master says: "Watch and pray, lest you enter into temptation" (Matt.26:41). So let everyone, when fighting against his own sinful desire, pray that he may not enter into temptation — that is, that he may not be drawn aside and enticed by it. But he does not "enter into temptation" if he conquers his sinful desire by a good will. However, the human will is not equal to the task, unless the Lord grants it victory in answer to its prayer that it may not enter into temptation. What could provide clearer evidence of God's grace than His answering our prayers in any such request we make? If our Saviour had only said, "Watch lest you enter into temptation," He would appear to have done nothing further than warn the human will. But since He added those words, "and pray", He showed that God helps us not to enter into temptation. These words are addressed to our free will: "My son, do not despise the chastening of the Lord" (Prov.3:11). But then the Lord says: "I have prayed for you that your faith may not fail" (Lk.22:32). You see, then, that we are assisted by grace, so that God's commands to our wills may not be useless.

On Grace and Free Will, 9

The Lord's prayer shows that we must not trust in free will

There are some people who presume so much on the free choice of the human will, they think the will need not sin, and that we require no divine assistance. They regard this choice of free will as belonging absolutely to our nature. An inevitable consequence of this is that we should not pray, "Lead us not into temptation" (Matt.6:13). That is, we should not ask *God* to save us from temptation, either when it deceives us and takes us by surprise in our ignorance, or when it pushes and urges us in our weakness. But how harmful, how destructive, how contrary to our salvation in Christ, not to rely on the Lord for such a blessing! How violently opposed to the religion in which we are instructed, and to the piety by which we worship God, if we thought that the petition "Lead us not into temptation" had been so emptily and uselessly inserted into the Lord's prayer! I cannot express my horror at such at idea.

On the Merits and Forgiveness of Sins, 2:2

If we can be righteous by free will, Christ died for nothing

If Adam is called the author of all sins that followed his own, because he was the first sinner of the human race, then why isn't Abel (rather than Christ) placed at the head of all the righteous, since he was the first righteous man? I am not referring here to the fate of infants dying in infancy. Let us take the case of a young man, or an old man, who has died in a country where he could not hear about Christ. Well, could such a man have become righteous by nature and by free will, or couldn't he? If the Pelagians argue that he could, then see what it is to "make the cross of Christ of no effect" (1 Cor.1:17). This is what we do, if we argue that apart from the cross, anyone can be justified by the law of nature and the power of his own will. We must also say then that "Christ died in vain" (Gal.2:21), since everyone might have achieved righteousness even if Christ had never died! And if people are unrighteous, it would (on this argument) be merely because they didn't want to be righteous, not because they were unable to be.

On Nature and Grace, 10

Chapter 3

Law and Grace

Do not be proud therefore, do not presume on your own strength, which is nothing; and you will understand why a good law was given by a good God, though it cannot give life. For the law was given for this purpose, that it might make you a little one instead of great — that it might show you that you had no strength to perform the law by your own power — and that thus, lacking help and destitute, you might fly to grace, saying, "Have mercy upon me, O Lord, for I am weak."

Augustine, *Expositions of the Psalms, 119:129*

"What, then, was the purpose of the law?" (Gal.3:19) The apostle Paul's question has often troubled the Church. So has Paul's answer — or what people have thought his answer was. I remember once reading a Christian publication which defined a Christian as "someone who is 100% committed to God", or something of the sort. It's the kind of loose statement that might make a superficial appeal to the young and the idealistic, especially if they think sin means killing people and virtue means smiling and singing choruses about loving each other. There is only one problem: the definition is pure Pelagianism, and if it were correct, there has never been a true Christian on the face of the earth. According to Scripture, sin actually means the slightest deviation from God's perfect law, even in my secret thoughts, feelings and desires. "From within, from out of the heart, come evil thoughts" (Mk.7:21). "There is no-one who does not sin" (1 Kings 8:46). "Cursed is everyone who does not abide by all things written in the book of the law, to perform them" (Gal.3:10). So having a 100% commitment to God means sinless perfection — absolute and unceasing ethical purity, in every single thought, every single feeling, every single desire, every single word, every single action....

It is slightly self-defeating to define Christians in such a way that they are defined out of existence. Or at least, defined out of earthly existence. The only "100% saints" are those in heaven, "the spirits of the righteous made perfect" (Heb.12:23). On earth they were "righteous" — justified by faith and in process of being sanctified — but not yet perfect. Far from perfect. "We all stumble in many ways" (Jam.3:2). Romantic idealism about the Christian life, as Augustine endlessly urged, is both harmful and stupid. If taken seriously, it reduces us to Soren Kierkegaard's scornful verdict that "Christianity does not exist." And surely then we can know that it is time to come out of the ivory tower, take off the rose-tinted glasses, and submit to a healthy, salty dose of biblical realism about Christian human nature.

Some, then, misunderstand the law — God's moral and spiritual requirements of obedience and holiness — as a way of life that is perfectly within the Christian's grasp. On the other side of the fence, there are Christians who will tell us that God's law is quite irrelevant to the true believer. Many of our ills, they declare, can be traced to our foolish attempts to take the law as a guide for how God wants His redeemed people to live. We must forget the law, forget the commandments, forget the tyrannous Old Testament legalism of "duty" and "ought"; we must simply wallow in New Testament grace. Comprehend this, and the secret of joy and victory is ours! What such purveyors of secrets about how to be a victorious Christian do not seem to realise is that they are rejecting the central Christian tradition concerning the law's positive function in the believer's life, a tradition which survived more or less unmolested until the birth of dispensationalism in the 19th century.[1]

With some people effectively defining Christians out of existence in their eagerness to exalt obedience to God's holy law, and others defining the law out of existence in their eagerness to exalt the Christian's experience of God's holy grace, it is wonderfully refreshing to turn to the sanity of a teacher like Augustine, who finds a home for both holy law and holy grace in the life of the real flesh-and-blood Christian man and woman.

The Pelagian view of the law had at least the merit of simplicity. God had given the law to be obeyed. If we obey it, we tread the path to heaven. In fact, the law is our guide to heaven. The more we sin, the more we need the law to point us back on the right way. If we speak of God's "grace", that means the help He gives our free will to obey Him; and that help is — the law! What about the gospel? Well, the good news that comes to us in Jesus Christ is that He is our perfect example of how to obey God's law. What an inspiration His example is to our faltering wills! And Christ's *teaching* helps us to obey even more easily, by making clear how enormous the stakes are: heaven if we get it right, hell if we go wrong. What good news!

Actually, it's catastrophically bad news, said Augustine. *No-one* will ever get to heaven this way. Such a view of the law would be fine if we ourselves were fine, if human nature were fine. But human nature is corrupt. Our wills are in deep wilful bondage to original sin. It is only because Pelagius disbelieves in original sin that he can take so rosy a view of the law as a route to heaven, so starry-eyed a view of our ability to obey it. The awful reality, maintained Augustine, is that putting the law together with a fallen human sinner is a bit like putting a beautiful woman in the same room as a chronic seducer to teach him morals. She will merely arouse his lawless desires. The more forbidden the pleasure, the more desirable it becomes to the

---

[1] Whoever dreamt up the "rapture" of the Church obviously decided to give it a trial run on the Ten Commandments first.

sinful heart. The law cannot save. Obedience to God's commands is not the highway to heaven.

Why then has God given the law? First and foremost, Augustine argued, *to reveal to the sinner the true extent of his corruption.* By setting forth God's holy commands in all their purity and clarity, the law shows what God requires of us; by stirring up and inciting our lawless passions, the law shows us just how fallen we are, how exceedingly sinful is our sin if it can respond so sinfully to God's holy commands; by declaring the full measure of God's holy hatred for sin, His righteous resolve to punish it in hell, the law makes us sigh and pine and cry for a Saviour. Who will deliver me from the plague of my sinful heart and the penalty it so richly deserves? Thanks be to God — through Jesus Christ our Lord!

The grace of the gospel, Augustine said, is not just the law in technicolour. The law *reveals* what is holy and righteous and good. But the law does not get down inside my will. It cannot take away my heart of stone with its "Do this" and "Do not do that." The law is not transforming, regenerating, sanctifying. But this is precisely what gospel grace is! The grace of God in Jesus Christ gets right inside me, down into the deepest depths of my fallen free will, and changes me from within. Grace means a gift freely given; and Christ's gift, the gift of all gifts, is the Holy Spirit Himself, the third person of the Trinity, to dwell in my heart and make me new and beautiful on the inside by forming Christ in me. So gospel grace works on a totally different principle from the law. The law demands; grace empowers. The law reveals a standard of righteousness outside us; grace inscribes it on our hearts. The law inflames and provokes our sinful passions; grace quenches them and puts them to death. The law condemns us to hell for our disobedience; grace rescues us from hell by the forgiveness of sins, purchased for us and applied to us by Christ crucified and risen.

So who is the true Christian? Not the moral and spiritual superman or superwoman beloved of Pelagius — they exist only in their own imaginations, because they do not really know what sin is, never having understood the depth of the law's demand. No, said Augustine, the true Christian is the imperfect, stumbling believer who "in all his sins accuses himself, and in all his good works praises God, counts himself a disgrace and gives to God the glory, and receives from God both the forgiveness of sins and a love of doing what is right" **(Against Two Letters of the Pelagians, 3:14)**.

Is there then any place for the law in a Christian's walk with God? Most certainly, answered Augustine. Although the law cannot give life, *life-giving grace puts this very law in our hearts*. Grace does not liberate us by giving us a license to be unholy; it liberates us *from* unholiness and inspires us to take pleasure in God's holy law. "Grace makes us lovers of the law," Augustine declared (**On Grace and Free Will, 38**). After all, the problem was never in the law, but in us. When God's free gift of the Holy Spirit gets to work inside us, He does for us what the law itself could never do, and that is to make us delight in God, delight in His holiness, delight in His holy commands. We still sin and are not yet perfected; but now, through the Spirit's indwelling, the basic direction of our wills is *towards* lawful obedience, not away from it. Carefree sinning against a law we hated is replaced by a lifelong struggle to obey a law we now love. And Augustine was piercingly clear that the law which the grace-justified believer seeks to obey is the Ten Commandments. (He had some sensational wobbles about the Sabbath, but ultimately held that this too retains its relevance to the New Testament Christian, as we shall see.) "Surely no-one will doubt," Augustine declared, "that God's law was necessary, not just for the people of that time [the Old Testament], but is also necessary for us today, for the right ordering of our life" (**Against Two Letters of the Pelagians, 3:10**).

Finally, Augustine protested passionately against the Pelagian view that there were different ways of salvation, depending on the historical period in which people lived. The Pelagians were the original dispensationalists, and Augustine was not impressed. "We must not therefore divide the times," he argued, "as Pelagius and his disciples do. They say that people first lived righteously by nature, then under the law, thirdly under grace" (**On the Grace of Christ and Original Sin, 2:30**). Of course, in one sense the Pelagians did not "divide the times" at all; they held that in all three "dispensations", it was really *law* that saved. Nature, law and grace were three manifestations of the one way of life — "Obey and live." Yet in another way, Pelagians did truly divide the times by restricting faith in Christ to the gospel dispensation. Augustine countered this by arguing that Christ-centred faith has always been the core and the heart of salvation from the moment Adam fell, up to the end of time. If Adam and Eve were saved, it was not by striving to obey the law in the power of free will; it must have been by faith in the Saviour promised to them by God before they were exiled from Eden — "the

Seed of the Woman shall bruise the head of the serpent" (Gen.3:15). Likewise Enoch, Noah, Abraham and all the patriarchs until Moses and the giving of the Ten Commandments: all saved by faith in the coming Seed. Likewise all godly Jews from Moses until John the Baptist: all saved by their forward-looking faith in the Messiah yet to come.

Augustine's point was that there is only one way of salvation, the way of faith in the Son of God Who destroys the works of the devil, and that there is therefore only one Church, only one body of the redeemed, all bound together in one grace, one gospel, one Mediator, the Lord Jesus Christ. The distinction between law and grace does not mean different justifications, different Churches, different classes of citizen in the Kingdom. From Adam to the world's end, everyone in heaven has arrived there by the same route: faith in the blood of the Lamb Who sits on the throne. There will be no conversations in glory in which one says, "I got here by the law of nature," and another, "I got here by way of Mount Sinai," and another, "I got here by the gospel," and another, "I got here by sinless perfection." All will be united in one theme: "Worthy is the Lamb that was slain, for with Your blood You purchased us for God from every tribe and tongue and people and nation." And all God's redeemed people, and the angels too, will shout "Amen!" throughout the ages of eternity.

****

Law and Grace

(a) The true function of the law

Mere knowledge of the law edifies no-one

Those Pelagian enemies of grace never try to lay subtler snares for a more vehement opposition to grace than when they praise the law (which is of course praiseworthy). But by their different turns of phrase, and various words, in all their arguments, they wish to say that the law *is* grace! For them, grace means the knowledge with which the Lord God helps us, by which we can *know* what our duty is. The true meaning of grace, however, is the love that God breathes into us, which enables us with a holy delight to *carry out* the duty that we know. For without love, the knowledge of the law does not build us up — it puffs us up. The apostle Paul quite openly says this: "Knowledge puffs up, but love builds up" (2 Cor.3:6). This saying of Paul is like the other one where he says, "The letter kills, but the Spirit gives life" (2 Cor.3:6). "Knowledge puffs up" corresponds to "the letter kills"; "love builds up" corresponds to "the Spirit gives life." For "the love of God has been poured out in our hearts by the Holy Spirit Who was given to us" (Rom.5:5).

So then, the mere knowledge of the law makes only a proud sinner [who thinks he can obey]. But by the gift of love, the sinner delights to be a doer of the law. We do not, then, cancel the law through faith; no, we establish the law, which by terrifying leads to faith. "The law brings about wrath" (Rom.4:15), and frightens the sinner, so that he turns to the fulfilment of the law's righteousness through Jesus Christ our Lord. In this way God's mercy bestows grace on the sinner.

Against Two Letters of the Pelagians, 4:11

By "grace", Pelagius means — the law!

Who can help wishing that Pelagius would tell us what he means by "grace"? Indeed, we have the strongest reason for desiring him to tell us what he means when he says, "grace does not consist merely in the law." But while we are hanging in suspense, please notice what else Pelagius has to tell us. "God helps us," he says, "by His teaching and revelation, when He opens the eyes of our hearts. He helps us by directing us to the future, so that we will not be overwhelmed by the present. He helps us by pointing out the devil's snares. He helps us by enlightening us with the manifold and indescribable gift of heavenly grace." Pelagius then finishes off his statement with a sort of self-vindication: "Does the man who says all this seem to you to be an enemy of grace? Does he not acknowledge both human free will and God's grace?"

And yet after all this, he has *still* not got beyond his extolling of the law and of teaching! Pelagius endlessly drives home the idea that "law and teaching" is the meaning of the grace that helps us. So he bolsters the idea he started with: "We admit that grace consists in the help of God." And "God's help" he defines as various incentives to right living: teaching, revelation, the opening of the heart's eyes, the unveiling of the future, the pointing out of the devil's wiles, the enlightenment of our minds by the manifold and indescribable gift of heavenly grace. All this, of course, so that we can learn the commands and promises of God. But what else is all this except to define God's grace as "law and teaching"? ...

In other passages, Pelagius asserts that a good will is formed within us, not by God's help, but from ourselves. Then he asks himself the following question from Paul's letter to the Philippians: "How is this consistent with the apostle's words, 'It is God Who works in you both to will and to do'" (Phil.2:13)? Then, to try to get around Paul's words, which he sees are flatly contradictory to his own theory, Pelagius says: "God works in us to will what is good and holy by rousing us from earthly desires and our love of the present world, to which we are devoted like senseless animals. And he rouses us by showing us the greatness of future glory and the promise of its rewards. By revealing wisdom to us, He stirs up our sluggish will to a longing for God, and thus persuades us to embrace everything that is good."

Now, what could be plainer than this? When Pelagius talks about the "grace" of God that "works within us to will what is good", all he means is "law and teaching"! For it is in the law and the teaching of the holy Scriptures that future glory is promised, along with its great rewards. "Teaching" also takes in the revealing of wisdom, and the directing of our wills to everything that is good. And if there seems to be a difference between "teaching" and "persuading" (or rather "exhorting"), even this is really part of "teaching", as we find it in the various discourses and letters of Scripture. For holy Scripture both teaches and exhorts; and in the process of teaching and exhorting, there is room for our own human work.

But we wish that Pelagius would at some point confess that grace does not merely *promise* future glory in all its greatness. No, grace also makes us *believe* in that glory and *hope* for it. We also want him to admit that grace does not just *reveal* wisdom, but also makes us *love* it. We desire him to acknowledge that grace does not just *recommend* everything that is good, but also *presses* it upon us until we *accept* it. For not everyone has faith when they hear the Lord in the Scriptures promising the kingdom of heaven. And not everyone is persuaded when they are counselled to come to Him Who says, "Come to Me, all you who labour" (Matt.11:28). But those who do have faith are those whom He has persuaded to come to Him. Christ taught this very clearly when He said, "No-one can come to Me unless the Father Who sent Me draws him" (Jn.6:44). And a little afterwards, speaking of unbelievers, He says: "Therefore I have said to you that no-one can come to Me unless it has been granted to him by My Father" (Jn.6:65). This is the grace which Pelagius ought to acknowledge, if he wishes not just to be called a Christian, but actually to be one!

On the Grace of Christ and Original Sin, 1:8 and 11.

Justification by the law is impossible

"But," the Pelagians say, "we do praise God as the Author of our righteousness, because He gave the law by whose teaching we have learned how we should live." They are paying no attention to Scripture: "By the deeds of the law, no flesh will be justified in His sight" (Rom.3:20). Justification by the law may be possible in the sight of human beings, but not in the sight of God Who looks into our very heart and inmost will. There, He sees that although the person who fears the law keeps a certain command, he would still rather do something else if it were allowed!

Some people will try to escape the force of Paul's teaching here by arguing that "the law" Paul mentions is the *ceremonial* law of the Old Testament, which contains many commands in the symbolic form of rituals, such as fleshly circumcision which infants were commanded to receive on the eighth day after birth. This interpretation is impossible; for after saying that no flesh will be justified in God's sight by the law, Paul immediately adds, "for by the law is the knowledge of sin" (Rom.3:20). Paul is speaking about that law of which he later declares, "I would not have known sin except through the law. For I would not have known covetousness unless the law had said, You shall not covet" (Rom.7:7). What does that mean, except that "by the law is the knowledge of sin"?

On the Spirit and the Letter, 14

The law cannot confer life

The Pelagians say, "We confess that even the old law, according to the apostle Paul, is holy and just and good, and that this could confer eternal life on those who kept its commandments, and lived righteously by faith, like the prophets and patriarchs and all the saints." By these words, very craftily expressed, they praise the law in opposition to grace. For certainly that law, although it was just and holy and good, could not confer eternal life on any of those men of God. It was faith in Christ that gave them life. For this faith works by love, not according to the letter that kills, but according to the Spirit that gives life.

In relation to this grace of God, the law was a kind of schoolmaster, leading people by deterring them from transgression, that so that they might arrive at the salvation which the law could not itself confer. The Pelagians may say, "the law was able to confer eternal life on the prophets and patriarchs, and all saints who kept its commandments." But the apostle Paul replies, "If righteousness comes through the law, then Christ died in vain" (Gal.2:21). "If the inheritance is by the law, then it is no longer by promise" (Gal.3:18). "If those who are of the law are heirs, faith is made void, and the promise is made of no effect" (Rom.4:14). "But that no-one is justified by the law in the sight of God is evident: for, 'The just live by faith.' But the law is not of faith: rather, 'The man that does these things shall live in them'" (Gal.3:11-12).

Against Two Letters of the Pelagians, 4:10

Law without grace is harmful

Clearly, then, Pelagius confesses God's grace in giving us the knowledge of our duty. But he does not confess the grace by which God enables and assists us to act. For the knowledge of the law, unless it is accompanied by the assistance of grace, merely serves to provoke transgression of God's commands. "Where there is no law," says Paul, "there is no transgression" (Rom.4:15). Again, "I would not have known covetousness unless the law had said, You shall not covet" (Rom.7:7).

Therefore it is simply not true that law and grace are the same thing. In fact, the law is worthless, indeed it is harmful, unless grace assists it! The real use of the law is this: it proves people guilty of transgression, and obliges them to flee to grace for deliverance and help in conquering their evil desires. The law commands rather than assists; it *reveals* the disease, but does not *heal* it. Indeed, the sickness which the law does not heal is actually made worse by the law, so that the cure of grace is more urgently and anxiously desired. For "the letter kills, but the Spirit gives life" (2 Cor.3:6). "For if there had been a law given which could have given life, truly righteousness would have been by the law" (Gal.3:21). To what extent, however, the law gives assistance, the apostle informs us when he says immediately afterwards: "The Scripture has concluded all under sin, so that the promise by faith in Jesus Christ might be given to those who believe" (Gal.3:22). Therefore, says the apostle, "the law was our schoolmaster in Christ Jesus" (Gal.3:24).

Now this very thing is useful to proud people, to be more firmly and manifestly "concluded under sin," so that no-one may presumptuously try to accomplish their justification by means of free will, as if they could do it by their own resources. No, let "every mouth be stopped, and all the world become guilty before God. For by the deeds of the law no flesh will be justified in His sight; for by the law is the knowledge of sin. But now the righteousness of God apart from the law is revealed, being witnessed to by the law and the prophets" (Rom.3:19-21). How then is it revealed apart from the law, if it is witnessed to by the law? For that very reason the phrase is not, "revealed apart from the law," but "the righteousness apart from the law," because it is "the righteousness of God" — that is, the righteousness which we have, not from the law, but from God. This is not the righteousness which, by reason of God's commanding it, causes us to fear through our knowledge of it; but rather this is the righteousness which, by reason of God's bestowing it, is held fast and maintained by us through our loving it, "so that he who glories, let him glory in the Lord" (1 Cor.1:31).

On the Grace of Christ and Original Sin, 1:9

The wicked make a bad use of the good law

The apostle wanted to show how harmful sin is, when grace does not help us; so he did not hesitate to say that the strength of sin is that very law by which sin is forbidden. "The sting of death is sin, and the strength of sin is the law" (1 Cor.15:56). Most certainly true! For forbidding something increases the desire for committing sin, if righteousness is not so loved that the desire for sin is conquered by that love. But unless divine grace helps us, we cannot love or delight in true righteousness. However, in case the law should be thought an evil thing, since it is called the strength of sin, the apostle (when discussing a similar question in another place) says, "The law indeed is holy, and the commandment holy, and just, and good. Was what is holy made death to me? God forbid. But sin, that it might appear as sin, worked death in me by what is good, so that by the commandment sin might become exceedingly sinful" (Rom.7:12-13). Exceedingly, he says, because the transgression is more vile when the law itself is despised through the increasing lust of sin.

Why have we thought it worthwhile to mention this? For this reason: when the law increases the lust of those who sin, that does not make the law itself an evil thing, so also when death increases the glory of those who suffer it [Christian martyrs], that does not make death itself a good thing. For the law is abandoned wickedly, and makes transgressors, while death is embraced for the truth's sake, and makes martyrs. And thus the law is indeed a good thing, because it is the prohibition of sin; and death is an evil thing, because it is the wages of sin. But as wicked persons make an evil use not only of evil, but also of good things, so the righteous make a good use not only of good, but also of evil things. Thus it comes to pass that the wicked make a bad use of the law, though the law itself is good; and the good die well, though death itself is an evil.

City of God, 13:5

The two righteousnesses: one of law, the other of grace

There are many who appear to do what the law commands, through fear of punishment, not through love of righteousness. Such righteousness is what the apostle calls "his own which is according to the law" (Phil.3:9) — so to speak, a thing commanded, not given. When, indeed, it has been given, it is not called our own righteousness, but God's, because it becomes our own only in the sense that God gives it to us. These are the apostle's words: "That I may be found in Christ, not having my own righteousness which is of the law, but that which is through faith in Christ, the righteousness which is from God by faith" (Phil.3:9).

So great, then, is the difference between law and grace, that although the law is undoubtedly of God, yet the righteousness which is "of the law" is not "of God"; rather, the righteousness which is accomplished by grace is "of God." The one is called "the righteousness of the law," because it is done through fear of the law's curse; while the other is called "the righteousness of God," because it is bestowed through the bounty of His grace, so that it is no longer a terrible but a pleasant commandment, as the prayer in the psalm says: "You are good, O Lord. Therefore in Your goodness, teach me Your righteousness" (Ps.119:68). That is, I may not be compelled like a slave to live under the law with fear of punishment; but rather, in the freedom of love may I be delighted to live with law as my companion. When the freeman keeps a commandment, he does it willingly. And whoever learns his duty in this spirit, does everything that he has learned ought to be done.

On the Grace of Christ and Original Sin, 1:14

Obeying out of fear of hell is not true obedience

In vain does anyone think he has gained the victory over sin, if he refrains from sin merely through fear of punishment. For although he does not perform the outward action to which an evil desire prompts him, the evil desire itself remains an unconquered enemy within the person. And who will be found innocent in God's sight, when they are willing to do the sin which is forbidden if you only remove the punishment which is feared? Consequently, even in the will itself, a person is guilty of sin if he wishes to do what is unlawful, but refrains from doing it because it cannot be done without punishment. For as far as he is concerned, he would prefer that there were no righteousness forbidding and punishing sins. And certainly, if he would prefer that there were no righteousness, who can doubt that he would abolish it altogether, if he could? How, then, can that person be called righteous who is such an enemy of righteousness that, if he had the power, he would abolish its authority, so that he might not be subject to its threats or penalties?

So then, a person is an enemy of righteousness if he refrains from sin only through fear of punishment. However, he will become the friend of righteousness if he refrains from sinning through love of righteousness, for then he will be really afraid to sin. For the person who only fears the flames of hell is afraid not of sinning, but of being burned! But the person who hates sin as much as he hates hell — that is the person afraid to sin. This is the "fear of the Lord" which "is pure, enduring for ever" (Ps.19:9). For the fear of punishment has torment, and has no place in love; and love, when it is perfect, casts it out (1 Jn.4:18).

Letter 145:4

The law makes us feel our need of grace

What object can Pelagius gain by saying that "law and teaching" are the grace by which God helps us to live righteously? If the law is going to help us at all, it must help us to feel our need of grace. Nobody is able to fulfil the law by means of the law. "Love is the fulfilment of the law" (Rom.13:10). And the love of God is not poured into our hearts by the law, but by the Holy Spirit Who was given to us (Rom.5:5). So the law points us to grace, in order that the law may be fulfilled by grace.

On the Grace of Christ and Original Sin, 1:10.

The law convicts us of our depravity

The law, by teaching and commanding what cannot be fulfilled without grace, demonstrates to a person his weakness, in order that the weakness thus revealed may take refuge in the Saviour. For by His healing, the will can do what in its feebleness it found impossible. So, then, the law leads us to faith; faith obtains the Spirit in fuller measure; the Spirit sheds love abroad within us; and love fulfils the law. For this reason the law is called a "schoolmaster" (Gal.3:24), under whose threats and severity "whoever shall call upon the name of the Lord will be saved. But how shall they call on Him in Whom they have not believed?" (Rom.10:13-14). Therefore to those who believe and call on the Lord, the life-giving Spirit is given, in case the letter without the Spirit kills them. But by the Holy Spirit Who is given to us, the love of God is shed abroad in our hearts, so that the words of the same apostle, "Love is the fulfilment of the law" (Rom.13:10), are accomplished.

So the law is good to the person who uses it lawfully. And a person uses it lawfully if he understands why it was given, and under the pressure of its threats, flees to grace, which sets him free. Whoever ungratefully despises this grace, by which the ungodly are justified, and trusts in his own strength, as if he could fulfil the law this way, is ignorant of God's righteousness. Trying to establish his own righteousness, he is not submitting himself to the righteousness of God; and thus the law becomes to him, not a help that leads to pardon, but the chain that fastens his guilt to him. Not that the law is evil, but sin produces death in such people by means of what is good. For the commandment merely provides an occasion for the self-righteous to sin more grievously, since through the commandment he knows how evil are the sins which he commits.

Letter 145:3

The law can be fulfilled only by grace

The Pelagians accuse us of saying that "the law of the Old Testament was given, not to justify the obedient, but to be the cause of greater sin." Clearly they do not understand what we teach about the law. We simply say what the apostle Paul says — and they don't understand him either! For who can say that someone who obeys the law is not justified, when he could not be obedient unless he already *were* justified? Our teaching is this: by the law God makes known what He wills people to do; by grace, He brings it about that the law is obeyed. "For not the hearers of the law," says the apostle, "are righteous before God, but the doers of the law will be justified" (Rom.2:13). Therefore the law makes hearers of righteousness, but grace makes doers. "For what was impossible to the law," says the same apostle, "in that it was weak through the flesh, God did by sending His Son in the likeness of sinful flesh, and for sin, and so condemned sin in the flesh, that the righteousness of the law might be fulfilled in us who walk not according to the flesh, but according to the Spirit" (Rom.8:3-4).

This is what we teach. Let the Pelagians pray that they may one day understand it, instead of arguing so that they never understand it. For it is impossible that the law should be fulfilled by the flesh, that is, by sinful presumption. Proud people are ignorant of the righteousness of God — that is, the righteousness that comes from God to a human being, that he may be righteous; they desire to establish their own righteousness, as if they could fulfil the law by their own will, without help from above. Thus they do not submit to the righteousness that comes from God (Rom.10:3-4). Therefore the righteousness of the law is fulfilled in those who walk, not according to the flesh — that is, according to human wisdom, ignorant of the righteousness of God and desiring to establish their own — but in those who walk according to the Spirit. But who walks according to the Spirit, except whoever is led by the Spirit of God? "For as many as are led by the Spirit of God, these are the sons of God" (Rom.8:14).

Therefore "the letter kills, but the Spirit makes alive" (2 Cor.3:6). And the letter of the law is not evil because it kills; rather, it convicts the wicked of transgression. "For the law is holy, and the commandment holy and just and good. Was, then," says Paul, "what is good made death to me? By no means; but sin, that it might appear to be sin, produced death in me by what is good, that sin might become sinful above measure, or a sin by the commandment" (Rom.7:12-13). This is what is the meaning of "the letter kills." "For the sting of death is sin, but the strength of sin is the law" (1 Cor.15:56) — because, by forbidding, the law increases the desires of sin. Thereby it kills a person, unless grace comes to his assistance and makes him alive.

Against Two Letters of the Pelagians, 3:2

(b) The undivided grace of God in Old and New Testaments

From Adam to Christ, there has only ever been one way of salvation

We are dealing with the matter of the two men [Adam and Christ]. By one of them, we are sold under sin, by the other we are redeemed from sins; by the one we have been plunged into death, by the other we are liberated into life. The first has ruined us in himself, by doing his own will instead of the will of his Creator; the second has saved us in Himself, by not doing His own will, but the will of Him who sent Him. The Christian faith properly consists in what concerns these two men. For "there is one God, and one Mediator between God and men, the man Christ Jesus" (1 Tim.2:5), because "there is no other name under heaven given to men, whereby we must be saved" (Acts 4:12), and "in Him God has given assurance to all people, in that He has raised Him from the dead" (Acts 17:31).

Now without this faith, that is to say, without a belief in the one Mediator between God and men, the man Christ Jesus; without faith in His resurrection by which God has given assurance to all, and which (of course) no-one could truly believe apart from His incarnation and death; without this faith, I say, in the incarnation and death and resurrection of Christ, Christian truth unhesitatingly declares that the ancient saints could not possibly have been cleansed from sin, so as to become holy, and justified by the grace of God....

Death indeed reigned from Adam until Moses (Rom.5:14), because it was not possible even for the law given through Moses to vanquish death. The law was not given, in fact, as something that could bestow life. It was given to those who were [spiritually] dead and in need of grace to give them life; it was given to show them that they were not only bowed down under the domination of inherited sin, but also convicted by the additional guilt of breaking the law itself. The purpose behind this was not that anyone should perish who by God's mercy understood this, even in that primitive age. No, the purpose was that he might seek God's help, destined though he was to punishment through the dominion of death, and proved guilty also through his own violation of the law. And so where sin abounded, grace has much more abounded, even the grace which alone delivers us from the body of this death.

Yet, despite this, even though the law which Moses gave was not able to liberate anyone from the dominion of death, there were even then men of God alive at the time of the law, who were not living under the terror, conviction and punishment of the law, but under the delight, healing and liberation of grace. There were some who said, "I was shaped in iniquity, and in sin my mother conceived me" (Ps.51:5), and, "There is no rest in my bones, because of my sins" (Ps.38:3), and, "Create in me a clean heart, O God, and renew a right spirit in my inward parts" (Ps.51:10), and, "Establish me with Your directing Spirit" (Ps.51:12), and, "Take not Your Holy Spirit from me" (Ps.51:11). There were some, again, who said: "I believed, therefore I have spoken" (Ps.116:10). For they too were cleansed by the self-same faith which cleanses us. That is why the apostle also says: "We have the same spirit of faith, as it is written, I believed, and therefore I have spoken; we also believe, and therefore speak" (2 Cor.4:13). This was the true faith that said, "Behold, a virgin shall conceive and bear a son, and they shall call His name Emmanuel, which is, being interpreted, God with us" (Isa.7:14, Matt.1:23)....

We must not therefore divide the times, as Pelagius and his disciples do. They say that people first lived righteously by nature, then under the law, thirdly under grace. By "nature" they mean the entire lengthy time from Adam until the giving of the law. "For then," say they, "the Creator was known by the guidance of reason; and the rule of living rightly was carried written in the human heart, not in the law of the letter, but of nature. But people's lives became corrupt; and then," they continue, "nature became tarnished and inadequate. So the law was added to it, by which as if by the moon, nature's original brightness was restored after its glow had been dimmed. But after the habit of sinning had prevailed too strongly among human beings, and the law was unequal to the task of healing it, Christ came; and the Physician Himself, through His own self, and not through His disciples, brought relief to the sickness at its most desperate development."

By this sort of argument, the Pelagians try to exclude the ancient saints from the grace of the Mediator. As if the man Christ Jesus were not the Mediator between God and those men, merely because He had not yet taken flesh of the Virgin's womb, and was not yet man at the time when those righteous men lived. Yet if this were true, the apostle would have said in vain: "Since by a man came death, by a man came also the resurrection of the dead; for as in

Adam all die, even so in Christ shall all be made alive" (1 Cor.15:21-22). According to the empty notions of these Pelagians, the Old Testament saints found their nature self-sufficient, and did not need the man Christ to be their Mediator to reconcile them to God. In that case, they will not be made alive in Him; they do not belong as members to His body, Who became human for the sake of humans. However, the Truth says through His apostles, "even as all die in Adam, even so shall all be made alive in Christ," and that the resurrection of the dead comes through the one man, even as death comes through the other man.

Which Christian will be bold enough to doubt that even those righteous ones who pleased God in the more remote periods of the human race are destined to attain to the resurrection of eternal life, and not eternal death, since they will be made alive in Christ? Who doubts that they are made alive in Christ, since they belong to the body of Christ? Who doubts that they belong to the body of Christ, since Christ is the head even to them? Who doubts that Christ is the head even to them, since there is but one Mediator between God and men, the man Christ Jesus? But this He could not have been to them, unless through His grace they had believed in His resurrection. And how could they have done this, if they had been ignorant that He was to come in the flesh, and if they had not by this faith lived a righteous and godly life?

Now, if the incarnation of Christ could be of no concern to them, on the basis that it had not yet taken place, it must follow that Christ's judgment can be of no concern to us, because it has not yet taken place. But if we will stand at the right hand of Christ through our faith in His judgment, which has not yet occurred but is still to come, it follows that those ancient saints are members of Christ through their faith in His resurrection, which had not in their day happened, but which was one day to occur.

On the Grace of Christ and Original Sin, 2:28-31

The Old Testament saints were saved by the grace of Christ

"We teach," says Julian, "that the saints of the Old Testament passed to eternal life after their righteousness was perfected here. By the love of virtue they departed from all sins. Those whom Scripture says committed any sin, nevertheless improved themselves, as we know."

Whatever virtue you may declare that the righteous of ancient times possessed, nothing saved them but their belief in the Mediator who shed His blood for the remission of their sins. For their own word is, "I believed, and therefore I spoke" (Ps.116:10). Thus the apostle Paul also says, "And we having the same Spirit of faith, as it is written, 'I believed, and therefore I have spoken'; we also believe, and therefore speak" (2 Cor.4:13). What is "the same Spirit," but that Spirit whom these righteous ones also had in saying such things?

The apostle Peter also says, "Why do you wish to put a yoke upon the Gentiles, which neither we nor our fathers have been able to bear? But, by the grace of the Lord Jesus Christ, we believe that we shall be saved, even as they" (Acts 15:10-11). You who are enemies of this grace do not wish us to believe that the ancients were saved by the same grace of Jesus Christ. No, you divide up the times as Pelagius does, in whose books this is taught; you say that before the law people were saved by nature, then by the law, lastly by Christ. So according to you, the blood of Christ was not necessary to those of the two former times, that is to say, before the law and under the law. Thus you make void what is said: "For there is one God and one Mediator between God and men, the man Christ Jesus" (1 Tim.2:5).

Against Two Letters of the Pelagians, 1:39

Old Testament saints were heirs of the New Testament

Which Catholic would say what the Pelagians accuse us of saying, that "the Holy Spirit did not help people to be virtuous in the Old Testament"? Unless, of course, we understand "the Old Testament" to mean the Covenant from Mount Sinai insofar as it "gives birth to bondage", as Paul says (Gal.4:24). However, the New Testament was foreshadowed by types in the Old. The people of God who at that time understood this, according to God's ordering of history, were indeed the stewards and bearers of the Old Testament, but Scripture shows them to be the heirs of the New. Shall we deny that David belongs to the New Testament when he says, "Create in me a clean heart, O God; and renew a right spirit within me" (Ps.51:10)? Or when he says, "He has set my feet upon a rock, and directed my steps; and he has put a new song in my mouth, even a hymn to our God" (Ps.40:2-3)?

Against Two Letters of the Pelagians, 3:6

Old Testament saints were children of the heavenly Jerusalem

Whether we are speaking of Abraham, or the righteous people before him or after him, even down to Moses himself, by whom was given the Covenant that gives birth to bondage from Mount Sinai, or the rest of the prophets after him, and the holy people of God up to John the Baptist — they are all children of the promise and of grace according to Isaac the son of the free woman. They are not children of the law, but of the promise, heirs of God and joint-heirs with Christ. Righteous Noah and the righteous folk of the earlier times, and whoever from that time was righteous up until the time of Abraham, whether we know about them or not — far be it from us to deny that they belong to the Jerusalem which is above, who is our mother, although they lived earlier in time than Sarah, who was the prophecy and type of the free mother herself. How much more evidently, then, must we count as children of the promise all who have pleased God, after the promise was declared to Abraham, that he should be called the father of many nations.

Against Two Letters of the Pelagians, 3:8

Predestination embraces all the saved in Christ, whenever they lived

This being the case, ever since the time when by one man sin entered into this world, and death through sin, and so it passed through to all people, up to the very end of this fleshly generation and perishing world, whose children beget and are begotten, there never has existed, and there never will exist, a human being in this life of ours concerning whom it could be said that he had no sin at all. The only exception is the one Mediator, who reconciles us to our Creator through the forgiveness of sins. Now this same Lord of ours has never yet refused, at any period of the human race, and right up to the last judgment He will never refuse, His healing to those whom He has predestined to reign with Himself in life eternal, in His most sure foreknowledge and future loving-kindness.

For before He was born in the flesh, underwent weakness in suffering, and displayed His power in His own resurrection, all who lived at that time He instructed in the faith of these future blessings, so that they might inherit everlasting life. Those who were alive at the very time when all these things were being accomplished in Christ, and who witnessed the fulfilment of prophecy, He instructed in the faith of blessings then actually present. And again, those who have since lived, and ourselves who are now alive, and all those who are yet to live, He does not cease to instruct in the faith of these blessings now past. It is therefore "one faith" (Eph.4:5) which saves all, who after their fleshly birth are born again of the Spirit; and this "one faith" terminates in Christ, the Judge of the living and the dead, Who came to be judged for us and to die. But the sacraments of this "one faith" are varied from time to time in order to signify it in a suitable way.

On the Merits and Forgiveness on Sins, 2:47

All legalists are "living under the Old Testament"

To live under the Old Testament "which gives birth from Mount Sinai to bondage" (Gal.4:24) symbolised by Hagar means receiving a law which is holy and just and good, and thinking that the bare letter of the law is enough to bring life. Such people do not seek the divine mercy to make them into doers of the law; they are ignorant of the righteousness that comes from God, desiring to establish their own righteousness, and therefore do not submit to the righteousness that God gives (Rom.10:3). Such were the multitude that grumbled against God in the wilderness, and made an idol, and those who even in the promised land itself committed fornication with strange gods. But this multitude, even in the Old Testament itself, were strongly rebuked.

Moreover, those Jews who at that time followed only after God's earthly promises, and who were ignorant of what those promises

signify under the New Testament, kept God's commandments with
the desire of gaining and the fear of losing those earthly promises.
Well, that was not true obedience; it was only a seeming obedience.
They had no faith in them that worked by love, but only an earthly
greed and fleshly fear. But someone who fulfils the commandments
from such motives fulfils them unwillingly, and does not obey them
in his heart. For he would really rather not obey them, if only he
could disobey and still have the things he desires and avoid the things
he fears. And he is guilty in his inward will; and it is here that God
the Lawgiver looks.

Such were the children of the earthly Jerusalem, about which the
apostle says, "For she is in bondage with her children" (Gal.4:25),
and belongs to the Old Testament "which gives birth to bondage
from Mount Sinai, which is Hagar" (Gal.4:24). Such too were those
who crucified the Lord, and persisted in the same unbelief. Such
today are their children, the great majority of Jews, although now
the prophesied New Testament has been made plain and confirmed
by the blood of Christ, and the gospel is made known from the river
where He was baptised and began His teachings, even to the ends of
the earth.

Against Two Letters of the Pelagians, 3:9

God's law is still necessary for New Testament believers

Surely no-one will doubt that God's law was necessary, not just for
the people of that time [the Old Testament], but is also necessary for
us today, for the right ordering of our life. True enough, Christ took
away from us that crushing yoke of many ceremonies, so that we
are not circumcised according to the flesh, we do not sacrifice victims
from our the cattle, we do not rest even from necessary works on the
Sabbath (although we keep the pattern of a seven day week), and
other such things. We keep these laws in a spiritual sense; the shadowy
symbols have been removed, and we see them in the light of the
realities they signified. But are we therefore to say, when the law
commands that whoever finds another man's lost property of any
kind should return it to him the owner, that this has no relevance to
us? And the law has many other things like this, teaching people to
live godly and upright lives.

Such teaching is especially found in the Ten Commandments themselves, contained in those two tables of stone — apart from the fleshly observance of the Sabbath, which signifies spiritual sanctification and rest.[2] For who can say that Christians ought not to keep the commands which tell us to serve the one God with religious obedience, not to worship an idol, not to take the Lord's name in vain, to honour one's parents, not to commit adulteries, murders, thefts, false witness, not to covet another man's wife, or anything at all that belongs to another? Who is so ungodly as to say that he does not keep those precepts of the law, because he is a Christian, and stands not under the law, but under grace?

Against Two Letters of the Pelagians, 3:10

Christ has not come to destroy the law

It is quite clear, and the New Testament leaves no doubt on the matter, what are the law and the prophets that Christ came not to destroy, but to fulfil. It was the law given by Moses which, through Jesus Christ, became grace and truth. The law given by Moses is that of which Christ says, "He wrote of Me" (Jn.5:46). For undoubtedly this is the law that was added so that the sin might abound — words which you often ignorantly quote as a reproach to the law. Read what is there said of this law: "The law is holy, and the commandment holy, and just, and good. Was then what is good made death to me? God forbid. But sin, that it might appear as sin, produced death in me by what is good" (Rom.7:12-13).

---

[2] Augustine was not exactly an anti-Sabbatarian in the modern sense of the term. However, he did make a sharp distinction between the Jewish Saturday Sabbath and the Christian Sunday, the Lord's day. The devout observance of Sunday he regarded as a Christian duty; believers were to observe and celebrate Sunday as a day especially dedicated to the service of God, just as the Levitical priests had served God through worship on the Jewish Sabbath. As Augustine said, "In the Old Covenant, the Sabbath was observed; in the New, the Lord's day" (**Expositions of the Psalms, 150:1**). He interpreted the Sabbath Commandment itself in a spiritual sense as referring to a spiritual resting from the "servile labours" of sin, in the redemptive freedom that Christ has purchased. Whenever Augustine says that Christians do not observe the Sabbath, he means a literal observance of the Saturday Sabbath. But he certainly expected Christians to observe the Lord's day.

The coming of the law made the sin abound, not because the law required what was wrong, but because the proud and self-confident incurred additional guilt as transgressors after they were made acquainted with the holy, and just, and good commandments of the law. The intent was that, being thus humbled, they might learn that only by grace through faith could they be set free from subjection to the law as transgressors, and be reconciled to the law as righteous people. So the same apostle says: "For before faith came, we were kept under the law, shut up until the faith came which was afterwards revealed. Therefore the law was our schoolmaster in Christ Jesus; but after faith came, we are no longer under a schoolmaster" (Gal.3:23-5). That is, we are no longer subject to the penalty of the law, because we are set free by grace.

Before we received in humility the grace of the Spirit, the letter of the law was only death to us, for it required an obedience which we could not render. Thus Paul also says: "The letter kills, but the Spirit gives life" (2 Cor.3:6). Again, he says: "For if a law had been given which could have given life, truly righteousness would have been by the law; but the Scripture has concluded all under sin, so that the promise by faith in Jesus Christ might be given to those who believe" (Gal.3:21-2). And once more: "What the law could not do, in that it was weak through the flesh, God did by sending His Son in the likeness of sinful flesh, so that by sin He might condemn sin in the flesh, in order that the righteousness of the law might be fulfilled in us, who do not walk according to the flesh, but according to the Spirit" (Rom.8:3-4).

Here we see Christ coming not to destroy the law, but to fulfil it. As the law brought the proud under the guilt of transgression, increasing their sin by commandments which they could not obey, so the righteousness of the same law is fulfilled by the grace of the Spirit in those who learn from Christ to be meek and lowly in heart; for Christ came not to destroy the law, but to fulfil it.

Reply to Faustus the Manichee, 19:7

The Ten Commandments must be kept by Christians

The apostle seems to reprove and correct those who were being persuaded to be circumcised, in such a way as to use the word "law" to mean circumcision itself and other similar legal observances, which Christians now reject as shadows of a future substance, although we still hold what those shadows figuratively promised. Still, at the same time Paul nevertheless would have us clearly understand that the law, by which he says no-one is justified, exists not merely in those sacramental institutions which contained symbolic promises; no, the law exists also in those works by which whoever has done them lives a holy life. Among these laws occurs this prohibition: "You shall not covet."

Now, to make our statement all the clearer, let us look at the Ten Commandments themselves. It is certain, then, that Moses on the mount received the law, so that he might deliver it to the people, written on tables of stone by the finger of God. It is summed up in these Ten Commandments, where there is no precept about circumcision, nor anything concerning those animal sacrifices which have ceased to be offered by Christians. Well now, apart from the observance of the Sabbath [see previous footnote p.107], I should like to be told what there is in these Ten Commandments which ought not to be kept by a Christian — whether it is the law forbidding the making and worshipping of idols, and of any other gods than the one true God, or the taking of God's name in vain, or prescribing honour to parents, or warning against fornication, murder, theft, false witness, adultery, or coveting other men's property? Which of these commandments would anyone say that the Christian ought not to keep?

On the Spirit and the Letter, 23

The Holy Spirit writes the Ten Commandments on our hearts

Having confirmed the disciples, and having stayed with them forty days, Christ ascended up into heaven, as these same persons were watching Him. And on the completion of fifty days from His resurrection, He sent to them the Holy Spirit (for so He had promised). By the Spirit's agency they were to have love shed abroad in their hearts, so that they might be able to fulfil the law, not only without the sense of its being burdensome, but even with a joyful mind. This law was given to the Jews in the Ten Commandments, which they call the Ten Words. And these commandments, again, are reduced to two, namely that we should love God with all our heart, with all our soul, with all our mind; and that we should love our neighbour as ourselves. For the Lord Himself has at once declared in the Gospel, and shown in His own example, that on these two precepts hang all the law and the prophets.

For it was the same in the instance of the people of Israel. From the day on which they first celebrated the passover in a ritual, slaying and eating the sheep, with whose blood their door-posts were marked to secure their safety — from that day, I repeat, the fiftieth day in succession was completed, and then they received the law written by the finger of God. Under this phrase [the finger of God], we have already stated that the Holy Spirit is signified. And in the same manner, after the suffering and resurrection of the Lord, who is the true passover, the Holy Spirit was sent personally to the disciples on the fiftieth day — not now, however, by tables of stone signifying the hardness of their hearts....

On the Catechising of the Uninstructed, 41

The Saturday Sabbath is the only ceremonial element in the Ten Commandments

It is for this reason that of all the Ten Commandments, the command concerning the Sabbath was the only one in which the thing commanded was figurative. The bodily rest of the Sabbath was a symbol which we have received as a means of our instruction, but not as a duty binding also upon us. For the Sabbath presents a figure of the spiritual rest, of which it is said in the Psalm, "Be still, and know that I am God" (Ps.46:10), and to which people are invited by the Lord Himself in the words, "Come to Me, all you who labour and are heavy laden, and I will give you rest. Take My yoke upon you, and learn from Me; for I am meek and lowly in heart. So shall you find rest for your souls" (Matt.11:28-9).

As for all the things prescribed in the other nine commandments, we are to yield to them an obedience which has nothing figurative in it. For we have been taught literally not to worship idols; and the precepts bidding us not to take God's name in vain, to honour our father and mother, not to commit adultery, or kill, or steal, or bear false witness, or covet our neighbour's wife, or covet anything that is our neighbour's — all these are devoid of figurative or mystical meaning, and are to be literally observed. But we are not commanded to observe the day of the Sabbath literally, in resting from bodily labour, as it is observed by the Jews. Even their observance of the prescribed rest is to be deemed worthy of contempt, except as it signifies another, namely, spiritual rest.

From this we may reasonably conclude, that all those things which are figuratively set forth in Scripture are powerful in stimulating that love by which we tend towards rest. For the only figurative or symbolic precept in the Ten Commandments is the one in which that rest is commended to us, which is desired everywhere, but is found sure and hallowed in God alone.

Letter 55:22

Christians have the same Ten Commandments as the Jews, but different promises

Expel from your hearts fleshly thoughts, that you may be truly under grace, that you may belong to the New Testament. This is why eternal life is promised in the New Testament. Read the Old Testament, and see that the same things were commanded to a people who were as yet fleshly. We have received the same commands. For to worship one God is also prescribed to us. "You shall not take the name of the Lord your God in vain" is also prescribed to us, which is the second commandment. "Observe the Sabbath-day" is prescribed to us more than to them, because we are commanded to observe it spiritually. For the Jews observe the Sabbath in a slavish manner, using it for luxury and drunkenness. How much better would their women be employed in spinning wool than in dancing on that day in the balconies! God forbid, my brothers, that we should call *that* an observance of the Sabbath! The Christian observes the Sabbath spiritually, by abstaining from the work of servants. For what is it to abstain from servile work? It is abstaining from sin. And how do we prove it? Ask the Lord. "Whoever commits sin is the servant of sin" (Jn.8:34). Therefore the spiritual observance of the Sabbath is indeed prescribed to us Christians.

And all those other commandments are more prescribed to us, and must be observed: "You shall not kill. You shall not commit adultery. You shall not steal. You shall not bear false witness. Honour your father and your mother. You shall not covet your neighbour's goods. You shall not covet your neighbour's wife." Are not all these things prescribed to us also? But ask what the reward is, and you will find it said [in the Ten Commandments]: "That your enemies may be driven forth before your face, and that you may receive the land which God promised to your fathers" (Deut.6:18-19). Because they were not able to comprehend invisible things, God held them by the visible. Why? To stop them perishing altogether, and slipping into idol-worship ...

The same things are commanded in the Ten Commandments as we Christians are commanded to observe; but the same promises are not made as to us. What is promised to us? Eternal life. "And this is eternal life, that they may know You, the only true God, and Jesus Christ Whom You have sent" (Jn.17:3). The knowledge of God is promised: that is, grace for grace. Brothers, we at present believe, but we do not see; for faith, the reward will be to see what we believe. The prophets knew this, but it was concealed before Christ came. For a certain sighing lover says in the Psalms: "One thing have I desired of the Lord, that I will seek after" (Ps.27:4). And do you ask what he seeks? For perhaps he seeks a land flowing with milk and honey in a physical sense, although this is to be spiritually sought and desired. Or perhaps he seeks the conquest of his enemies, or the death of foes, or the power and riches of this world. For he glows with love, and sighs greatly, and burns and pants. Let us see what he desires: "One thing have I desired of the Lord, that I will seek after." What is it that he seeks after? "That I may dwell in the house of the Lord all the days of my life." And suppose that you dwell in the house of the Lord: from what source will your joy there be derived? "That I may behold the beauty of the Lord."

Sermons on John, 3:19-20

The Lord's day: the proper day of church worship and the Lord's supper

In Troas, through the necessity of his departure being close at hand, Paul's sermon was prolonged until midnight. It was the first day of the week, which is called the Lord's day — from this phrase we understand that Paul was not with Jews, but with Christians. We also understand this when the narrator himself says they were gathered together for the purpose of breaking bread (Acts 20:6-7). And indeed this is the best method of management, that all things should be allotted to their proper times and be done in order, in case they become muddled up in perplexing entanglements, throwing our human minds into confusion.

On the Work of Monks, 21

Chapter 4

The Incarnation and Atonement

Christ was named the Mediator between God and human beings. He stood between the immortal God and mortal humanity, as being Himself both God and human, Who reconciled humanity to God. He continued to be what He was [God], but became also what He was not [man]. And the same Person is for us at once the centre of our faith in things that are created, and the truth in things that are eternal.

*Augustine, **Harmony of the Gospels, 1:53***

Anselm of Canterbury, one of Augustine's greatest and most winsome disciples in the Middle Ages, wrote a book called **Cur deus homo** — "Why God became man." It turned out to be one of the theological masterpieces of all time. Anselm would certainly have found plenty of material in Augustine for his masterpiece.

The sheer wonder of the eternal and almighty God actually becoming a human being, without in any way ceasing to be the eternal and almighty God, was something that haunted Augustine's soul with unceasing amazement and heart-piercing thankfulness. In his writings, it is almost as if he cannot stop talking about it. For the bishop of Hippo, the incarnation was no mere preface to the atonement: it was itself an essential part of our salvation. When God took human nature from the Virgin Mary, this act had a saving significance in its own right, although without the cross it would have been insufficient for our liberation from sin and Satan. Evangelicals today are usually strong on the atonement but weak on the incarnation; we can learn from Augustine here.

Augustine taught that the incarnation was essential to our sharing in the very life of God. Salvation is more than the forgiveness of sins; it also involves being filled with the holiness and immortality of God Himself, in our souls and our bodies too (ultimately in resurrection glory). The early Church fathers called this "deification" — "becoming divine", or even "becoming gods". Today this has an eerie New Age ring to it, but the fathers were not New Agers, and did not think that all human beings are God by nature. What they meant was something quite different. According to Augustine and the other fathers, God the Creator remains the one and only true God, the unique source of divine life and light; but He graciously chooses to enter into the closest possible union with His redeemed creatures, so that we become "partakers of the divine nature" (2 Pet.1:4). The life, the glory, the energy of God come streaming into us; we become alive with a divine vitality — "the life of God in the soul of man", as Henry Scougal famously put it in the title of the book through which George Whitefield was largely converted. How is this entrance of the divine life into human nature possible? Because God has become one of us, a true human being, in the person of Jesus the Creator-Redeemer. Jesus is the God-man: fully and truly human, fully and truly divine, in one and the same person.

So we find Augustine reasoning as follows. I am a sinful and mortal man, bound by the chains of depravity and death. But Christ is different. His human nature has never been corrupted by sin, and never could be. He is the Holy One. Further, Christ cannot die, unless He voluntarily chooses to undergo death; and even then, death cannot hold Him — He bursts from the tomb. He is the Living One. Why is Christ so different to me? *Because He is God in the flesh.* The second person of the Trinity, the everlasting Son of the everlasting Father, has taken to Himself our nature, wrapped Himself in a human soul and a human body. By so doing, He has transfused His divine life and glory into the human nature He took. (Or to use the language of the fathers, Christ "deified" His human nature.) So here is a man who is God. In Christ the God-man, human nature has become something that it was not before: it has (O wonder of wonders!) become *God's* human nature. God now has a human soul; God now has a human body. In Christ, human nature is now alive with the shining, creative, immortal life of the One Who made and upholds the cosmos.

And that life can be mine. Christ is human; I too am human; therefore there is a bond between Christ and me. We are of the same race, the same human substance. What He did to His human nature by taking it into union with His divine person, He can do for mine too. That holiness and life and glory which have filled His humanity to overflowing — He wants to share them with me. By the Holy Spirit, the God-man joins me to Himself, and the divine energy that pervades His humanity comes pouring into mine. I am alive again! Alive with the life of Christ — alive with the life of God! His holiness heals me of my sinfulness; His resurrection life carries me safely through death to immortality. Thanks be to God for His indescribable gift, the Word Who became flesh of our flesh and bone of our bone, and dwelt among us, full of grace and truth, radiant with the transforming glory of the Father's Only-begotten!

These are the central thoughts about the incarnation that lie behind the various musings of Augustine in the quotations that follow. Incidentally, the notion of "salvation by deification through the incarnation" is often said to be an Eastern thought, or even an Eastern Orthodox thought, which has no place in Western thinking. Well, Augustine of Hippo, the ultimate Western father, is full of it. The Eastern Orthodox usually don't like Augustine (because they don't like his views on the enslaved will and predestination), but they won't be able to find much wrong with his perpetual exposition of 2 Peter 1:4.

That brings us to the atonement. Augustine glories in the incarnation; no less does he glory in the Incarnate One's cross. He was under no delusions about the incarnation being adequate in itself to redeem fallen sinners. Issues of justice had to be settled, and they were settled not when the Son of God took human life upon Himself, but rather when He freely laid down that life in the dust of death. Not that Augustine believed this was the only possible way that God could have removed our guilt and freed us from Satan; but Augustine held that the way of the cross was the best, the wisest, the most fitting way. Most Evangelicals since the 17th century have maintained that the cross was in fact the only possible way. But we need not quarrel with Augustine over this, since he insisted so strongly that God *did* choose this way — and so having chosen it, it is the only *actual* way of salvation that we will find through the length, breadth, height and depth of God's universe.

Two thoughts dominate Augustine's treatment of the atonement. First, and more often, he views the human predicament as one of *bondage to Satan*. Through our sin, Satan has (in a sense) acquired rights over us. That is, God's justice has delivered us over into the powerful domain of the dark angel whom we chose to follow instead of God, our true Lord. That is part and parcel of the punishment of sin. How then shall we be released from this deserved slavery to Satan? God could have snapped His fingers and liberated us by power alone; but that, said Augustine, would not have been fitting. We came into subjection to Satan by a moral act — Adam's rebellion; therefore we must be liberated by a moral act, not a mere exercise of superior force. Satan was given dominion over us when the first Adam disobeyed; he loses his dominion by the obedience of the second Adam. The Father commands the Messiah to lay down His life. Jesus obeys. When *we* die, it is by necessity — we are doomed to die, we cannot help it. But when Jesus dies, it is an act of the freest obedience by the King of life Who need not have died at all.

More than this, the *way* Jesus dies is critical to our liberation. He allows Himself to be put to death by Satan. True, Satan does not visibly appear and murder Jesus with his own hands. He acts through others — Judas Iscariot, Annas, Caiaphas, Pontius Pilate, the mocking soldiers, the self-righteous Pharisees, the howling mob.

They are Satan's instruments. But Satan has no *right* to kill Jesus. The devil may have the power of death over us (Heb.2:14), but not over the sinless Son of God. So in putting Christ to death, Satan has overstepped the rightful limits of his dominion. Now it becomes a righteous thing in God to say to Satan, "Because you put to death My sinless Son, over Whom you had no rights, I am going to set free the debtors over whom I did give you rights. If their sin made it a matter of justice that they should become your captives, your murder of the Sinless One makes it a matter of justice that you should now be stripped of your captives. For they are bound to My Son, the Second Adam, by the ties of a common humanity." And so by a moral act — not by superior power, but by humble obedience to the Father's will, culminating in a freely accepted death He does not deserve — Christ plunders Satan of the spoils of human souls. In Augustine's words: "certainly it is in harmony with justice that we, whom the devil held as debtors, should be dismissed free by believing in Him Whom the devil put to death without any debt. In this way, we are said to be justified in the blood of Christ; in this way, His innocent blood was shed for the forgiveness of our sins" (**On the Trinity, 13:18**).

I suppose Evangelicals today might find all this a somewhat strange and alien way of looking at the atonement. However, it was widespread among the early Church fathers. And it does have its merits. Chiefly, it takes Satan seriously. We are more accustomed to thinking that on the cross, Christ did something *for us*. Augustine is saying that Christ did something for us by doing something *to Satan* — the Redeemer struck out at Satan on the cross, and crushed the serpent's head. And that is why the cross is liberating for us. In this view, the cross is not just a transaction between Christ, the Father and human sinners, but between Christ, the Father, human sinners, *and Satan*. In the light of texts like Gen.3:15, Jn.12:31, Col.2:15 and Heb.2:14-15, is this not worthy of consideration?

Augustine's other main thought about the atonement will be far more familiar to us. He teaches that Christ took upon Himself the punishment of our sins, so as to set us free from punishment. "In bearing our punishment, He died in the flesh which He took; so likewise, while ever blessed in His own righteousness, He was cursed for our offences, in the death which He suffered in bearing our punishment" (**Against Faustus the Manichee, 14:6**). This "penal substitution" view of the atonement is often said (by the ignorant) to be something the Protestant Reformers dreamt up. Well, if it frequented their dreams, it may have been because they'd been reading Augustine. Penal substitution is found equally clearly in other great fathers of the early Church, notably Athanasius who expounds it at some length in his masterpiece **On the Incarnation of the Logos**, chapters 3-10. If Liberals, Modernists and others scoff at you for daring to believe in substitutionary atonement, it is a comforting thought that you are in good company. They are scoffing at Augustine and Athanasius too. Not to mention the prophets and apostles.

Finally, I have gathered some quotations illustrating Augustine's acceptance of "particular redemption" — that Christ died with the specific intention of redeeming the elect, those predestined to eternal life, rather than the whole human race indiscriminately. It is often called the doctrine of "limited atonement", a phrase I have never liked. (Would we speak about our belief in a "limited heaven" because not everyone goes there?) Honesty compels me to say that Augustine does not seem consistent in his views on the extent of the atonement. The quotations here clearly teach particular redemption. Others could be found that appear equally clearly to teach universal redemption. Since this question was not one that Augustine actually tackled in a deliberate systematic manner, I feel no inclination to try to harmonise his various utterances. I think I will leave it up to Augustine's Lord and Saviour to call him to account for "every careless word". However, Augustine was obviously quite happy on occasion to set forth Christ's death as offered particularly, specifically and expressly for the elect, and even to deny that He offered it for the non-elect. So down crashes another witless myth, that particular redemption was never taught by any Christian theologian until Calvinism came along. How wonderful Church history is.

****

The Incarnation and Atonement

(a) The Incarnation

Christ is both God and Man at the same time

Therefore Christ Jesus, the Son of God, is both God and man. He is God before all worlds; He is man in our world. He is God, because He is the Word of God (for "the Word was God," Jn.1:1); and He is man, because in His one person the Word was joined with a body and a rational soul. Therefore, so far as He is God, He and the Father are one; so far as He is man, the Father is greater than He. For when He was the only Son of God, not by grace, but by nature, He became the Son of man so that He might be also full of grace. He Himself unites both natures in His own identity, and both natures constitute one Christ; because, "being in the form of God, He thought it not robbery to be" what He was by nature, "equal with God." But "He made Himself of no reputation, and took upon Himself the form of a servant," without losing or lessening the form of God (Phil.2:6-7). And, accordingly, He was both made less than God and remained equal with God, being both of these in one person, as has been said; but He was one of these as the Word, and the other as man. As the Word, He is equal with the Father; as man, He is less than the Father. He is one Son of God, and at the same time Son of man; He is one Son of man, and at the same time Son of God. He is not two Sons of God, a divine and human one, but one Son of God: God without beginning, man with a beginning — our Lord Jesus Christ.

Enchiridion, 35

God's manifold wisdom in providing a Mediator

We could not have been redeemed, even through the man Christ Jesus, the one Mediator between God and men, unless He were also God. Now when Adam was created, he was a righteous man and had no need of a mediator. But when sin had opened a wide gulf between God and the human race, it was expedient that a Mediator should reconcile us to God, and procure even for our bodies a resurrection to eternal life, and that this Mediator should be born, and live, and die, without sin, unique among the human race. Thus human pride was exposed and healed through the humility of God, so that the human race might be shown how far it had departed from God, when God became incarnate to bring it back. Further, an example was set to disobedient humanity in the God-man's life of obedience. The fountain of grace was opened up by the Only-begotten taking upon Himself the form of a servant, a form which had no preceding merit. A pledge of the resurrection of the body which is promised to the redeemed was given in the Redeemer's own resurrection. The devil was subdued by the same nature which he boasted he had deceived; and yet human nature was not glorified, lest pride should again spring up. In short, all these advantages which the thoughtful can perceive and describe, or perceive without being able to describe, flow from the transcendent mystery of the person of the Mediator.

Enchiridion, 108

The Word became flesh

Now of this Mediator it would occupy too much space to say anything at all worthy of Him. Indeed, to say what is worthy of Him does not lie in human power. For who will explain in consistent words this single statement, that "the Word became flesh, and dwelt among us" (Jn.1:14), so that we may believe in the only Son of God the Father Almighty, born of the Holy Spirit and the Virgin Mary? The meaning of the Word becoming flesh is not that the divine nature was *changed into* flesh, but that the divine nature *assumed* our flesh. And by "flesh" we are here to understand "human nature", the part being put for the whole, as when it is said: "By the deeds of the law shall no flesh be justified" (Rom.3:20), that is, no human being. For we must believe that no part was lacking in that human nature which the Word put on, save that it was a nature wholly free from every taint of sin. It was not such a nature as is conceived between the two sexes through carnal lust, which is born in sin, and whose guilt is washed away in regeneration; but it was such as it befitted a Virgin to bring forth, when the mother's faith, not her lust, was the condition of conception.[1]

Enchiridion, 34

Flesh means human nature, body and soul

It is the belief of all of us, to whom to live is Christ, that humanity was taken to Himself by the Word of God, not surely without a rational soul, as certain heretics will have it. And yet we read, "The Word became flesh" (Jn.1:14). What shall we understood here by "flesh", but humanity? "And all flesh shall see the salvation of God" (Lk.3:6). What does this mean, but all human beings? "To You shall all flesh come" (Ps.65:2). What is this, but all human beings? "You have given to Him power over all flesh" (Jn.17:2). What is this, but all human beings? "By the works of the law no flesh will be justified" (Rom.3:20). What is this, but no human being will be justified?

On Continence, 11

Christ did not have a *sinful* human nature

He goes on to add, "And the Word became flesh, and dwelt among us" (Jn.1:14); as much as to say, "A great thing indeed has been done among us, even that we are born again of God to God, when previously we had been born of the flesh to the world, although created by God Himself. But a far more wonderful thing has been done so that, although it belonged to us by nature to be born of the flesh, we might by the divine goodness be born of God. For in order that so great a blessing might be imparted to us, He who was in His

---

[1] By Mary's faith being the condition of Christ's conception, Augustine is referring to Mary's response to the angel Gabriel's message: "Behold the Lord's maidservant. Let it be to me according to your word" (Lk.1:38). This was the obedience of faith. Luke makes it clear in Lk.2:21 that Jesus was not conceived in Mary's womb until *after* she had submitted in faith to God's choice of her. In that sense, faith not lust was the channel of Christ's conception.

own nature born of God, granted it in mercy that He should also be born of the flesh."

Nothing less is meant by the passage, "And the Word became flesh, and dwelt among us." By this, he says in effect, it has been accomplished that we who were born of the flesh as flesh, by being afterwards born of the Spirit, may be spirit and may dwell in God. For God, Who was born of God [the Son eternally born of the Father in the Trinity], by being afterwards born of the flesh, became flesh, and dwelt among us. The Word Who became flesh existed in the beginning, and was God with God. But at the same time He shared in our inferior condition, in order that we might share in His higher state. He took a kind of middle way in His birth of the flesh. For we indeed were born in sinful flesh, but He was born in the *likeness* of sinful flesh (Rom.8:3). We were born not only of flesh and blood, but also of the will of man, and of the flesh; but He was born only of flesh and blood, not of the will of man, nor of the will of the flesh, but of God. We were therefore born to die on account of sin; He was born to die on our account without sin.

So also, just as His inferior circumstances, into which He descended to us, were not in every detail exactly the same as our inferior circumstances, in which He found us here; so our superior state, into which we ascend to Him, will not be quite the same as His superior state, in which we will there find Him. For we by His grace are to be made the sons of God, whereas He was eternally by nature the Son of God. We, when we are converted, cleave to God, though not as His equals; Christ never turned away from God, and remains ever equal to God. We are *partakers* of eternal life; Christ *is* eternal life. Christ alone, therefore, having become man, but still continuing to be God, never had any sin. He did not assume sinful flesh, though born of sinful flesh from His mother. For the flesh He took from her, He either cleansed *in order* to take it, or cleansed *by* taking it.[2]

On the Merits and Forgiveness of Sins, 2:38

---

[2] So Augustine believed the Virgin Mary was "sinful flesh".

By sharing our mortal humanity, the Mediator enables us to share in His immortal and blessed divinity

If, as is much more probable and credible, all human beings are miserable so long as they are mortal, we must seek an intermediary who is not only human, but also God. Such an intermediary, by interposing His blessed mortality, can bring humans out of their mortal misery to a blessed immortality. In this intermediary, two things are required: He must *become* mortal, but He must not *continue* mortal. He did become mortal, not by making the divinity of the Word weak, but by assuming the weakness of flesh. Yet He did not continue mortal in the flesh, but raised it from the dead; for it is the very fruit of His mediation that those for whose redemption He became the Mediator should not abide eternally in bodily death. Therefore it suited the Mediator between us and God to have both a temporary mortality and a permanent blessedness. By means of what is temporary He became like mortals, so that He might transfer them from mortality to what is permanent....

Humanity, then, is mortal and miserable, and far removed from the immortal and the blessed. What medium shall we choose by which we may be united to immortality and blessedness? The immortality of the demons, which might have some charm for us, is a miserable immortality; the mortality of Christ, which might offend us, exists no longer. In the immortality of the demons, there is the fear of an eternal misery; but in the mortality of Christ, death (which could not be eternal) can no longer be feared, and blessedness (which is eternal) must be loved. The immortal and miserable mediator [a demon] interposes himself to prevent us from passing to a blessed immortality; for the thing that hinders such a change, namely, misery, continues in him. But the mortal and blessed Mediator interposed Himself, in order that, having passed through mortality, He might make mortals into immortals (showing His power to do this in His own resurrection). Further, He raises us from our misery to the blessed company from whose number He had Himself never departed.

There is, then, a wicked mediator, who separates friends, and a good Mediator, who reconciles enemies. And those who separate are numerous, because the multitude of the blessed are blessed only by their participation in the one God. The evil angels are deprived of this participation, and are therefore miserable. They interpose to hinder rather than to help us to this blessedness, and by their very number prevent us from reaching that one good that makes us blessed. To obtain this, we need not many mediators, but one Mediator, the uncreated Word of God, by whom all things were made, and in partaking of Whom we are blessed.

I do not say that He is Mediator because He is the Word; for as the Word, He is supremely blessed and supremely immortal, and therefore far from miserable mortals. But He is Mediator in His humanity. For by His humanity, He shows us that, in order to obtain that blessed and blissful good, we need not seek other mediators to lead us through successive steps to final attainment. Rather, the blessed and blissful God, having Himself become a partaker of our humanity, has afforded us ready access to participation in His divinity. For in delivering us from our mortality and misery, He does not lead us to the immortal and blessed angels, so that we should become immortal and blessed by participating in their angelic nature. No, He leads us straight to the Trinity, by participating in which the angels themselves are blessed. Therefore, when the Word chose to be in the form of a servant, and lower than the angels, so that He might be our Mediator, He still remained higher than the angels, in the form of God. He was Himself at the same time the way of life on earth, and life itself in heaven.

City of God, 9:15

The incarnation and cross were the best way God could have chosen

There are those who say, "What, did God have no other way by which He might free human beings from the misery of this mortality? Was it necessary for Him to will that the Only-begotten Son, God co-eternal with Himself, should become man, by putting on a human soul and flesh, and being made mortal to endure death?" In response, it is not enough simply to assert that the way by which God chooses to free us through the Mediator between God and human beings, the man Christ Jesus, is good and suitable to the dignity of God. We must show also, not indeed that no other way was *possible* to God (to His power all things are equally subject), but that there neither was nor need have been any other way more *appropriate* for healing our misery,

For what was so necessary for the building up of our hope, and for liberating the minds of mortals from despair of immortality, cast down by the condition of mortality itself, than that it should be demonstrated to us at how great a price God valued us, and how greatly He loved us? But what is more manifest and plain in the great proof of this? The Son of God, unchangeably good, remaining what He was in Himself, received from us and for us what He was not [human nature]. Without any loss of His own nature, and graciously choosing to enter into fellowship with ours, He bore our evils, without any evil deserving of His own. And then with free generosity He bestowed His own gifts upon us. Now we believe how much God loves us; now we hope for what we despaired of, without anything in us that deserved good — indeed, with much in us that already deserved evil!

On the Trinity, 13:13

The incarnation honours both flesh and spirit, man and woman

With a view to our restoration and salvation, and with the goodness of God acting in this purpose, our changeable nature has been taken to Himself by the unchangeable Wisdom of God. So we also have faith in those temporal things which have been done with saving effect on our behalf, believing in the Son of God Who was born of the Virgin Mary through the Holy Spirit. For by the gift of God, that is, by the Holy Spirit, such great humility on the part of so great a God was shown to us, that He deemed it worthy of Himself to take to Himself the entire nature of humanity in the womb of the Virgin. He inhabited our material body so that it sustained no harm in being taken to Himself, and kept it without any harm thereafter.

This pre-planned act of God carried out in time is in many ways craftily assaulted by the heretics. But if anyone grasps the Catholic faith, and believes that the entire nature of humanity was taken to Himself by the Word of God, (that is to say, body, soul and spirit), he has a sufficient defence against those persons. For surely, since that taking of our nature was carried out on behalf of our salvation, one must be on his guard. For if a person believes that there is something belonging to our nature which was not included in the Word's taking of our nature, this "something" will fail to be included in the salvation!

Consider this: with the exception of the shape of the bodily members, which has been imparted to the varieties of living creatures with differences adapted to their different kinds, humanity is no different from the cattle but in the possession of a rational spirit, which is also called mind. How is that faith healthy, then, which maintains the belief that the Wisdom of God assumed that part of us which we hold in common with the cattle [flesh], but did not assume that which is brightly illumined by the light of wisdom, and which is humanity's peculiar gift [mind and spirit]? Moreover, those persons are also to be abhorred who deny that Mary was the earthly mother of our Lord Jesus Christ. For in reality, God's plan of salvation honoured both sexes, the male and the female at the same time. God has made it plain that He doesn't care only for the sex which He took to Himself [male human nature]. No, He also cares for that other sex by which He took the first to Himself, because He bore the nature of the man, and in that nature He was born of the woman.

On Faith and the Creed, 8-9

Why the virgin birth?

Certainly, in order to be a human Mediator between God and humans, God could have taken it upon Himself to be man from some other source, and not from the race of Adam who enslaved the human race by his sin. After all, God did not create the first-created man out of someone else's race. Therefore God was able, either in this way, or in any other way He pleased, to create yet another man, by whom the conqueror of the first man might be conquered. However, God judged it better to take humanity upon Himself from the very race that had been conquered, and in their humanity to conquer the enemy of the human race. And yet He judged it best to do this from a Virgin, whose act of conception was preceded, not by the flesh, but by the spirit — not by lust, but by faith. For in this conception, the lustful desire of the flesh did not intervene, by which the rest of human beings, who derive original sin, are propagated and conceived. No, it was holy virginity that became pregnant — not by conjugal intercourse, but by faith. Lust was utterly absent.

Consequently, what was born in this way from the root of the first man shared only in the origin of race, but not its guilt. For there was born, not a nature corrupted by the virus of transgression, but the only remedy of all such corruptions. There was born, I say, a Man Who had absolutely no sin, and never would have. Through Him, human beings who could not be born without sin would be born again and so be freed from sin. For although marital chastity makes a right use of the carnal desire which is in our bodily members, yet such desire is liable to involuntary arousals. This shows that it could not have existed at all in paradise before the entrance of sin; or if it did exist, it was not then the sort of desire that sometimes resists the will. But that is what we now feel it to be. In rebellion against the control of the mind, even where there is no question of begetting children, carnal desire works in us and incites us to sexual intercourse. If people yield to it, it is satisfied by an act of sin; if they do not yield, it is suppressed by an act of denial. Who could doubt that both these things were absent from paradise before sin entered? For the chastity that existed in paradise never did anything indecent, nor did the pleasure that existed in paradise experience anything disturbing.[3]

It was necessary, therefore, that this carnal lust should be entirely absent, when the offspring of the Virgin was conceived. For in Him the author of death was to find nothing worthy of death, and yet was to slay Him in order that he might be conquered by the death of the Author of life. The conqueror of the first Adam, who held the human race captive, was to be conquered by the second Adam. The devil was to lose the Christian race, brought out of the human race in freedom from human guilt, through Him who was not involved in the guilt, although He belonged to the race. In this way the deceiver was conquered by that very race which he had conquered by means

---

[3] Augustine is simply making the point that in us, sexual desire is often irrational, rebellious, extravagant, and very hard to bring under proper discipline and control. It cannot have been like that in Adam and Eve in the state of innocence. If they did have sexual relations before the fall, it did not give them a "disturbing" pleasure that undermined their rationality and self-control.

of guilt. And this was so done, in order that human nature may not be lifted up, but "that he that glories should glory in the Lord." For he who was conquered was only man; and he was conquered, because he lusted proudly to be a god. But He Who conquered was both man and God. Therefore He conquered, being born of a Virgin, because God in humility was not the Governor of that man [Jesus], as He is of other saints, but was His Father. These great gifts of God, and whatever else there are, which it would take too long for us at this point to inquire and to discuss, could not exist unless the Word had become flesh.

On the Trinity, 13:23

God was born of flesh that we might be born of God

So that human beings might be born of God, God was first born of them. For Christ is God, and Christ was born of us. It was only a mother, indeed, that He sought upon earth; for He had already a Father in heaven. He by Whom we would be created was [eternally] born of God, and He by whom we would be re-created was born of a woman. Do not marvel, then, O man, that you are made a child of God by grace, or that you are born of God according to His Word. The Word Himself first chose to be born of a human being, so that you might be born of God for salvation. Say to yourself, "Not without reason did God wish to be born of a human being. It was because He counted me of some importance, that He might make me immortal, and for my sake be born as a mortal man." Therefore, after John had said, "born of God" (Jn.1:13), in case we should be filled with amazement and trembling at such grace — grace so great as to exceed belief, that humans are born of God — as if assuring you, he says, "And the Word became flesh, and dwelt among us" (Jn.1:14). Why, then, do you marvel that humans are born of God? Consider God Himself, born of humans: "And the Word became flesh, and dwelt among us."

Because "the Word became flesh, and dwelt among us," by His very nativity He made an eye-salve to cleanse the eyes of our heart, and to enable us to see His majesty by means of His humility. Therefore "the Word became flesh, and dwelt among us." He healed

our eyes; and what follows? "And we beheld His glory." No-one
can see His glory unless they are healed by the humility of His flesh.
Why were we unable to see? Consider, dearly beloved, and see what
I say. There had dashed into the human eye, as it were, dust and
earth; it had wounded the eye, and it could not see the light. That
wounded eye is anointed; by earth it was wounded, and earth [Christ's
flesh] is applied to it for healing. For all eye-salves and medicines
are derived from the earth. By dust you were blinded; by dust [Christ's
flesh] you are healed. Flesh had wounded you; flesh heals you. The
soul had become carnal by consenting to the affections of the flesh;
and so the eye of the heart was blinded. But "the Word became
flesh." The Physician made an eye-salve for you.

And so He came by flesh to extinguish the vices of the flesh, and
by death to slay death; therefore this took place in you, that as "the
Word became flesh," so you might be able to say, "And we beheld
His glory." What sort of glory? The glory of a son of man? That
was His humility, not His glory. But what vision is granted to human sight when it is cured by means of His flesh? "We beheld His
glory, the glory as of the Only-begotten from the Father, full of
grace and truth."

Sermons on John, 2:15-16

Christ and Mary

Why, then, did the Son say to the mother, "Woman, what have I to
do with you? My hour is not yet come"? (Jn.2:4) Our Lord Jesus
Christ was both God and man. According as He was God, He had
no mother; according as He was man, He had. Mary was the mother,
then, of His flesh, of His humanity, of the weakness which for our
sakes He took upon Himself. But the miracle which He was about to
do, He was about to do according to His divine nature, not according
to His weakness: according to the nature in which He was God, not
according to the nature in which He was born weak. However, the
weakness of God is stronger than human beings. His mother then
demanded a miracle of Him; but He, about to perform divine works,
did not in that respect acknowledge a human womb. So He said in
effect, "That nature in Me which works a miracle was not born of

you. You did not give birth to My divine nature. But because My weakness was born of you, I will acknowledge you at the time when that same weakness shall hang upon the cross."

This, indeed, is the meaning of "My hour is not yet come." For it was in that hour [of His death] that He acknowledged the one who, in truth, He always did know. He knew His mother in the decree of predestination, even before He was born of her. Even before, as God, He created the woman from whom, as man, He was Himself to be created, He knew her as His mother. But at a certain hour, in a mystery, He did not acknowledge her; and at a certain hour which had not yet come, again in a mystery, He does acknowledge her. For He acknowledged her, when that to which she gave birth was dying. That by which Mary was made [the divine nature] did not die, but that which was made from Mary died [Christ's human nature]. It was not the eternity of the divine nature, but the weakness of the flesh, that was dying. He gave that answer, therefore, making a distinction in the faith of believers, between *Who* came, and *how* He came. For while He was God and the Lord of heaven and earth, He came by a mother who was a woman. As far as He was Lord of the world, Lord of heaven and earth, He was, of course, the Lord of Mary too; but in that nature of which it is said, "born of a woman, born under the law" (Gal.4:4), He was Mary's son. The same person was both the Lord of Mary and the son of Mary; the same person was both the Creator of Mary and created from Mary.

Do not marvel that He was both son and Lord. For just as He is called the son of Mary, so likewise is He called the son of David — indeed, son of David because son of Mary. Hear the apostle openly declaring, "He was made of the seed of David according to the flesh" (Rom.1:3). Hear Him also declared to be the Lord of David; let David himself declare this: "The Lord said to my Lord, Sit on my right hand" (Ps.110:1). And this verse Jesus Himself brought forward to the Jews, and refuted them from it (Matt.22:42-5). How then was He both David's son and David's Lord? He was David's son according to the flesh, David's Lord according to His deity; so also He was Mary's son according to the flesh, and Mary's Lord according to His majesty. Now as she was not the mother of His divine nature, while it was by His divinity that the miracle she asked for would be performed, therefore He answered her, "Woman, what have I to do with you? But do not think that I deny you are My mother: My hour is not yet come. For in that hour I will acknowledge you, when the weakness of which you are the mother comes to hang on the cross."

Let us prove the truth of this. When the Lord suffered, the same gospel-writer who knew the mother of the Lord, and who has given us to know about her in this marriage feast — the same, I say, tells us, "There was standing near the cross the mother of Jesus; and Jesus says to His mother, Woman, behold your son! and to the disciple, Behold your mother!" (Jn.19:25-6). He commits His mother to the care of the disciple, because He is about to die before she dies, and to rise again before her death. The man commits her, a human being, to a man's care.

Sermons on John, 8:9

Predestination shines at its brightest in the Man Christ Jesus

The most illustrious light of predestination and grace is the Saviour Himself, the Mediator between God and men, the Man Christ Jesus. I ask you, by what preceding merits of its own, whether of works or of faith, did the human nature in Christ procure for itself that it should Christ's human nature? Answer me, I beg you! The human nature of Jesus: on what basis did it deserve to be assumed into unity of person with the Word co-eternal with the Father, and so to be the only-begotten Son of God? Was it because any kind of goodness in Jesus' human nature preceded its assumption by the Word? What did His human nature do before this? What did it believe before this? What did it ask before this, that it should attain to this unspeakable excellence? Was it not by the act and the assumption of the Word that the man Jesus began to be the only Son of God, from the very instant that He began to exist as a man? Did not that woman, full of grace, conceive this man *as* the only Son of God? Was He not born as the only Son of God, born of the Holy Spirit and the Virgin Mary, not of the lust of the flesh, but by God's distinctive gift? Was it to be feared that as He matured in age, this man would sin by free will? Was the human will of Christ not free on that account? In fact, it was much more free in proportion to the greater impossibility of His becoming the slave of sin! Certainly, it was not by virtue of any preceding virtues of its own that human nature in Christ — that is to say, our nature — specially received all those specially admirable gifts, and any others that may most truly be said to be distinctive to Him.

Let anyone here answer back to God if he dare, and say, Why was *my* human nature not chosen to be united with the Word in the incarnation? And if he should hear, "O man, who are you that answer back against God?" (Rom.9:20), let him not at this point restrain himself. Let him increase his impudence and say, "How is it that I hear this, 'Who are you, O man?' For I am what I hear — that is, I am a man, and Christ of Whom I speak is also a man. So why shouldn't I also be the same as He is? For it is by grace that His human nature is so great. Why is a different grace given to Him and to me when we share a common human nature? Surely there is no respect of persons with God!" I say, not what Christian man, but what madman will say this?

On the Predestination of the Saints, 30

The incarnation is the highest proof of sovereign grace

Now here the grace of God is displayed with the greatest power and clearness. For what merit had the human nature of the man Christ earned, that it should in this unparalleled way be taken up into the unity of the person of God's only Son? What goodness of will, what goodness of desire and intention, what good works, had gone before, which made Christ's humanity worthy to become one person with God? Had He even *existed* as a man previously to this? Had He earned this unprecedented reward, that He should be thought worthy to become God? Assuredly not! From the very first moment that He began to exist as a man, He was none other than the very Son of God, the only Son of God, the Word Who became flesh. Therefore He was God. Just as each individual human being unites in one person a body and a rational soul, so also Christ in one person unites the Word and human nature.

Now on what basis was this unheard of glory conferred on human nature, a glory which, as there was no preceding virtue, was of course entirely of grace? Those who looked at the matter soberly and honestly might here behold a clear manifestation of the power of God's free grace, and might understand that they are justified from their sins by the same grace which made the man Christ Jesus free from the possibility of sin. And so the angel, when he announced to Christ's mother the coming birth, saluted her thus: "Hail, you who are full of grace"; and shortly afterwards, "You have found grace with God" (Lk.1:28,30). Now Mary was said to be full of grace, and to have found grace with God, because she was to be the mother of her Lord — indeed, the mother of the Lord of all flesh. But, speaking of Christ Himself, the gospel-writer John, after saying, "The Word became flesh, and dwelt among us," adds, "and we beheld His glory, the glory as of the Only-begotten of the Father, full of grace and truth" (Jn.1:14). When he says, "The Word became flesh," this is "full of grace"; when he says, "the glory of the Only-begotten of the Father," this is "full of truth." For the Truth Himself was the Only-begotten of the Father, not by grace but by nature; but He took our humanity upon Him by grace, and united it with His own person, so that He Himself became also the Son of Man.

Enchiridion, 36

Incarnation and atonement: the link

"The light shines in darkness, and the darkness did not comprehend it" (Jn.1:5). Now the "darkness" is the foolish minds of human beings, made blind by vicious desires and unbelief. In order that the Word, by Whom all things were made, might care for these and heal them, "The Word became flesh, and dwelt among us" (Jn.1:14). For our enlightenment is a sharing in the Word, namely, in that "life which is the light of human beings" (Jn.1:4). However, for this sharing we were utterly unfit, and fell short of it, on account of the uncleanness of sins. Therefore we had to be cleansed.

And the only cleansing of the unrighteous and of the proud is the blood of the Righteous One, and the humbling of God Himself, so that we might be cleansed through Him. He became what we are by nature [human], and what we are not by sin [perfectly human], in order that we might contemplate God, which by nature we are not. For by nature we are not God; by nature we are human, and by sin we are not righteous. Therefore God became a righteous man, and interceded with God for sinful humanity. For the sinner is not akin to the righteous, but the human is akin to the human. Therefore by joining to us the likeness of His humanity, He took away the unlikeness of our unrighteousness; and by becoming sharer of our mortality, He made us sharers in His divinity. For the death of the sinner springs from the necessity of condemnation, and is deservedly abolished by the death of the Righteous One which springs from the free choice of His compassion ...

On the Trinity, 4:4

Christ incarnate: the humble God

Therefore, it was mainly for this purpose that Christ came, that human beings might learn how much God loves them, and that they might learn this, so that they might be kindled to love Him by Whom they were first loved. Christ's purpose was also to teach human beings to love their neighbours, at the command and example of Him Who became our neighbour, because He loved us when, instead of being a neighbour to Him, we were dwelling far off. Again, all divine Scripture, which was written before the event, was written with the view of signifying in advance the Lord's coming; and whatever has been committed to writing in times subsequent to these, and established by divine authority, is a record of Christ, and admonishes us concerning love.

It is manifest, then, that on those two commands — love to God and love to our neighbour — hang all "the law and the prophets" which, at the time when the Lord spoke to that effect, were the only holy Scripture then written. But the same is true of all those books of divine literature which have been written at a later period for our health, and committed to remembrance. Therefore, in the Old Testament the New lies veiled, and in the New Testament the Old lies revealed. According to the veiling, carnal people understood things in a carnal fashion, and have been under the dominion, both then and now, of a fear of punishment. According to the revealing, on the other hand, spiritual people understand things in a spiritual fashion, and have been made free through the love with which they have been gifted. Among them we reckon those who once knocked in piety and found hidden things opened to them, and those who now seek in no spirit of pride, in case even things uncovered should be closed to them.

Consequently, since there is nothing more opposed to love than envy, and since pride is the mother of envy, the Lord Jesus Christ, the God-man, is both a manifestation of divine love towards us, and an example of human humility among us, so that our greatly swollen egos might be cured by a greater counteracting remedy. For here is great misery — a proud human being! But here is greater mercy — a humble God! Take this love, therefore, as the goal that is set before you, to which you must refer all that you say. And whatever you tell [as a teacher in the Church], tell it in such a way that he to whom you are speaking may believe when he hears, may hope when he believes, may love when he hopes.

On the Catechising of the Uninstructed, 8

(b) The Atonement

Christ the Mediator takes away God's wrath

And so the human race was lying under a just condemnation, and all human beings were the children of wrath. Of this wrath it is written: "All our days are passed away in Your wrath; we spend our years as a tale that is told" (Ps.90:9). Of this wrath also Job says: "Man that is born of a woman is of few days, and full of trouble" (Job 14:1). Of this wrath also the Lord Jesus says: "He that believes in the Son has everlasting life: and he that does not believe the Son shall not see life, but the wrath of God abides on him" (Jn.3:36).[4] He does not say that God's wrath *will* come, but it "abides on him." For every human being is born with it; therefore the apostle says: "We were by nature the children of wrath, even as others" (Eph.2:3).

---

[4] These are actually the words of John the Baptist.

Now, human beings were lying under this wrath on account of their original sin, and this original sin was the more heavy and deadly in proportion to the number and magnitude of the actual sins that were added to it. This is why there was need for a Mediator, that is, a reconciler, who by the offering of one sacrifice, of which all the sacrifices of the law and the prophets were types, should take away this wrath. Therefore the apostle says: "For if, when we were enemies, we were reconciled to God by the death of His Son, much more, being reconciled, we shall be saved by His life" (Rom.5:10).

When God is said to be angry, we do not attribute to Him such a disturbed feeling as exists in the mind of an angry man; but we call His *just displeasure against sin* by the name *anger*, a word transferred by analogy from human emotions. But our being reconciled to God through a Mediator, and receiving the Holy Spirit, so that we who were enemies are made sons ("For as many as are led by the Spirit of God, they are the sons of God," Rom.8:14): this is the grace of God through Jesus Christ our Lord.

Enchiridion, 33

The necessity of the atonement: mankind's subjection to Satan

By the justice of God (in some sense) the human race was delivered into the power of the devil. The sin of the first man passed over originally into all males and females in their birth through conjugal union, and the debt of our first parents bound all their offspring. This delivering up is first signified in Genesis, where it was said to the serpent, "You shall eat dust" (Gen.3:14). And then it was said to the man, "Dust you are, and to dust you shall return" (Gen.3:19). In the words, "to dust you shall return," the death of the body is announced, because Adam would not have experienced that either, if he had continued to the end upright as he was made. But since it is said to him whilst still living, "Dust you are," it is shown that the whole man was changed for the worse. For "Dust you are" is much the same as, "My spirit shall not always remain in these men, for that they also are flesh" (Gen.6:3).

Therefore it was at that time shown, that Adam was delivered to the devil, since it had been said to the serpent, "You shall eat dust."

But the apostle declares this more clearly, where he says: "And you who were dead in trespasses and sins, in which in time past you walked according to the course of this world, according to the prince of the power of the air, the spirit that now works in the children of unfaithfulness; among whom we also had our conversation in times past, in the lusts of our flesh, fulfilling the desires of the flesh and of the mind; and were by nature the children of wrath, even as others" (Eph.2:1-3). The "children of unfaithfulness" are the unbelievers; and who is not this before he becomes a believer? And therefore all humans are originally under the prince of the power of the air, "who works in the children of unfaithfulness." And what I have expressed by "originally" is the same that the apostle expresses when he speaks of himself and the rest who "by nature" were the same as others. "By nature" means human nature as it has been depraved by sin, not as it was created upright from the beginning.

But the way in which the human race was thus delivered into the power of the devil ought not to be so understood as if God did this, or commanded it to be done. Rather, He only permitted it, yet He permitted it justly. For when He abandoned the sinner, the author of the sin immediately entered. Yet certainly God did not abandon His own creature so totally as not to reveal Himself to mankind as God in creating and giving life, and in the midst of penal evils bestowing also many good things upon evil humans. For He has not in anger shut up His tender mercies. Nor did He dismiss man from the law of His own power, when He permitted him to be in the power of the devil. For even the devil himself is not separated from the power of the Almighty, or even from His goodness. For how do even the evil angels exist in whatever manner of life they have, except through Him who gives life to all things? So then, the commission of sins subjected the human race to the devil through the just anger of God. Yet doubtless the forgiveness of sins rescues man from the devil through the merciful reconciliation of God.

On the Trinity, 13:16

Christ triumphed over Satan by the cross

The devil received outwardly the power of slaying the Lord in the flesh, but in so doing, his inward power, by which he held us prisoner, was slain. For it was brought about that the bonds of many sins in many deaths were loosed, through the one death of One Who had committed no sin. The Lord therefore offered His death for us, though He was under no obligation to die, so that the death which we deserved might inflict on us no harm. For He was not stripped of the flesh by obligation to any authority, but He stripped Himself. For doubtless He who was capable of not dying, if He chose not to, did actually die because He chose to. And thus He made a spectacle of principalities and powers, openly triumphing over them in Himself; for by His death, the one and most real sacrifice was offered up for us. In this way, He cleansed, abolished, and extinguished whatever fault there was, by which principalities and powers held us justly captive to pay the penalty of death. Then by His own resurrection He also called us, whom He predestined to a new life; and those whom He called, He justified; and those whom He justified, He glorified. And so the devil, in that fleshly death itself, lost mankind, whom he possessed by an absolute right, seduced as mankind was by its own consent…

And so the Son of God graciously chose to become our friend in the fellowship of death – the death to which the enemy [Satan] was not subject, so that he thought himself better and greater than ourselves. For our Redeemer says, "Greater love has no man than this, that a man lay down his life for his friends" (Jn.15:13). Therefore the devil thought himself superior to the Lord Himself, since the Lord in His sufferings yielded to him. For we must understand the Psalm to refer to Christ, "For You have made Him a little lower than the angels" (Ps.8:5). He was Himself put to death, although innocent, by the unjust one [the devil] acting against us as if it were by just right. In this way, by a most just right, He overcome the devil, and so led captive the captivity brought about through sin. He freed us from a just captivity on account of sin, by blotting out the handwriting, and through His own righteous blood unrighteously shed He redeemed us — us who were to be justified although we were sinners.

On the Trinity, 4:17

The Good Merchant

My brothers, let us long for the life of Christ, seeing that we hold as a pledge the death of Christ. How shall He not give us His good things, Who has suffered our evil things? In this our earth, in this evil world, what abounds but to be born, to labour, and to die? Examine thoroughly the human condition, and convict me if I lie. Consider all people, whether they are in this world for any other end than to be born, to labour, and to die. This is the merchandise of our country; these things abound here. To such merchandise did that Merchant descend. And every merchant gives and receives — gives what he has, and receives what he lacks; when he buys anything, he gives money, and receives what he buys. So Christ too in His commerce gave and received. But what did He receive? What abounds here — to be born, to labour, and to die. And what did He give? To be born again, to rise again, and to reign for ever.

O Good Merchant, buy us! Yet why should I say buy us, when we ought to give You thanks that You *have* bought us? You deal out our price to us; we drink Your blood — thus You deal out to us our price. And we read the Gospel, our title deed. We are Your servants, we are Your creatures; You have made us, You have redeemed us. Anyone can buy a servant for himself, but he cannot create one. The Lord has both created and redeemed His servants: created them, that they might exist; redeemed them, that they might not be captives for ever. For we fell into the hands of the prince of this world, who seduced Adam, and made him his servant, and began to possess us as his slaves. But the Redeemer came, and the seducer was overcome.

And what did our Redeemer do to him who held us captive? For our ransom, Jesus held out His cross as a trap; He placed in it His blood as a bait. The devil indeed had the power to shed the Redeemer's blood, but he did not attain to drink it. And because he shed the blood of Him who was no debtor, the devil was commanded to release the debtors; he shed the blood of the Innocent One, so he was commanded to withdraw from the guilty. Jesus truly shed His blood for this purpose, that He might wipe out our sins. That by which the devil held us fast was cancelled by the Redeemer's blood. For the devil held us captive only by the bonds of our own sins. They were the prisoner's chains. The Redeemer came, He bound the strong one with the bonds of His suffering; He entered into his house, that is, into the hearts of those in whom the devil dwelt, and took away his vessels. We are his vessels. The devil had filled us with his own bitterness. This bitterness too he pledged to our Redeemer in the gall. Satan had filled us then as his vessels; but our Lord seized Satan's vessels, made them His own, emptied out the bitterness, and filled them with sweetness. Let us then love Him, for He is sweet. "Taste and see that the Lord is sweet" (Ps.34:8). He is to be feared, but to be loved still more.

Sermons on the Gospels, 80:2-3

Original sin and the atonement

A man and a man: a man brings death and a man brings life. Thus says the apostle: "Since, indeed, by a man came death, by a man also comes the resurrection of the dead" (1 Cor.15:21). By which man came death, and by which man came the resurrection of the dead? Do not make haste: he goes on to say, "For as in Adam all die, so also in Christ shall all be made alive" (1 Cor.15:22). Who belong to Adam? All who are born of Adam. Who belong to Christ? All who were born through Christ. Why are all in sin? Because no-one was born except through Adam. But they were born of Adam by necessity, arising from condemnation; to be born through Christ is of will and grace.[5] People are not compelled to be born through Christ; but they were not born of Adam because they wished it. All, however, who are born of Adam are sinners with sin; all who are born through Christ are justified, and righteous not in themselves, but in Christ. For in themselves, if you ask, they belong to Adam; but in Christ, if you ask, they belong to Christ. Why? Because He, the Head, our Lord Jesus Christ, did not come with the inheritance of sin; but He came nevertheless with mortal flesh.

---

[5] "Born of will and grace" points to the fact that the new birth has an element of willingness that is lacking from fleshly birth. We become human beings by nature without our consent; we become Christians by grace with our consent – hence "of will and grace". Of course, Augustine thought that the consent was *itself* a sovereign gift of grace. "No-one can come to Me unless the Father draws him" (Jn.6:44); and the Father draws us precisely by making us willing.

Death was the punishment of sins; in the Lord was the gift of mercy, not the punishment of sin. For the Lord had nothing on account of which He should justly die. He Himself says, "Behold, the prince of this world comes, and finds nothing in Me." Why then do You die? "But that all may know that I do the will of my Father, arise, let us go from here" (Jn.14:30-31). The Lord did not have in Himself any reason why He should die, and yet He died; you have such a reason, and do you refuse to die? Do not refuse to bear with a calm mind what you deserve, when the Lord did not refuse to suffer so that He might deliver you from eternal death.

A man and a man! But the one was nothing but man; the other was God-man. The one was a man of sin, the other a man of righteousness. You died in Adam; rise in Christ — for both are made yours. Although you have now believed in Christ, render nevertheless what you owe through Adam. But the chain of sin will not hold you eternally, for the temporal death of your Lord killed your eternal death.

Sermons on John, 3:12-13

Christ was "made sin" for us

Jesus was begotten and conceived, then, without any indulgence of carnal lust, and therefore brought with Him no original sin, and by the grace of God was joined and united in a wonderful and unspeakable way in one person with the Word, the Only-begotten of the Father, a Son by nature, not by grace, and therefore having no sin of His own. Nevertheless, on account of the likeness of sinful flesh in which He came, He was called sin, so that He might be sacrificed to wash away sin. For under the Old Covenant, *sacrifices* for sin were called *sins*.[6] And He, of whom all these sacrifices were

---

[6] The commentator Adam Clarke remarks that the word "sin" in 2 Cor.5:21, where Paul says that God made Christ to be sin, "signifies a sin-offering, or sacrifice for sin, and answers to the chattaah and chattath of the Hebrew text; which signifies both sin and sin-offering in a great variety of places in the Pentateuch. The Septuagint translates the Hebrew word by $\alpha\mu\alpha\rho\tau\iota\alpha$ (sin) in ninety-four places in Exodus, Leviticus, and Numbers, where a sin-offering is meant." See Clarke's commentary on the whole Bible at this place, and other commentaries on 2 Corinthians.

types and shadows, was Himself truly made sin. Hence the apostle, after saying, "We implore you in Christ's stead, be reconciled to God," immediately adds: "for He has made Him to be sin for us who knew no sin, that we might be made the righteousness of God in Him" (2 Cor.5:20-21). He does not say, as some incorrect copies read, "He Who knew no sin committed sin for us," as if Christ had Himself sinned for our sakes; but Paul says, "Him Who knew no sin" (that is, Christ), God "has made to be sin for us." That is, God to Whom we are to be reconciled has made Him a *sacrifice* for our sins, by which we might be reconciled to God.

He, then, was made sin, just as we are made righteousness, not in ourselves, but in Him (our righteousness being not our own, but God's); Christ was made sin, not His own, but ours — not in Himself, but in us. He thus showed, by the likeness of sinful flesh in which He was crucified, that though sin was not in Him, yet that in a certain sense He died to sin, by dying in the flesh which was the likeness of sin. He also showed that although He Himself had never lived the old life of sin, yet by His resurrection He typified our new life springing up out of the old death in sin.

Enchiridion, 41

Christ's sacrifice destroys the separating wall of sin

You heard when the apostle was read: "We are ambassadors," he says, "for Christ, as though God were exhorting you by us; we beseech you in Christ's stead," — that is, as if Christ were beseeching you, and for what? — "to be reconciled to God" (2 Cor.5:20). If the apostle exhorts and beseeches us to be reconciled to God, then we were God's enemies. For no-one is reconciled unless from a state of hostility. And we have become God's enemies not by nature, but by sin. From the same source that we are the servants of sin, we are the enemies of God. God has no enemies in a state of freedom. They must be slaves; and slaves will they remain, unless delivered by Him to whom they wished by their sins to be enemies. Therefore, says be, "We beseech you in Christ's stead to be reconciled to God." But how are we reconciled, except by the removal of what separates between us and Himself? For He says by the prophet, "He has not made the ear heavy that it should not hear; but your iniquities have separated between you and your God" (Isa.59:1-2).

So then, we are not reconciled, unless what is in the midst is taken away, and something else is put in its place. For there is a separating medium, and, on the other hand, there is a reconciling Mediator. The separating medium is sin; the reconciling Mediator is the Lord Jesus Christ: "For there is one God and Mediator between God and men, the man Christ Jesus" (1 Tim.2:5). To take away the separating wall, which is sin, that Mediator has come, and the priest has Himself become the sacrifice. He was made a sacrifice for sin, offering Himself as a whole burnt-offering on the cross of His passion. Therefore the apostle, after saying, "We beseech you in Christ's stead to be reconciled unto God" — as if we had said, How shall we be able to be reconciled? — goes on to say, "He has made Him," that is, Christ Himself, "Who knew no sin to be sin for us, that we may be the righteousness of God in Him" (2 Cor.5:21). By "Him," he means Christ Himself, our God, "Who knew no sin." For He came in the flesh, that is, in the likeness of sinful flesh, but not in sinful flesh, because He had no sin at all; and therefore He became a true sacrifice for sin, because He Himself had no sin.

But perhaps, through some special perception of my own, I have said that sin is a sacrifice for sin. Let those who have read it be free to acknowledge it; let not those who have not read it be backward; let them not, I say, be backward to read, that they may be truthful in judging. For when God gave commands about the offering of sacrifices for sin (in which sacrifices there was no actual expiation of sins, but the shadow of things to come), the self-same sacrifices, the self-same offerings, the self-same victims, the self-same animals, which were brought forward to be slain for sins, and in whose blood Christ's blood was prefigured, are themselves called sins by the law. This is true to such an extent that, in certain passages, it is written in these terms, that the priests, when about to sacrifice, were to lay their hands "on the head of the sin", that is, on the head of the victim about to be sacrificed for sin. Such sin, then — that is, such a sacrifice for sin — was our Lord Jesus Christ made, "Who knew no sin."

Sermons on John, 41:5-6

The death of death in the death of Christ

Jesus came down and died, and by that death delivered us from death. Being slain by death, He slew death. And you know, brethren, that this death entered into the world through the devil's envy. "God did not make death," says Scripture, "nor delights He in the destruction of the living; but He created all things to exist." But what does it say here? "But by the devil's envy, death entered into the whole world" (Wisdom 1:2).[7] To the death offered for our contemplation by the devil, man would not come by force; for the devil did not have the power of forcing, but only of cunning to persuade. If you had not consented, the devil would have brought in nothing; your own consenting, O man, led you to death. Mortals are born from that which is mortal; from being immortals, we have become mortals. From Adam all humans are mortal; but Jesus the Son of God, the Word of God, by Whom all things were made, the only Son equal with the Father, became mortal: "for the Word became flesh, and dwelt among us" (Jn.1:14). Jesus endured death, then; but He impaled death on the cross, and mortal humans are delivered from death.

The Lord calls to mind a great matter, which was done figuratively among the Jews of old: "And as Moses," He says, "lifted up the serpent in the wilderness, so must the Son of man be lifted up, so that everyone who believes in Him may not perish, but have everlasting life" (Jn.3:15). Here is a great mystery, as those who read know. Let them hear again, both those who have not read and those who have forgotten what perhaps they had heard or read. The people of Israel had fallen helplessly in the wilderness by the bite of serpents; they suffered a great calamity by many deaths. For it was the stroke of God, correcting and scourging them that He might instruct them. In this was shown a great mystery, the symbol of a thing to come: the Lord Himself testifies in this passage, so that no-one can give another interpretation than that which the Truth indicates concerning itself.

---

[7] Augustine thought the apocryphal book of Wisdom was part of the Old Testament canon. Jerome, the most learned of the early Church fathers, demonstrated that the apocryphal books were never recognised as canonical by the Jews, and should be rejected by Christians too, since we have no warrant to add any book to the established Jewish Old Testament.

Now Moses was ordered by the Lord to make a bronze serpent, and to raise it on a pole in the wilderness, and to admonish the people Israel, that, when anyone had been bitten by a serpent, he should look to that serpent raised up on the pole. This was done. People were bitten; they looked and were healed. What are the biting serpents? Sins, arising from the mortality of the flesh. What is the serpent lifted up? The Lord's death on the cross. For since death came by the serpent, it was symbolised by the image of a serpent. The serpent's bite was deadly; the Lord's death is life-giving. A serpent is gazed on that the serpent may have no power. What is this? A death is gazed on, that death may have no power! But whose death? The death of Life. If this may be said, the death of Life! Yes, it may be said, but said wonderfully. But should it not be spoken, seeing it was a thing done? Shall I hesitate to utter what the Lord has graciously chosen to do for me? Is not Christ the Life? And yet Christ hung on the cross. Is not Christ Life? And yet Christ was dead. But in Christ's death, death died! Life, put to death, slew death; the fullness of Life swallowed up death; death was absorbed in the body of Christ.

So also shall we say in the resurrection, when we triumphantly sing, "Where, O death, is your victory? Where, O death, is your sting?" (1 Cor.15:55). Meanwhile, brethren, that we may be healed from sin, let us now gaze on Christ crucified. For "as Moses," He says, "lifted up the serpent in the wilderness, so must the Son of man be lifted up, so that whoever believes in Him may not perish, but have everlasting life." Just as those who looked on that serpent did not perish by the serpent's bites, so those who look in faith on Christ's death are healed from the bites of sins. But those [Jews] were healed from death to merely temporal life; whereas here He says, "that they may have everlasting life." So there is this difference between the figurative image and the real thing: the symbol procured temporal life; the reality that it symbolised procures eternal life.

Sermons on John, 12:10-11

Christ took our penalty

How can the Pelagians say it was only death that passed upon us by means of Adam? For if we die because Adam *died*, but Adam died because he *sinned*, they are saying that the punishment is passed on without the guilt! That means that innocent infants are punished with an unjust penalty by deriving death without deserving death. But the Catholic faith affirms this exclusively of the one and only Mediator between God and mankind, the man Christ Jesus, Who for our sake stooped down to undergo death — that is, the penalty of sin — Himself being without sin. As He alone became the Son of Man, in order that we might become through Him sons of God, so He alone, on our behalf, undertook punishment without deserving it, that we through Him might obtain grace without deserving it.

Against Two Letters of the Pelagians, 4:6

"Cursed is everyone who is hanged on a tree"

Christ has no sin in the sense of deserving death, but for our sakes He "bore sin" in the sense of the death that came upon human nature through sin. This is what hung on the tree; this is what was cursed by Moses (Deut.21:23). Thus death was condemned so that its reign might cease, and was cursed that it might be destroyed. By Christ's taking our sin in this sense, its condemnation is our deliverance, while to remain in subjection to sin is to be condemned.

What does Faustus find strange in the curse pronounced on sin, on death, and on human mortality, which Christ bore on account of human sin, though He Himself was sinless? Christ's body was derived from Adam, for His mother the Virgin Mary was a child of Adam. But God said in Paradise, "On the day that you eat, you shall surely die" (Gen.2:17). This is the curse which hung on the tree. You can deny that Christ was cursed if you deny that He died! But the person who believes that Christ died, and acknowledges that death is the fruit of sin, and is itself called sin, will understand who it is that is cursed by Moses, when he hears the apostle saying, "For our old man is crucified with Him" (Rom.6:6). The apostle boldly says of Christ, "He was made a curse for us" (Gal.3:13). For he could also venture to say, "He died for all" (2 Cor.5:14). "He died," and "He was cursed," are the same. Death is the effect of the curse; and all sin is cursed, whether it means the action that deserves punishment, or the punishment that follows. Christ, though guiltless, took our punishment, that He might cancel our guilt and do away with our punishment. These things are not my opinions, but are affirmed constantly by the apostle, with an emphasis sufficient to rouse the careless and to silence the disputers....

Exemption from Adam's curse implies exemption from his death. But Christ endured death as a human being, and on humanity's behalf. So also, though He was the Son of God — ever living in His own righteousness, but dying for our offences — He submitted as a human being, and on humanity's behalf, to bear the curse which accompanies death. In bearing our punishment, He died in the flesh which He took; so likewise, while ever blessed in His own righteousness, He was cursed for our offences, in the death which He suffered in bearing our punishment. And these words "everyone" ["Cursed is everyone that is hanged on a tree"] are intended to check the ignorant impertinence which would deny that this curse has any reference to Christ; for since the curse goes along with death, denying the curse would lead to the denial of the true death of Christ.

The believer in the true doctrine of the gospel will understand that Moses does not reproach Christ when he speaks of Him as "cursed" — not in His divine majesty — but as hanging on the tree as our substitute, bearing our punishment. This is no reproach to Christ, any more than the Manichees praise Him when they deny that He had a mortal body and suffered real death. In the curse of the prophet, there is praise of Christ's humility; in the pretended esteem of the heretics, there is a charge of falsehood. If, then, you deny that Christ was cursed, you must deny that He died; and then you have to take up the argument, not with Moses, but with the apostles. Confess that Christ died, and you may also confess that He, without taking our sin, took its punishment.

Reply to Faustus the Manichee, 14:3-7

Lord Jesus, You have suffered for us

He contracted Himself; He lessened Himself, so to speak. "For being in the form of God, He emptied Himself, taking the form of a servant" (Phil.2:6-7). What does this mean, that He conformed Himself alive to the dead? Do you ask what this is? Hear the apostle: "God sent His Son" (Rom.8:3). What does it mean that He conformed Himself to the dead? Let Paul tell us this, let him go on and declare it again: "In the likeness of sinful flesh" (Rom.8:3). This is to conform Himself alive to the dead: to come to us in the likeness of sinful flesh, but not in actual sinful flesh. Humanity lay dead in sinful flesh; the likeness of sinful flesh conformed Himself to humanity. For He died, though He had no reason to die. He died, the only One to be "free among the dead" (Ps. 88:5), since the whole of human flesh was indeed sinful flesh. And how should this flesh rise again, unless He Who had no sin, conforming Himself to the dead, came in the likeness of sinful flesh? O Lord Jesus, You have suffered for us, not for Yourself; You had no guilt, yet endured its punishment, that You might remove both the guilt and the punishment.

Sermons on the Gospels, 86:6

Christ paid our debt

And, as if it were said to Him, Why do You die, if You have no sin to merit the punishment of death? He immediately added, "But that the world may know that I love the Father, and as the Father gave me commandment, even so I do: arise, let us go from here" (Jn.14:30-31). For He was sitting at table with those who were similarly occupied. But "let us go," He said. Where to? To the place where He Who had nothing in Him deserving of death was to be delivered up to death. But He had the Father's commandment to die, as the very One of Whom it had been foretold, "Then I paid for what I did not take away" (Ps.69:4). And so He was appointed to pay death to the full, while owing it nothing, and to redeem us from the death that was our due. For Adam had seized on sin as a prey, when in a deceived state of mind he arrogantly stretched forth his hand to the tree, and tried to invade the incommunicable name of the Godhead which was not permitted to him. But the Son of God was endowed with this Godhead by nature, and not by robbery.

Sermons on John, 79:2

Through the cross, Christ achieves salvation by righteousness, not merely by power

What, then, is the righteousness by which the devil was conquered? The righteousness of Jesus Christ. And how was the devil conquered? Because he found in Christ nothing worthy of death, and yet he killed Him. And certainly it is in harmony with justice that we, whom the devil held as debtors, should be dismissed free by believing in Him whom the devil put to death without any debt. In this way, we are said to be justified in the blood of Christ; in this way, His innocent blood was shed for the forgiveness of our sins. This is why He calls Himself in the Psalms, "Free among the dead" (Ps. 88:5). For only a dead person is free from the debt of death. Thus also in another psalm He says, "Then I paid for what I did not take away" (Ps.69:4). By "what I did not take away" he means sin, because sin is something unlawfully taken away. Thus also He says with the mouth of His own flesh, as we read in the Gospel: "For the prince of this world comes, but he has nothing in me," that is, no sin; but "that the world may know that I obey the commandment of the Father — arise, let us go from here" (Jn.14:30-31). And thus He proceeds to His suffering, so that for us debtors He might pay what He Himself did not owe.

Would the devil be conquered by this right of supreme justice, if Christ had willed to deal with him merely by power, not by righteousness? But Christ refrained from doing what was merely *possible* to Him, in order that He might first do what was *fitting*. And so it was necessary that He should be both man and God. For unless Christ had been man, He could not have been put to death. But unless He had been God, human beings would not have believed that He was refraining from doing what He could – they would have believed that He was not able to do what He wished! Further, if Christ had not been God, His death would not make us think that He set a higher value on righteousness than power; it would make us think that He lacked power. However, Christ suffered for us the fate that belonged to humanity, because He was human; but if He had been unwilling to suffer it, it would have been within His power not to suffer, because He was also God.

Righteousness was therefore made more acceptable in Christ's humility, because the great power that was in His divine nature would have been able to avoid suffering in humility, if He had been unwilling to suffer. Thus by this powerful One Who died, righteousness was commended, and power was promised, to us weak mortals. For He did one of these two things by dying, the other by rising again. What is more righteous than to suffer even the death of the cross for the sake of righteousness? And what is more powerful than for Christ to rise from the dead, and to ascend into heaven with that very flesh in which He was put to death? Thus Christ conquered the devil first by righteousness, and afterwards by power. He conquered him by righteousness, because Christ had no sin, and was put to death by the devil most unjustly. But Christ also conquered him by power, because having been dead He returned to life, never to die again.

Christ indeed would have conquered the devil by power, if the devil had not been able to slay Him at all. However, it belongs to a greater power to conquer death itself by rising again, than to avoid death by living. But here is the true reason why it is by the blood of Christ that we are justified, when we are rescued from the devil's power through the forgiveness of sins: it is to ensure that Christ conquers the devil by righteousness, not by power. For Christ was crucified, not through immortal power, but through the weakness which He took upon Him in mortal flesh. Of this weakness the apostle says, "the weakness of God is stronger than men" (1 Cor.1:25).

On the Trinity, 13:18

Christ's atoning death covers our imperfections

Because even for those who are under grace it is difficult in this mortal life to keep perfectly what is written in the law, "You shall not covet," Christ obtains pardon for us as our Priest by the sacrifice of His flesh. And in this also He fulfils the law; for where we fail through weakness, our defect is supplied by His perfection — He being the Head, while we are His members. Thus John says: "My little children, these things write I to you, that you may not sin. But if anyone sins, we have an Advocate with the Father, Jesus Christ the righteous: He is the propitiation for our sins" (1 Jn.2:1-2).

Reply to Faustus the Manichaean, 19:7

How great a price that blood was worth!

Why then should the death of Christ not have occurred? Or rather, why should that death not have been chosen above all else to occur, passing by other countless ways which He who is omnipotent could have employed to free us? For in that death, nothing was diminished or changed from Christ's divinity, and so great a benefit was conferred upon human beings, from the humanity which He took upon Him. A temporal death, which He did not owe, was offered by the eternal Son of God, Who was also the Son of Man, by which He freed us from an eternal death which we owed. The devil held fast our sins, and through them trapped us deservedly in death. But Christ discharged our sins, having none of His own, when He was led by the devil to an undeserved death. How great a price that blood was worth! For the devil slew Christ for a time by a death which was not owed; his reward is that no-one who has put on Christ can be detained by the devil in the eternal death which was their due.

Therefore "God commends His love towards us, in that, while we were yet sinners, Christ died for us. Much more then, being now justified in His blood, we shall be saved from wrath through Him" (Rom.5:8-9). Justified, he says, in His blood — obviously, justified in that we are freed from all sin. And we are freed from all sin, because the Son of God, who knew no sin, was slain for us. Therefore "we shall be saved from wrath through Him." He means the wrath of God, which is nothing else but righteous retribution. For the wrath of God is not like human wrath, a disturbance of the mind. Rather it is the wrath of Him to Whom Holy Scripture says in another place, "But You, O Lord, mastering Your power, judge with calmness" (Wisdom 12:18).[8]

If, therefore, the righteous retribution of God has received such a name, what can be the right understanding of the reconciliation of God, unless such wrath comes to an end? For we were not enemies of God, except as sins are enemies of righteousness. Once those sins are forgiven, such hostility comes to an end, and those whom He Himself justifies are reconciled to the Just One. And yet certainly He loved them even while still enemies, since "He spared not His own Son, but delivered Him up for us all" (Rom.8:32), when we were still enemies. And therefore the apostle has rightly added: "For

---

[8] See previous footnote.

if, when we were enemies, we were reconciled to God by the death of His Son," by which that forgiveness of sins was accomplished, "much more, being reconciled, we shall be saved by His life" (Rom.5:10).

Reconciled by His death — saved by His life! For who can doubt that He will give His life for His friends, for whom He gave His death when they were His enemies? "And not only so," he says, "but we also rejoice in God, through our Lord Jesus Christ, by whom we have now received the atonement" (Rom.5:11). "Not only," he says, "shall we be saved," but "we also rejoice" — not in ourselves, but "in God", nor through ourselves, "but through our Lord Jesus Christ, by whom we have now received the atonement," as we have argued above.

Then the apostle adds, "Therefore, as by one man sin entered into the world, and death by sin; and so death passed upon all men, in whom all have sinned;" *etc.* (Rom.5:12). Here he disputes at some length concerning the two men. On the one hand there is the first Adam, through whose sin and death we, his descendants, are bound by hereditary evils, so to speak. On the other hand there is the second Adam, who is not only man, but also God; by His payment for us of what He did not owe, we are freed from the debts both of our first father and of ourselves. Further, since on Adam's account the devil held captive all who were begotten through Adam's corrupted carnal lust, it is righteous that on account of the second Adam the devil should lose all who are regenerated through His immaculate spiritual grace.

On the Trinity, 13:21

Christ's incarnation and cross remove death and God's wrath and bring us grace and immortality

Carnal thought does not grasp what I say. Let it put understanding to one side for a moment, and begin by faith; let it hear what follows: "He who believes in the Son has everlasting life: and he who does not believe the Son shall not see life, but the wrath of God abides on him" (Jn.3:36). He does not say, "The wrath of God comes to him," but, "The wrath of God abides on him." All that are born mortals have the wrath of God upon them. What wrath of God? That wrath which Adam first received. For when the first man sinned, and heard the sentence, "You shall die the death," he became mortal; and so we began to be born mortal, and we have been born under the wrath of God. From this stock came the Son, yet without sin, and He was clothed with our flesh and mortality. If He shared with us in the wrath of God, are we slow to share with Him in the grace of God? Whoever, then, will not believe the Son, on him "the wrath of God abides." What wrath of God? That of which the apostle says, "We also were by nature the children of wrath, even as the rest" (Eph.2:3). All are therefore children of wrath, because all are born through the curse of death. Believe in Christ, made mortal for your sake, so that you may receive Him, the Immortal; and when you have received His immortality, you will no longer be mortal. He lived, you were dead; He died that you should live. He has brought us the grace of God, and has taken away the wrath of God. God has conquered death, lest death should conquer mankind.

Sermons on John, 14:13

If Christ died for us, why do believers still have to die?

He might, however, have also granted to believers that they should not experience bodily death. But if He had done this, although it might have been added a certain happiness to the flesh, the fortitude of faith would have been lessened. For people have such a fear of death, they would declare Christians happy merely because of their immunity from dying. Consequently, for the sake of that life which is to bring such happiness after death, no-one would hasten to the grace of Christ by virtue of contempt for death itself. Rather, with a view to removing the trouble of death, they would resort to a more luxurious mode of believing in Christ.

Therefore, He has bestowed more grace than this on those who believe on Him; yes, He has undoubtedly conferred a greater gift on them! What great trouble would it have been for a person, on seeing that people did not die when they became believers, himself also to believe in order that he might not die? But how much greater a thing it is, how much braver, how much more praiseworthy, to believe in such a way that, although one is sure to die, he can still hope to live for evermore hereafter! Ultimately, this blessing will be bestowed upon some at the last day, that they will not experience death itself, but in a sudden change will be caught up together with the resurrected in the clouds to meet Christ in the air, and so they shall ever live with the Lord.

And it is right that it should be these believers [at the time of Christ's return] who receive this grace [of escaping death]. For after them, there will be no more people to be led to faith; for then faith would not be by the hope of what is unseen, but by the love of what is seen. Such faith is weak and nerveless. In fact, it must not be called faith at all, since faith is defined like this: "Faith is the firmness of those who hope, the clear proof of things which they do not see" (Heb.11:1). Accordingly, in the same Letter to the Hebrews where this passage occurs, after listing in the following sentences certain heroes who pleased God by their faith, he says: "These all died in faith, not having received the promises, but seeing them afar off, and greeting them, and confessing that they were strangers and pilgrims on the earth" (Heb.11:13). And then afterwards he concludes his eulogy of faith in these words: "And these all, having obtained a good report through faith, did not indeed receive God's promises; for they foresaw better things for us, and that without us they could not themselves become perfect" (Heb.11:39-40). Now this would be no praise for faith, nor (as I said) would it be faith at all, if believing meant pursuing rewards which could be seen — in other words, if believers were granted the reward of immortality in this present world.

On the Merits and Forgiveness of Sins, 2:50

The wonderful exchange

He died, because it was expedient that by His death, He might kill death. God died, in order that an exchange might be accomplished by a kind of heavenly contract, so that humanity might not see death. For Christ is God; but He did not die in that nature in which He is God. For the same person is God and man; God and man is one Christ. The human nature was taken upon Him, in order that we might be changed for the better. He did not degrade the divine nature down to the level of the lower nature; rather, He took to Himself what He was not, but without losing what He was.

Since then He is both God and man, choosing that we should live by what was His, He died in what was ours. For He had nothing Himself by which He could die; nor had we anything by which we could live. For what was He who had nothing by which He could die? "In the beginning was the Word, and the Word was with God, and the Word was God" (Jn.1:1). If you seek for anything in God by which He may die, you will not find it. But we all die, we who are flesh — humans carrying about sinful flesh. Seek for that by which sin may live; it has nothing. So then, He could not have death in what was His own, nor could we have life in what was ours; but we receive life from what is His, while He receives death from what is ours.

What an exchange! What has He given, and what has He received? People who trade enter into commercial intercourse in order to exchange things. For ancient commerce was only an exchange of things. A man gave what he had, and received what he did not have. For example, he had wheat, but had no barley; another had barley, but no wheat; the former gave the wheat which he had, and received the barley which he lacked. How simple it was that the larger quantity should make up for the cheaper sort! So then another man gives barley, to receive wheat. Another gives lead, to receive silver, only he gives much lead against a little silver. Another gives wool, to receive a ready-made garment. And who can enumerate all these exchanges? But no one gives life to receive death!

Not in vain, then, did the voice of the Physician speak as He hung upon the tree [Augustine is commenting on "Father, forgive them!" Lk.23:34]. Because the Word could not die [in His divine nature], "the Word became flesh, and dwelt among us" in order that He might die for us. He hung upon the Cross, but in the flesh. There was the lowliness, which the Jews despised; there was the love by which the Jews were delivered. For them was it said, "Father, forgive them, for they know not what they do." And that voice was not in vain. He died, was buried, rose again, having passed forty days with His disciples, He ascended into heaven, He sent the Holy Spirit on those who waited for the promise. They were filled with the Holy Spirit, Whom they had received, and began to speak with the tongues of all nations. Then the Jews who were present, amazed that unlearned and ignorant people, whom they had known as brought up among them with one tongue, should in the name of Christ speak in all tongues, were astonished. They learnt from Peter's words where this gift came from. The One Who hung upon the tree gave it! He gave it, the One Who was mocked as He hung upon the tree, so that from His throne in heaven He might bestow the Holy Spirit. Those for whom He had said, "Father, forgive them, for they know not what they do," heard and believed. They believed, they were baptised, and their conversion was accomplished. What conversion? By faith they drank the blood of Christ, which in fury they had shed.

Sermons on the Gospels, 30:5

Without Christ, I would utterly despair

The true Mediator, Whom in Your secret mercy You have pointed out to the humble, and sent forth so that by His very example they might learn the same humility — that "Mediator between God and men, the man Christ Jesus" (1 Tim.2:5), appeared between mortal sinners and the immortal Just One. He shared the mortality of humans, and the justice of God. For the reward of righteousness is life and peace; therefore by means of righteousness conjoined with God, Christ cancelled the death of justified sinners, which He chose to share in common with them. Thus He was pointed out to holy men of old, in order that they might be saved through faith in His future suffering, even as we are saved through faith in His past suffering. For He was Mediator in His humanity; but as the Word He was not Mediator, because as the Word He is equal to God — He is God with God, and (together with the Holy Spirit) the one God.

How much You have loved us, good Father, in sparing not Your only Son, but delivering Him up for us wicked people! How much You have loved us, since for our sakes He Who thought it no robbery to be equal with You, "became obedient unto death, even the death of the cross" (Phil.2:8). He alone was "free among the dead" (Ps.88:5),[9] having the power to lay down His life, and the power to take it back again. For us He was, in Your eyes, both Victor and Victim; indeed, He was the Victor precisely by being the Victim. For

---

[9] This is the literal translation of the phrase in Ps.88:5, which is variously rendered "forsaken among the dead" (NASB) and "set apart among the dead' (NIV) in English.

us He was, in Your eyes, both Priest and Sacrifice; indeed, He was the Priest precisely by being the Sacrifice. By being born of You, and serving us, He made those who were slaves into Your sons. Rightly, then, is my hope strongly fixed on Him, so that You will heal all my diseases by Him who sits at Your right hand and makes intercession for us. Without Him, I would utterly despair. For my infirmities are numerous and great; yes, how numerous and great they are! But Your medicine is greater. We might think that Your Word was removed from fellowship with human beings, and despair of ourselves, if He had not "become flesh and dwelt among us" (Jn.1:14).

Terrified by my sins and the burden of my misery, I had resolved in my heart, and meditated flight into the wilderness. But You forbade me, and strengthened me, saying that Christ "died for all, that those who live should no longer live for themselves, but for Him Who died for them" (2 Cor.5:14). Behold, O Lord, I cast my care upon You, that I may live, and "behold wondrous things out of Your law" (Ps.119:18). You know my lack of skill and my infirmities; teach me, and heal me! Your only Son — He "in Whom are hidden all the treasures of wisdom and knowledge" (Col.2:3) — has redeemed me with His blood. Let not the proud speak evil of me, because I consider my ransom, and eat it and drink it, and share it with others; and being poor, desire to be satisfied from Him, together with those who "eat and are satisfied, seeking and praising the Lord" (Ps.22:26).

Confessions, 10:68-70

The difference between Christ's death and ours

Christ had the power to lay down His life, and to take it back again; but we have no power to live as long as we wish, and we must die, however unwillingly. He, by dying, immediately slew death in Himself; we, by His death, are delivered from death. His flesh underwent no corruption; ours, after undergoing corruption, will at the end of the world be clothed by Him with incorruption. He had no need of us, in order to work out our salvation; without Him, we can do nothing. He gave Himself as the vine, to us the branches; apart from Him, we can have no life. Lastly, although [Christian] brothers die for brothers, yet no martyr's blood is ever shed for the forgiveness of the sins of his brothers, as was the case in what Christ did for us. In this respect He bestowed nothing on us for our imitation, but something for congratulation. In so far, then, as the martyrs have shed their blood for their brothers, to that extent they have exhibited such tokens of love as they themselves perceived at the table of the Lord. Yet however one might imitate Christ in dying, no-one could imitate Him in redeeming.

Sermons on John, 84:2

Condemned in Adam, justified in Christ

Therefore Christ asked to be baptised in water by John, not that any iniquity of His might be washed away, but that He might manifest the depth of His humility. For baptism found in Him nothing to wash away, as death found in Him nothing to punish; so that it was in the strictest justice, and not by the mere violence of power, that the devil was crushed and conquered. For he had most unjustly put Christ to death, though there was no sin in Him to deserve death. Therefore it was most just that through Christ, the devil should lose his grip on those who by sin were justly subject to the bondage in which he held them. Christ submitted, then, to both of these, that is, both baptism and death, not through a pitiable necessity, but of His own free pity for us. He did this as part of the arrangement by which, even as one man brought sin into the world, that is, upon the whole human race, so one man was to take away the sin of the world.

But there is this difference: the first man brought *one* sin into the world, but this man [Christ] took away not only that one sin, but all that He found added to it. Hence the apostle says: "The gift is not like what came through the one that sinned: for the judgment was from one sin, resulting in condemnation, but the free gift is from many offences, resulting in justification" (Rom.5:16). For it is evident that the one sin which we bring with us by nature would, even if it stood alone, bring us under condemnation; but the free gift justifies a person from many offences. For each human being, in addition to the one sin which, in common with all his kind, he brings with him by nature, has committed many sins that are strictly his own.

But what Paul says a little after, "Therefore, as through one offence, judgment came upon all men resulting in condemnation, even so through one act of righteousness, the free gift came upon all men resulting in justification of life" (Rom.5:18), shows clearly enough that there is no-one born of Adam but is subject to condemnation, and that no-one, unless he is new-born in Christ, is freed from condemnation.

Enchiridion, 49-51

Christ's death is our invincible confidence before Satan

"For You will bless the righteous man" (Ps.5:12). This is blessing, to glory in God, and to be indwelt by God. Such sanctification is given to the righteous. But in order that they may be justified, they must first be called; and this calling is not from their merit, but from the grace of God. "For all have sinned, and lack the glory of God" (Rom.3:23). "For those whom He called, He also justified; and those whom He justified, He also glorified" (Rom.8:30). Since then calling is not from our merit, but from the goodness and mercy of God, he went on to say, "O Lord, with the shield of Your good will You have crowned us" (Ps.5:12). For God's good will goes before our good will, to call sinners to repentance. And these are the weapons by which the enemy is overcome, against whom it is said, "Who will bring any accusation against God's elect?" (Rom.8:33). Again, "if God is for us, who can be against us? He Who spared not His Only Son, but delivered Him up for us all" (Rom.8:32). "For if, when we were enemies, Christ died for us; much more being reconciled, we shall be saved from wrath through Him" (Rom.5:9). This is the unconquerable shield, by which the enemy is driven back, when he suggests despair of our salvation through the multitude of tribulations and temptations.

Commentary on the Psalms, 5:18

The Church itself is offered to God in the sacrifice of Christ

A true sacrifice is every work that is done in order that we may be united to God in holy fellowship; it has a reference to that supreme good and supreme end in which alone we can be truly blessed. And therefore even the mercy we show to others, if it is not shown for God's sake, is not a sacrifice. For, though made or offered by a human being, sacrifice is a divine thing, as those who called it *sacrifice* meant to indicate. Thus a human being himself, consecrated in the name of God, and vowed to God, is a sacrifice in so far as he dies to the world that he may live to God. For this is a part of that mercy which each man shows to himself; as it is written, "Have mercy on your soul by pleasing God" (Ecclesiasticus 30:24).[10] Our body, too, is a sacrifice when we chasten it by temperance, if we do this as we ought, for God's sake, that we may not yield our members as instruments of unrighteousness for sin, but instruments of righteousness for God. Exhorting to this sacrifice, the apostle says, "I beseech you, therefore, brethren, by the mercy of God, that you present your bodies a living sacrifice, holy, acceptable to God, which is your reasonable service" (Rom.12:1) ...

True sacrifices, then, are works of mercy to ourselves or others, done with a reference to God. And works of mercy have no other object than the relief of distress or the conferring of happiness. But there is no happiness apart from that good of which it is said, "It is good for me to be very near to God" (Ps.73:28). So it follows that the whole redeemed city, that is to say, the congregation or community of the saints, is itself offered to God as a sacrifice through the great High Priest. He offered Himself to God in His passion for us, so that we might be members of this glorious Head, according to the form of a servant. For it was this servant-form that He offered, and in this He was offered, because it is according to His servant-form that He is Mediator. In this servant-form He is both our Priest and our Sacrifice.

Accordingly, when the apostle had exhorted us to present our bodies a living sacrifice, holy and acceptable to God, our reasonable service, and not to be conformed to the world, but to be transformed

---

[10] Augustine thought that the apocryphal book of Ecclesiasticus was part of the Old Testament canon. See footnote 7.

in the renewing of our mind, that we might prove what is that good, and acceptable, and perfect will of God, that is to say, the true sacrifice of ourselves, he then says, "For I say, through the grace of God given to me, to everyone that is among you, not to think of himself more highly than he ought to think, but to think soberly, according as God has dealt to every man the measure of faith. For, as we have many members in one body, and all members do not have the same office, so we, being many, are one body in Christ, and every one members one of another, having gifts differing according to the grace that is given to us" (Rom.12:3-6).

This is the sacrifice of Christians: we, being many, are one body in Christ. And this also is the sacrifice which the Church continually celebrates in the sacrament of the altar, known to the faithful, in which she teaches that she herself is offered in the offering she makes to God.[11]

City of God, 10:6

Christ's incarnation and cross show that we must not be ashamed of flesh or of dying

Thus the good and true Mediator showed that it is sin which is evil, and not the substance or nature of flesh. For He could without sin both assume and retain our flesh (together with a human soul), and

---

[11] Augustine teaches that in the "sacrament of the altar" (the Lord's Supper), the Church "offers" to God (presents before Him) not some human offering of our own, but the once-for-all sacrifice of Christ. In other words, we plead before God the one true offering which He has first given to us by His sovereign grace — the perfect all-sufficient sacrifice of His incarnate Son — praying that God will accept us on the ground of this unique sacrifice. (This is what we do inwardly and spiritually by faith at all times; in the Lord's Supper, we do it outwardly, visibly and symbolically too.) In thus pleading the one true offering of Christ, we ourselves are offered to God, and become living sacrifices. Augustine's moral point is that we cannot truly be united with Christ in His sacrifice without sacrificing ourselves to God. The effect of Christ's death in us is our own death to self and sin, so that we become one body of love, devoted to one another, in and through our self-sacrificing Head. The priesthood of all believers means the self-sacrifice of all believers to one another in Christ's love. This is the truth that is made real in the Lord's Supper.

lay it down in death, and change it to something better by resurrection. Furthermore, death itself is the punishment of sin; and yet He submitted to it for our sakes without sin. He thereby showed us that we must not try to escape death by committing sin, but rather, if opportunity serves, endure it for righteousness' sake. For Christ was able to expiate sins by dying, because when He died it was not for sin of His own.

City of God, 10:24

The blood of Christ unites angels with humans in one Church

What is the organisation of that supremely happy society in heaven? What are the differences of rank which explain the fact that all are called by the general name "angels", as we read in the Letter to the Hebrews, "but to which of the angels did God say at any time, 'Sit on my right hand?'" (Heb.1:13), for this form of expression is evidently designed to embrace all the angels without exception; and yet we find that there are some called "archangels"? Are the archangels the same as those called "hosts", so that the expression, "Praise Him, all His angels: praise Him, all His hosts" (Ps.148:2), is the same as if it had been said, "Praise Him, all His angels: praise Him, all His archangels"? What are the various meanings of those four names under which the apostle seems to embrace the whole heavenly company without exception, "whether thrones, or dominions, or principalities, or powers" (Col.1:16)? Let those who are able to do so answer these questions, if they can also prove their answers to be true. As for me, I confess my ignorance. I am not even certain upon this point: whether the sun, and the moon, and all the stars, do not form part of this same society, though many consider them merely luminous bodies, without either sensation or intelligence ...

This part of the Church, then, which is made up of the holy angels and the hosts of God, will become known to us in its true nature, when, at the end of the world, we will be united with it in the common possession of everlasting happiness. But the other part, which is separated from it, and wanders as a stranger on the earth, is better known to us, because we ourselves belong to it — it is composed of human beings, and we too are human beings. This section of the Church has been redeemed from all sin by the blood of a Mediator Who had no sin, and its song is: "If God is for us, who can be against us? He that spared not His own Son, but delivered Him up for us all" (Rom.8:31-2). Now it was not for the angels that Christ died. Yet what was done for the redemption of humanity through His death was in a sense done for the angels. For the barrier which sin had erected between humans and the holy angels is removed, and friendship is restored between them, and by the redemption of humanity the gaps which the great apostasy left in the angelic host are filled up.

And, of course, the holy angels, taught by God, in the eternal contemplation of Whose truth their happiness consists, know how great a number of the human race are to supplement their ranks, and fill up the full tally of their citizenship. Therefore the apostle says that "all things are gathered together in one in Christ, both which are in heaven and which are on earth" (Eph.1:10). Things in heaven are gathered together when what was lost from heaven in the fall of the angels is restored from among human beings; and things on earth are gathered together, when those who are predestined to eternal life are redeemed from their old corruption. And thus, through that single sacrifice in which the Mediator was offered up, the one sacrifice of which the many victims under the law were types, heavenly things are brought into peace with earthly things, and earthly things with heavenly. Therefore, as the same apostle says: "For it pleased the Father that in Him all fullness should dwell; and, having made peace through the blood of His cross, by Him to reconcile all things to Himself: by Him, I say, whether things in earth, or things in heaven" (Col.1:19-20).

Enchiridion, 58 & 61-62

(c) The Extent of the Atonement

Christ died for the sheep

The Jews put this question to Christ (Jn.10:24), chiefly in order that, if He said, "I am Christ," they might, in accordance with the only meaning they attached to such a name — that He was of the seed of David — slander Him with aiming at the kingly power. But there is more than this in His answer to them. They wished to slander Him with claiming to be the Son of David. He replied that He was the Son of God! How? Listen: He answered them, "I tell you, and you do not believe. The works that I do in My Father's name, they bear witness of Me. But you do not believe, because you are not of My sheep" (Jn.10:25-6). You have already learned above who the sheep are. Be sheep, all of you! They are sheep through believing, sheep in following the Shepherd, sheep in not despising their Redeemer, sheep in entering by the door, sheep in going out and finding pasture, sheep in the enjoyment of eternal life. What did He mean, then, in saying to them, "You are not of my sheep"? He meant that He saw them predestined to everlasting destruction, not won to eternal life by the price of His own blood.

Sermons on John, 48:4

Christ suffered for those predestined to life

Who can count up all the blessings we enjoy? If I were to try to detail and describe only these few which I have generally indicated, such a list would fill a volume. And all these are merely the comfort of the wretched and the condemned, not the rewards of the blessed. What then will these rewards be, if such are the blessings of a condemned state? What will God give to those whom He has predestined to life, Who has given such things even to those whom He has predestined to death? What blessings will He pour forth in the blessed life upon those for whom, even in this state of misery, He has been willing that His only-begotten Son should endure such sufferings even to death? Thus the apostle reasons concerning those who are predestined to that kingdom: "He that spared not His own Son, but delivered Him up for us all, how shall He not with Him also give us all things?" (Rom.8:32). When this promise is fulfilled, what will we be? What blessings will we receive in that kingdom, since already we have received Christ's dying as the pledge of them?

City of God, 22:24

Not one perishes for whom Christ died

If Christ died for those only who with clear intelligence can discern these things, our labour in the Church is almost spent in vain. In fact, however, crowds of common people, possessing no great strength of intellect, run to the Physician in the exercise of faith. Consequently they are healed by Christ and Him crucified, so that "where sin has abounded, grace may much more abound" (Rom.5:20). So it comes to pass in wonderful ways, through the depths of the riches of God's wisdom and knowledge and His unsearchable judgments, that some who do discern between the physical and the spiritual in their own nature, and pride themselves on this attainment, despise the foolishness of preaching by which those who believe are saved. Thus they wander far from the only path that leads to eternal life. But on the other hand, because not one perishes for whom Christ died, there are many who glory in the cross of Christ, and do not step off that same path, despite their ignorance of those things which some investigate with the most profound shrewdness. Thus these ones attain to eternity, truth, and love — that is, to that enduring, clear, and full happiness, in which all things are plain to those who abide there, and see, and love.

Letter 169:4

By dying for the elect, Christ saves them from eternal death

It is not difficult to see that the devil was conquered, when He Who was slain by him rose again. But it is something more, and requires a more profound comprehension, to see that the devil was conquered when he thought he had conquered, that is, when Christ was slain. For the reason why His blood was poured out was for the forgiveness of our sins, since it was the blood of Him Who had no sin at all. So then, the devil deservedly held captive those guilty of sin, whom he bound by the condition of death; but he deservedly lost them through Him Who was guilty of no sin, Who therefore was undeservedly touched by the punishment of death. The strong man was conquered by this righteousness, and bound with this chain, so that his vessels might be taken from him, which along with himself and his angels had been vessels of wrath while they were with him, but are now turned into vessels of mercy ...

In this redemption, the blood of Christ was given (as it were) as a price for us. By accepting this price, the devil was not enriched, but bound, so that we might be released from his bonds. Consequently, not one of those whom Christ, Himself free from all debt, has redeemed by pouring out His own blood which He did not owe as a debt, will be involved with the devil in the meshes of sins, or delivered to the destruction of the second and eternal death. Rather, those who belong to the grace of Christ, foreknown and predestined and elected before the creation of the world, will die only to the degree Christ Himself died for them, *i.e.* only by fleshly death, not by spiritual death.

On the Trinity, 13:19

"World" can mean the Church

"If you were of the world," He says, "the world would love its own" (Jn.15:19). He speaks, of course, of the whole Church, which by itself He often calls by the name of "the world": as when it is said, "God was in Christ, reconciling the world to Himself" (2 Cor.5:19). And this also: "The Son of man came not to condemn the world, but that the world through Him might be saved" (Jn.3:17). And John says in his epistle: "We have an advocate with the Father, Jesus Christ the righteous: and He is the propitiation for our sins; and not for ours only, but also for those of the whole world" (1 Jn.2:1-2). The whole world then is the Church, and yet the whole world hates the Church. The world therefore hates the world, the hostile world hates the reconciled world, the condemned world hates the saved world, the polluted world hates the cleansed world. But that world which God is in Christ reconciling to Himself, which is saved by Christ, and has all its sins freely pardoned by Christ, has been chosen out of the other world that is hostile, condemned, and defiled. For out of that mass, which has all perished in Adam, the vessels of mercy are formed; and these make up that world of reconciliation which is hated by the world which belongs to the vessels of wrath, formed out of the same mass and prepared for destruction.

Finally, after saying, "If you were of the world, the world would love its own," He immediately added, "But because you are not of the world, but I have chosen you out of the world, therefore the world hates you." And so these men were themselves of that [sinful] world. But in order that they might no longer belong to it, they were chosen out of it. They were chosen, through no merit of their own, for no good works of theirs had gone before; and not by nature, which through free will had become totally corrupted at its source. No, they were chosen gratuitously, that is, by actual grace. For He Who chose the world out of the world, created for Himself, instead of finding, what He should choose. For "there is a remnant saved according to the election of grace. And if by grace," he adds, "then is it no more by works: otherwise grace is no longer grace" (Rom.11:5-6).

Sermons on John, 87:3

The "world" Christ came to save is the Church

See, that which persecutes is called the "world". Let us test whether that which suffers persecution is also called "the world". What! Are you deaf to the voice of Christ who speaks, or rather to Holy Scripture which testifies, "God was in Christ reconciling the world to Himself" (2 Cor.5:19)? "If the world hates you, know that it first hated Me" (Jn.15:18). See, the "world" hates. What does it hate? It hates — the "world"! What "world"? "God was in Christ reconciling the world to Himself." The condemned "world" persecutes; the reconciled "world" suffers persecution. The condemned "world" is all that is *outside* the Church; the reconciled "world" *is* the Church. For He says, "The Son of Man came not to judge the world, but that the world through Him may be saved" (Jn.3:17). Now in *this* world, the holy, good, reconciled, saved world (or rather, still to be saved, and now saved in hope, "for we are saved in hope," Rom.8:24) — in this world, I say, that is in the Church which wholly follows Christ, He has said as having universal application, "Whoever will follow Me, let him deny himself" (Mk.8:34).

Sermons on the Gospel, 46:8-9

The whole world whose sins Christ propitiated is the world of the faithful

What is "the world"? The world, when used in a bad sense, means lovers of the world. When the term is used in praise, the world is heaven and earth, and the works of God that are in them; as it is said, "And the world was made by Him" (Jn.1:10). Also, the world is the fullness of the earth, as John himself has said, "Not only for our sins is He the propitiation, but of the whole world" (1 Jn.2:2). Here he means, the world of all the faithful who are scattered throughout the whole earth.

Sermons on 1 John, 5:9

The "all" for whom Christ died and rose again are those whom Paul no longer knows according to the flesh — those destined for resurrection

"The love of Christ," we read, "constrains us, because we judge thus, that if one died for all, then all died; and He died for all, that those who live should no longer live for themselves, but for Him Who died for them, and rose again. Therefore from now on we know no man after the flesh; and though we have known Christ after the flesh, yet now from now on we know Him no longer" (2 Cor.5:14-16). The words, "those who live should no longer live for themselves, but for Him Who died for them, and rose again," show plainly that the resurrection of Christ is the ground of the apostle's statement. To live not for themselves, but for Christ, must mean to live not according to the flesh, in the hope of earthly and perishable goods, but according to the spirit, in the hope of resurrection — a resurrection already accomplished in Christ.

Of those, then, for whom Christ died and rose again, and who live no longer for themselves, but for Him, the apostle says that he knows no-one according to flesh, on account of the hope of future immortality to which they were looking forward — a hope which in Christ was already a reality. So, though Paul has known Christ according to the flesh, before Christ's death, now he knows Him no longer; for Paul knows that He has risen, and that death has no more dominion over Him. And because in Christ we are all even now what Christ is, according to hope, though not in reality, Paul adds: "Therefore if anyone is in Christ, he is a new creation: old things have passed away; behold, all things have become new. And all things are of God, who has reconciled us to Himself by Christ" (2 Cor.5:17).

What the new creation — that is, the people renewed by faith — hopes for, it possesses already in Christ; and the hope will hereafter be actually made real. As regards this hope, old things have passed away, because we are no longer in the times of the Old Testament, expecting a temporal and fleshly kingdom of God; and all things have become new, making the promise of the kingdom of heaven, where there shall be no death or corruption, the ground of our confidence. But in the resurrection of the dead it will not be as a matter of hope, but in reality, that old things will pass away, when the last enemy, death, will be destroyed; and all things will become new when this corruptible has put on incorruption, and this mortal has put on immortality.

This has already taken place in Christ, whom Paul accordingly, in reality, knew no longer according to the flesh. But it was not yet in reality, but only in hope, that Paul knew no-one after the flesh of those for whom Christ died and rose again. For, as he says to the Ephesians, we are already saved by grace. The whole passage is to the purpose: "But God, who is rich in mercy, because of His great love with which He loved us, even when we were dead in sins, has quickened us together with Christ, by Whose grace we have been saved" (Eph.2:4-5). The words, "has quickened us together with Christ," correspond to what he said to the Corinthians, "that those who live should no longer live for themselves, but for Him that died for them and rose again." And in the words, "by Whose grace we have been saved," he speaks of the thing hoped for as being already accomplished.

Reply to Faustus the Manichee, 2:8

Christ the High Priest prays only for the "world' of the predestined

For you see here that He Who had said, "I do not pray for the world"

(Jn.17:9), now prays for the world that it may believe (Jn.17:21). For there is a "world" of which it is written, "That we might not be condemned with the world" (1 Cor.11:32). For that world, Christ does not pray, for He is fully aware to what it is predestined. But there is another "world" of which it is written, "For the Son of man came not to condemn the world, but that the world through Him might be saved" (Jn.3:17). And so the apostle also says, "God was in Christ, reconciling the world unto Himself" (2 Cor.5:19). It is for this world that Christ prays, saying, "That the world may believe that You have sent me" (Jn.17:23).

Sermons on John, 110:2

Chapter 5

The New Life in Christ

"Can we possibly, without utter absurdity, maintain that there first existed in anyone the good virtue of a good will, to entitle him to the removal of his heart of stone? How can we say this, when all the time this heart of stone itself signifies precisely a will of the hardest kind, a will that is absolutely inflexible against God? For if a good will comes first, there is obviously no longer a heart of stone."

Augustine, *On Grace and Free Will, 29*

"For we are now speaking of the desire for goodness. If they want to say that this begins from ourselves and is then perfected by God, let them see how they can answer the apostle when he says, 'Not that we are sufficient of ourselves to claim anything as coming from us, but our sufficiency is from God'" (2 Cor. 3:5)

Augustine, *Against Two Letters of the Pelagians, 2:18*

Richard was a fairly recent convert to the Augustinian understanding of grace. One Sunday, he visited a church where the preacher seemed to go out of his way to show the congregation how utterly dependent on God they were for their spiritual life. There can be no self-reliance, he declared, no looking to ourselves; all goodness, all holiness flow from God to us. Why, even the very faith by which we believe and trust in God is itself His gift to sinners! "This is good," Richard thought. "The man has clearly grasped the sovereignty of grace in salvation. Augustine would be pleased with him." But alas, Richard's verdict was premature. Suddenly the sermon went sensationally contrary to Scripture. After all the extolling of God as the giver of faith, the preacher added: "But of course, even though faith is God's gift, we have to accept the gift by our free wills. We can refuse it if we choose. It's up to us." By the time it was all over, Richard left church feeling rather deflated. "It's up to us" seemed a strange note on which to conclude a celebration of God's grace.

Richard was right to feel deflated. If it is ultimately "up to us" to make sure we accept the divine gift of faith, then manifestly God is *not* the giver of *all* our spiritual virtues (which is what the preacher in the church Richard was visiting had started out by saying). Apparently, I have something in me, some act of my own, which reaches out and grasps God's kind offer of faith. What is this "something"? It can't be faith, because faith is what God is offering to give me. I don't know how the preacher would have described this mysterious "something". Repentance, perhaps? Can I repent by my own will, and God then crowns my cake of repentance with the icing of faith? But where did the repentance come from? If I can repent by my own will, why can't I believe and trust by my own will? Doesn't the same Scripture that says *faith* is God's gift (Eph.2:8, Phil.1:29) also say that *repentance* is His gift (Acts 5:31, 2 Tim.2:25)? Maybe the preacher would have acknowledged that repentance is God's gift. But probably it would then have fared no better than faith. Probably the preacher would have said, "But of course, even though repentance is God's gift, we have to accept the gift by our free wills. We can refuse it if we choose. It's up to us."

What is it in me that accepts repentance, then? A spiritually softened heart, perhaps? But if I can soften my own heart by my own will (or does that mean "soften my will by my own will"?), why can't I repent by my own will, or believe by my own will? And doesn't the same Scripture that says *faith* and *repentance* are God's gifts also say that *the heart of flesh* is His gift (Deut.30:6, Ezek.36:26-27)? Maybe the preacher would have acknowledged that the heart of flesh is God's gift too. But probably it would then have fared no better than faith and repentance. Probably the preacher would have said, "But of course, even though the heart of flesh is God's gift, we have to accept the gift by our free wills. We can refuse it if we choose. It's up to us."

What is it in me that accepts the heart of flesh, then? Is it ... But we have been here before, and by now it is getting a touch silly. Like some bizarre spiritual board game, we are constantly going one square forwards and two squares backwards. And somehow, we always end up on a square that says, "It's up to us."

Augustine's theology of the new life in Christ was really just a way of saying, *"It's not up to us."* Our new life in Christ comes from Christ. From its first stirrings to its final consummation, it comes from Christ. Faith, repentance, the softened heart, and any other virtue that can be named — they all come from Christ. Our conversion comes from Christ. Our regeneration comes from Christ. Our spiritual illumination comes from Christ. Our desire for Christ comes from Christ. Our seeking after Christ comes from Christ. As that great Italian Augustinian, Thomas Aquinas, was to teach 800 years after Augustine's death, *nothing comes before grace*. All the things that we might think make us ready for grace are themselves the work of grace. If we insist on talking about "accepting grace", even the acceptance of grace is created in us by grace.

The truth about grace, then, is both simple and radical. The first brick in the foundation of our salvation is laid in us by Christ, just as the last tile on the roof will be. He creates us afresh. He begets us again. He raises us from the dead. At no point can we take any credit to ourselves. No true Christian has the slightest wish to take any credit to himself or herself. That is why, as I said in the Introduction, all God's redeemed children are Augustinians when they pray. They may be Semi-Pelagians in their heads, but their twice-born hearts know better, and when they speak to their God, they give Him all the praise, gratitude and glory for saving them. *Lex orandi lex credendi:* the law of praying is the law of believing.

Of course, if Augustine is right in his understanding of what the Bible says about the bondage of our fallen wills, it follows that our spiritual regeneration must *necessarily* come only and utterly from Christ. Left to our own devices, all we ever do is sin; for we love created things, not the Creator, and our lives are built on that false love. There is no beauty in Christ that we should desire Him. We are too busy desiring other things. That is why "It's up to us" is such a tragically hopeless recipe for any kind of salvation. Scripture describes our salvation as a new creation, a rebirth, a resurrection. Yet God did not say to a non-existent universe, "I'm offering to create you, but it's up to you to accept the offer." Parents do not say to non-existent children, "We're offering to conceive you, but it's up to you to accept the offer." The Lord did not say to Lazarus, "I'm offering to resurrect you from the tomb, but it's up to you to accept the offer." The depth and horrible complexity of our corruption make just as futile any "It's up to you" scheme of salvation. If indeed it is "up to us," whether in the Pelagian sense (obey the law and win heaven!) or the Semi-Pelagian sense (accept the offer of salvation!), then *no-one will ever be saved.* As Benjamin Warfield commented, a gospel of "Whosoever will" is not much good in a world of universal "Won't!"

Augustine knew that however daintily it is dressed, however carefully it is qualified, however tiny the amount it leaves to us to contribute to our own salvation, "It's up to us" is always a counsel of hellish despair for sinners deceived and broken and exhausted and blinded and driven mad and killed by sin. He would have none of it, either for himself, or for his flock, or for the Church Catholic. The bishop of Hippo sang loud and clear with his theological mind the song of confession and praise that every saved heart knows well:

"It's not up to us! We were dead in our transgressions and sins, in which we used to live when we followed the ways of the world. We were under the power of the prince of this world, the spirit who is now at work in the children of disobedience. We lived among them. We gratified the cravings of the flesh and followed its desires and thoughts. We were by nature the children of wrath, like the rest. But God, Who is rich in mercy, because of the great love with which He loved us, made us alive with Christ, even when we were dead in transgressions. By grace we have been saved. By grace, through faith — and this not from ourselves, it is the gift of God. No works. No-one can boast. God Who said, 'Let light shine out of darkness!' caused His light to shine in our hearts, giving us the light of the knowledge of the glory of God, shining in the face of Christ. We were foolish, obstinate, deluded, the slaves of various cravings and pleasures, spending our lives in malice and envy, hateful ourselves and hating one another. But the kindness and love of God our Saviour

The Triumph of Grace

dawned upon us, and He saved us, not in consequence of righteous things we did, but because of His mercy. Yes, He saved us, by the washing of regeneration and renewing by the Holy Spirit, Whom He poured out on us richly through Jesus Christ our Saviour. By grace we are justified. We are new creations in Christ. The old has passed away. The new has come. All this is from God, Who has reconciled us to Himself through Christ. Thanks be to God!"[1]

****

The New Life in Christ

A definition of grace

The grace of God through Jesus Christ our Lord must be understood as follows: grace is the only thing that delivers human beings from evil; without it, they do absolutely nothing good, whether in thought, or in will and emotion, or in action. Grace not only makes known to people what they ought to do, but also enables them to perform with love the duty that they know.

The apostle Paul certainly asked God to inspire the Corinthians with this good will and action when he said, "Now we pray to God that you do no evil, not that we should appear to be approved, but that you should do what is good" (2 Cor.13:7). Who can hear this and not wake up and confess that the Lord God is the One Who turns us away from evil so that we do good? For the apostle does not say, "We admonish, we teach, we exhort, we rebuke." He says, "We pray to God that you do no evil, but that you should do what is good." Of course, he was also in the habit of speaking to them, and doing all those things which I have mentioned — he admonished, he taught, he exhorted, he rebuked. But he knew that all these things which he was openly doing in the way of planting and watering were of no avail, unless He Who secretly gives the increase answered his prayer on the Corinthians' behalf. For as the same teacher of the

---

[1] Eph.2:1-10, 2 Cor.4:6, Tit.3:3-7, 2 Cor.5:17-18.

Gentiles says, "Neither he who plants is anything, nor he who waters, but God Who gives the increase" (1 Cor.3:7).

On Rebuke and Grace, 3

Two more definitions

Listen to the apostle Paul when he says, "Love is the fulfilment of the law" (Rom.13:10). How do we obtain the love? By the grace of God. By the Holy Spirit. For we could not have it from ourselves, as if we created it for ourselves. Love is the gift of God. And a great gift it is! For the apostle says, "The love of God has been poured out in our hearts by the Holy Spirit Who was given to us" (Rom.5:5).

Sermons on John, 17:6

For them [the Pelagians], grace means the knowledge with which the Lord God helps us, by which we can *know* what our duty is. The true meaning of grace, however, is the love that God breathes into us, which enables us with a holy delight to *carry out* the duty that we know.

Against Two Letters of the Pelagians, 4:11

No-one has any right to God's grace

The grace of Christ, without which neither infants nor adults can be saved, is not bestowed on account of any virtues, but is given gratuitously, which is why it is called "grace". As Paul says, "being justified freely through His blood" (Rom.3:24). So those who are not liberated by grace are indeed justly condemned — those who are not yet able to hear, those who are unwilling to obey, or again those who did not receive (at the time when their youth made them unable to hear) that washing of regeneration, which they might have received and through which they might have been saved. All these are justly condemned, because they are not without sin, either the sin that they have derived from their birth, or the sin that they have added from their own misconduct. "For all have sinned" whether in Adam or in themselves "and come short of the glory of God" (Rom.3:23).

The entire mass of humanity, therefore, becomes liable to punishment. And if the deserved punishment of condemnation were inflicted on all, it would without doubt be righteously inflicted. Consequently, those who are delivered from punishment by grace are called, not vessels of their own virtues, but "vessels of mercy" (Rom.9:23). Whose mercy? God's — the One Who sent Christ Jesus into the world to save the sinners whom He foreknew, and predestined, and called, and justified, and glorified. Now, who could be so madly insane as to fail to give inexpressible thanks to the mercy which liberates whom it chooses? The person who correctly appreciated the whole subject could not possibly blame the justice of God if He utterly condemned all people absolutely.

On Nature and Grace, 4-5

There is no true goodness in us prior to our conversion

You [Julian of Eclanum] think that a person is helped by the grace of God in a good work, in such a way that grace does nothing to stir up his will towards that good work. Your own words sufficiently declare this. For why have you failed to say that a person is aroused by God's grace to a good work, as you have indeed said that he is aroused to evil by the suggestions of the devil? Why have you merely said that a person is always "helped" in a good work by God's grace? As if by his own will, and without any grace of God, he undertook a good work, and *then* was divinely helped in the work itself, on account of the virtues of his good will. In that case, grace is rendered as something due, rather than given as a gift — and so grace is no longer grace. But this is what, in the Palestinian verdict [the synod of Diospolis — see Introduction], Pelagius with a deceitful heart condemned, namely, that the grace of God is given according to our virtues.

Tell me, please, what good Paul willed while he was still Saul, when he was in fact willing great evils, breathing out slaughter as he went, in a horrible darkness of mind and madness, to destroy Christians? What virtues of Saul's good will prompted God to convert him by a marvellous and sudden call from those evils to good things? What shall I say, when Paul himself cries, "Not by works of righteousness that we have done, but according to His mercy He saved us" (Tit.3:5)? And what about that saying of the Lord which I have already mentioned, "No one can come to Me" — that is, "believe in Me" — "unless it has been granted to him by My Father" (Jn.6:65)? Is faith given to the person who is already willing to believe, in recognition of the virtues of his good will? Or rather, is not the will itself stirred up from above, as in the case of Saul, *in order* that he may believe, even though he is so hostile to the faith that he persecutes believers?

Indeed, how has the Lord commanded us to pray for those who persecute us? Do we pray that the grace of God may reward them for their good will? Do we not rather pray that the evil will itself may be changed into a good one? Surely the saints whom Saul was persecuting prayed for Saul, that his will might be converted to the faith which he was destroying; and they did not pray in vain. Indeed, the obviously miraculous nature of Saul's conversion made it clear that it originated in heaven. How many enemies of Christ at the present day are suddenly drawn to Him by God's secret grace! And let me set down this word from the gospel: "No-one can come to Me, unless the Father Who sent me draws him" (Jn.6:44). What would Julian not have said against me, if it were not for that verse? As it is, he is rousing himself, not against me, but against Christ Who spoke these words. For He does not say, "unless He leads him," which would have allowed us to think that the person's will went beforehand. But who is "drawn," if he was already willing? And yet no-one comes unless he *is* willing. Therefore in wondrous ways a person is drawn into a state of willingness, by Him who knows how to work within the very hearts of human beings. Not that unwilling people are made to believe, which cannot be. Rather, unwilling people are made willing.

Against Two Letters of the Pelagians, 1:37

The proud Pelagian takes the credit for his own goodness

What good does it do the Pelagians to praise free will by saying, "grace assists everyone's good resolution"? We could accept this without hesitation as being said in a Catholic spirit, if they did not attribute *worthiness* to the good resolution. For that would mean that God's assistance was now a wage paid as a debt to this worthiness — and that is no longer grace. They need to understand and confess that even that good resolution itself, which grace then comes and assists, could not have existed in a person if grace had not gone before it. How can there be a good resolution in someone without the mercy of God going first, since it is the good will which is itself prepared by the Lord?

When the Pelagians say that "grace assists everyone's good resolution," and then add, "yet grace does not infuse the love of virtue into a heart that resists," even this might be understood in a right sense, except that we know what they really mean. For in the case of the heart that resists, God's grace itself first of all makes the heart willing to hear the divine call; and then, the heart no longer resisting, grace kindles the desire for virtue. So then, in everything where anyone does anything in accordance with God, God's mercy works first. And this our adversaries will not confess, because they choose to be not Catholics, but Pelagians. For it gives much delight to a proud ungodliness to think that, even when a person is forced to acknowledge that the Lord has given him something, it was not given as a gift, but paid in return for something. In this way, the children of destruction, not of the promise, think that they have made themselves good, and that God has repaid the self-made virtuous the reward they deserve for their work.

This is the pride that has blocked up the ears of the Pelagians' hearts, so that they do not hear, "For what do you have that you did not receive?" (1 Cor.4:7) They do not hear, "Without Me you can do nothing" (Jn.15:5). They do not hear, "Love is from God" (1 Jn.4:7). They do not hear, "God has dealt out to each one a measure of faith" (Rom.12:3). They do not hear, "The Spirit breathes where He wills" (Jn.3:8), and, "Those who are led by the Spirit of God, they are the sons of God" (Rom.8:14). They do not hear, "No-one can come to Me, unless it has been granted to him by My Father" (Rom.8:14). They do not hear what Ezra writes, "Blessed is the Lord of our fathers, Who has put into the heart of the king to glorify His house which is in Jerusalem" (Ezra 7:27). They do not hear what the Lord says through Jeremiah, "And I will put My fear into their heart, so that they will not depart not Me. Yes, I will visit them to make them good" (Jer.32:40-41).

And especially they do not hear that word spoken by Ezekiel the prophet, where God fully shows that He does not make people good (that is, obedient to His commands) because He is moved by worthy qualities in them. No, He repays people good for evil, by doing this for His own sake, and not for theirs. For He says, "Thus says the Lord God: I do not do this for your sake, O house of Israel, but for My holy name, which you have profaned among the nations, where you went. And I will sanctify My great name, which has been profaned among the nations, which you have profaned in the midst of them; and the nations shall know that I am the Lord, says the Lord God, when I shall be sanctified in you before their eyes. For I will take you from among the nations, and gather you out of all the countries, and will bring you into your own land. And I will sprinkle clean water upon you, and you shall be clean: from all your filthiness, and from all your idols, I will cleanse you. A new heart also I will give you, and a new spirit I will put within you; and I will take away the stony heart out of your flesh, and I will give you a heart of flesh. And I will put My Spirit within you, and cause you to walk in My statutes, and you shall keep My ordinances, and do them" (Ezek.36:22-27).

Against Two Letters of the Pelagians, 4:13-14

God is the source of the new heart and Christian obedience

What does the putrid flesh of humanity have left to puff itself up with, and to refuse to glory in the Lord? Whatever it claims it has done to achieve virtue by its own effort, so that God must then reward it — against all such claims it shall be answered, it shall be exclaimed, it shall be contradicted, "I do it; but for My own holy name's sake; I do not do it for your sakes, says the Lord God" (Ezek.36:22). Nothing so overthrows the Pelagians when they say that the grace of God is given according to our virtues. (In fact, Pelagius himself condemned this view, although he did not embrace the correct one — he was just afraid of the Eastern judges.)[2] Nothing so overthrows

---

[2] At the synod of Diospolis. See Introduction.

the arrogance of people who say, "We do it, that we may by our
virtues establish a basis for God to work." It is not Pelagius that
answers you, but the Lord Himself: "I do it, and not for your sakes,
but for My own holy name's sake." For what good can you do out of
a heart that is not good? But in order that you may have a good
heart, He says, "I will give you a new heart, and I will put a new
spirit within you" (Ezek.36:26).

Can you say, "We will first walk in His righteousness, and will
observe His judgments, and will act in a worthy way, so that He will
give His grace to us"? But what good would you evil people do?
And how would you do those good things, unless you were yourselves
good? But Who causes people to be good? Only He Who said, "And
I will visit them to make them good," and, "I will put my Spirit
within you, and will cause you to walk in my righteousness, and to
observe my judgments, and do them" (Ezek.36:27). Are you asleep?
Can't you hear Him saying, "I will cause you to walk, I will make
you to observe," lastly, "I will make you to do"? Really, are you still
puffing yourselves up? We walk, true enough, and we observe, and
we do; but it is God Who makes us to walk, to observe, to do. This
is the grace of God making us good; this is His mercy going before us.

Against Two Letters of the Pelagians, 4:15

Without Me, you can do nothing

The Pelagians think they have good grounds for accusing us of false
teaching when we say, "God inspires an unwilling and resisting person
with the desire," not for any very great good, but "even for imperfect
good." Possibly, then, they themselves are keeping open a place for
grace (at least in some sense) by thinking as follows: a person can
have the desire for good without grace, but only for imperfect good;
he could not easily have the desire for perfect good even with grace,
but without grace he could not desire perfect good at all.

But actually, even this view sees God's grace as being given
according to our virtues (which Pelagius, in the church synod in the
East, condemned, merely from the fear of being condemned). For if
the desire for good begins from ourselves without God's grace, virtue
itself will have begun — and to this virtue, the assistance of grace

then comes, as if it were owed. Thus God's grace is not bestowed freely, but is given according to our virtue. However, in order that he might provide a reply to the future Pelagius, the Lord does not say, "Without Me, it is with difficulty that you can do anything," but He says, "Without Me, you can do nothing" (Jn.15:5). And, that He might also provide an answer to these future heretics, in that very same Gospel saying He does not say, "Without me you can bring nothing to perfection," but "do" nothing. For if He had said "bring nothing to perfection", they might say that God's help is necessary, not for beginning good, which rests with ourselves, but for perfecting it. But let them hear the apostle too. For when the Lord says, "Without Me you can do nothing," in this one word He comprehends both the beginning and the ending. The apostle, indeed, as if he were an expounder of the Lord's saying, distinguishes both [beginning and ending] very clearly when he says, "Because He who has begun a good work in you will perfect it even to the day of Christ Jesus" (Phil.1:6).

Against Two Letters of the Pelagians, 2:18

From first beginnings to final completion, salvation is by grace

Since these things are so, everything that is commanded to human beings by the Lord in the holy Scriptures, for the sake of testing human free will, is either something we begin to obey by God's goodness, or is demanded in order to show us our need of grace to do it. Indeed, a person does not even begin to be changed from evil to good by the first stirrings of faith, unless the free and gratuitous mercy of God produces this in him…. So, therefore, we should think of God's grace as working from the beginning of a person's changing towards goodness, even to the end of its completion, so that he who glories may glory in the Lord. For just as no-one can bring goodness to perfection without the Lord, so no-one can begin it without the Lord.

Against Two Letters of the Pelagians, 2:23

Pelagius turns grace into a reward for human goodness

Then again, whatever it is that Pelagius means by "grace," he says
is given even to Christians according to their virtues, although (as I
have already mentioned above), when he was in Palestine, in his
truly remarkable vindication of himself, he condemned those who
hold this opinion! Now these are his words: referring to non-
Christians, he says, "In these, the good of their created condition is
naked and defenceless." Then he adds: "In those, however, who
belong to Christ, there is defence afforded by Christ's help." You
see it is still uncertain what this "help" is, according to the remark
we have already made on the same subject. Pelagius goes on, however,
to say of those who are not Christians: "They deserve judgment and
condemnation, because they possess free will whereby they could
come to have faith and deserve God's grace, but they make a bad
use of the freedom which has been granted to them. But as for those
who by the right use of free will merit the Lord's grace, and keep
His commandments—these deserve to be rewarded."

Now it is clear; he says grace is bestowed according to worthiness
(whatever he means by grace, which he does not make clear). For
when he speaks about people deserving reward because they make a
good use of their free will, so that they merit the Lord's grace, he
asserts in fact that a debt is paid to them. What, then, becomes of
the apostle's saying, "Being justified freely by His grace"
(Rom.3:24)? And what of his other statement too, "By grace you
are saved" (Eph.2:8)? In this verse, Paul prevents us from supposing
that salvation is by works, by expressly adding, "by faith." And
even further, in case anyone imagines that faith itself is of human
origin independently of the grace of God, the apostle says: "And
that not of yourselves; for it is the gift of God."

On the Grace of Christ and Original Sin, 1:34

The Pelagians call it "fate"; we call it "grace"

I was carefully meditating about why the Pelagians think they have
a trump card when they accuse us of teaching "fate" under the name
of grace. So I first of all looked into their statements on the matter.
They thought they could bring this objection against us: "Under the

name of grace, they teach fate, for they say that unless God inspired an unwilling and resisting person with the desire for good (even an imperfect good), he would not be able to cease from evil, nor to embrace good." Then a little later, they assert their own beliefs, which I also examined: "We confess that baptism is necessary for all ages, and that grace assists the good resolutions of everybody. But grace does not infuse the love of virtue into a reluctant soul, because there is no favouritism with God."

From these words of theirs, I perceived that the Pelagians think (or wish others to think) that we "teach fate under the name of grace" merely because we say that God's grace is not given in respect of our virtues, but according to God's own most merciful will. For He said, "I will be gracious to whom I will be gracious, and will show mercy to whom I will show mercy" (Rom.9:15). And by way of consequence, Scripture adds, "Therefore it is not of him who wills, nor of him who runs, but of God Who shows mercy" (Rom.9:16). Here, anyone might be equally foolish in thinking or saying that the apostle teaches fate! But these Pelagians sufficiently lay themselves open to accusation. For when they slander us by saying that we "maintain fate under the name of grace", because we say that God's grace is not given on account of our virtues, beyond a doubt *they* confess that they themselves say that grace *is* given on account of our virtues!

Against Two Letters of the Pelagians, 2:10

The effective transforming teaching of the Holy Spirit

The kind of teaching we are talking about is spoken of by the Lord when He says: "Everyone who has heard and learned from the Father comes to Me" (Jn.6:45). So if someone does not come to Christ, we cannot correctly say of him, "he has heard and learned that he ought to come to Christ, but he is not willing to do what he has learned." It is indeed absolutely improper to apply such a statement to God's method of teaching people by grace. For if, as the Truth says, "Everyone who has learned comes," it follows, of course, that whoever does *not* come has *not* learned. But who can fail to see that a person's coming or not coming is by the choice of his will? If a person does not come to Christ, he has simply made his choice not

to come. But if he *does* come, it cannot be without assistance —
such assistance that he not only *knows* what it is he ought to do, but
actually *does* what he knows.

And so, when God teaches, it is not by the letter of the law, but
by the grace of the Spirit. Moreover, He teaches so that whatever a
person learns, he not only sees it with his perception, but also desires
it with his choice, and accomplishes it in action. By this method of
divine instruction, our very choosing itself, and our very performance
itself, are assisted, and not merely our natural "capacity" of willing
and performing. For if nothing but this "capacity" of ours were
assisted by this grace, the Lord would have said, "Everyone that has
heard and learned from the Father may possibly come to Me." This,
however, is not what He said. His words are these: "Everyone who
has heard and learned from the Father comes to Me."

Now Pelagius says that the possibility of coming lies in our nature.
Or as we even found him attempting to say some time ago, it lies in
grace (whatever that may mean according to him), as when he says,
"grace assists our capacity of coming to Christ." But he holds that
our *actual* coming to Christ lies in our own will and act. Now just
because a person *may* come to Christ, it does not follow that he
actually comes, unless he has also willed and acted to come. But
everyone who has learned from the Father not only has the possibility
of coming, but actually comes! And in this result are already included
the use of the capacity, the affection of the will, and the effect of the
action.

On the Grace of Christ and Original Sin, 1:27

Only those taught by the Father come to Christ

Accordingly, our only Master and Lord Himself, when He had said
what I previously mentioned — "This is the work of God, that you
believe in Him whom He has sent" (Jn.6:29) — says a little afterwards
in the same discourse, "I said to you that you also have seen Me and
have not believed. All that the Father gives Me will come to Me"
(Jn.6:37). What is the meaning of "will come to Me" but "will believe
in Me"? But it is the Father's gift that this happens. Moreover, a
little later Jesus says, "Do not murmur among yourselves. No-one
can come to Me unless the Father Who sent Me draws him; and I

will raise him up at the last day. It is written in the prophets, 'And they will all be taught by God.' Everyone who has heard from the Father, and has learned, comes to Me" (Jn.6:43-5). What is the meaning of "Everyone who has heard from the Father, and has learned, comes to Me," except that there is no-one who fails to come to Me if they hear from the Father and learn? For if everyone who has heard from the Father, and has learned, comes, then certainly everyone who does *not* come has *not* heard from the Father! For if he had heard and learned, he would come. No-one has heard and learned, and yet has failed to come. But everyone, as the Truth declares, who has heard from the Father, and has learned, comes.

This teaching in which the Father is heard, and teaches to come to the Son, is far removed from the senses of the flesh. The Son Himself is also involved in this teaching, because He is the Father's Word by which He teaches; and He does not do this through the ear of the flesh, but the ear of the heart. The Spirit of the Father and of the Son is also, at the same time, involved in this teaching; He, too, teaches, and does not teach separately, for we have learned that the workings of the Trinity are inseparable. And that is certainly the same Holy Spirit of Whom the apostle says, "We, however, having the same Spirit of faith" (2 Cor.4:13). But this teaching is especially ascribed to the Father, because the Only-begotten is begotten from Him, and the Holy Spirit proceeds from Him, of which it would be tedious to argue more elaborately. I think that my work in fifteen books on the Trinity which God is, has already reached you.

No, this instruction in which God is heard and teaches is very far removed, I say, from the senses of the flesh. We see that many come to the Son because we see that many believe in Christ; but when and how they have heard and learned this from the Father, we do not see. It is true that this grace is exceedingly secret, but who doubts that it is grace? This grace, therefore, which is invisibly bestowed on human hearts by the divine gift, is not rejected by any hard heart — because it is given for the purpose of first taking away the hardness of the heart! When, therefore, the Father is heard within, and teaches, so that a person comes to the Son, He takes away the heart of stone and gives a heart of flesh, as He has promised in the declaration of the prophet. He thus makes them children and vessels of mercy which He has prepared for glory.

On the Predestination of the Saints, 13

Free will and a good will both come from God

It is not enough simply to have choice of will, which is freely turned in this direction and that, and belongs among those natural gifts which a bad person may use badly. We must also have a *good* will, which belongs among those gifts which it is impossible to use badly. This impossibility is given to us by God; otherwise I do not know how to defend what Scripture says: "What do you have that you did not receive?" (1 Cor.4:7) For if God gives us a *free* will, which may still be either good or bad, but a *good* will comes from *ourselves*, then what comes from ourselves is better than what comes from God! But it is the height of absurdity to say this. So the Pelagians ought to acknowledge that we obtain from God even a good will.

It would indeed be a strange thing if the will could stand in some no-man's-land, where it was neither good nor bad. For we either love righteousness, and this is good; and if we love it more, this is better. If we love it less, this is less good; or if we do not love righteousness at all, it is not good. And who can hesitate to affirm that, when the will does not love righteousness in any way at all, it is not only a bad will, but even a totally depraved will? Since therefore the will is either good or bad, and since of course we do not derive the bad will from God, it remains that we derive from God a good will. Otherwise, since our justification[3] proceeds from a good will, I do not know what other gift of God we ought to rejoice in. That, I suppose, is why it is written, "The will is prepared by the Lord" (Prov.8:35, Septuagint). And in the Psalms, "The steps of a man will be rightly ordered by the Lord, and His way will be the choice of his will" (Ps.37:23). And what the apostle says, "For it is God Who works in you both to will and to do of His own good pleasure" (Phil.2:13).

On the Merits and Forgiveness of Sins, 2:30

---

[3] By "justification" Augustine means the total experience of being forgiven and then made progressively holy. This definition of justification sprang from the fact that the New Testament Greek word for "justify" (*dikaioo*) was translated into Latin as *iustificare*, which — by a plausible mistake — Augustine interpreted as "to make righteous". Actually *dikaioo* means to *declare* righteous. It refers to God's bestowal of an objective status of acceptance, not the inner process of sanctification. This confusion about justification was one of Augustine's less happy legacies to the Western Church. It took the Reformation to set things right on this score.

What we need is love

We maintain that God does not only create a person with a free will, and give teaching by which he is instructed how he ought to live. We say further that the human will is so divinely aided in the pursuit of righteousness, that a person receives the Holy Spirit. And the Spirit forms in his mind a delight in, and a love of, that supreme and unchangeable good which is God, even now while he is still "walking by faith" and not yet "by sight" (2 Cor.5:7). By this gift to him of the Spirit as the pledge, as it were, of the free gift [of eternal life], he conceives an ardent desire to cling to his Creator, and burns to enter into a state of participation in that true light, so that he may enjoy blessing from the One to Whom he owes his existence. A person's free will, indeed, avails for nothing except to sin, if he does not know the way of truth. And even after his duty and his true goal begin to become known to him, he still fails to do his duty, or to set about it, or to live rightly, unless he also takes delight in it and feels a love for it. Now, in order to win our affections to what is right, God's "love is shed abroad in our hearts," not through the free-will which arises from ourselves, but "through the Holy Spirit Who is given to us" (Rom.5:5).

On the Spirit and the Letter, 5

God's grace works in us sovereignly to produce a godly will

Some might interpret "It is not of him who wills, nor of him who runs, but of God Who shows mercy" (Rom.9:16), in this sense — that salvation comes from both, that is, both from the human will and from the mercy of God. In that case, we must understand the saying, "It is not of him who wills, nor of him who runs, but of God Who shows mercy," as if it meant that the human will alone is not sufficient, unless the mercy of God goes with it. But then it would follow that the mercy of God alone is not sufficient, unless the human will goes with it! Therefore, if we may rightly say, "it is not of man who wills, but of God Who shows mercy," because the human will by itself is not enough, why may we not also rightly put it the other way round: "It is not of God Who shows mercy, but of man who wills," because the mercy of God by itself is not sufficient? Surely, no Christian will dare to say this, "It is not of God Who shows mercy, but of man who wills," in case he openly contradicts the apostle!

So it follows that the true interpretation of the saying, "It is not of him who wills, nor of him who runs, but of God Who shows mercy," is that the entire work belongs to God, Who both makes the human will righteous, and prepares it in this way for His assistance, and then assists it when it is prepared. For human righteousness of will precedes many of God's gifts, but not all of them; and it must itself be included among those gifts which it does not precede. We read in Holy Scripture, both that God's mercy "shall meet me" (Ps.59:10), and that His mercy "shall follow me" (Ps.23:6). Mercy goes before the unwilling person to make him willing; it follows the willing person to make his will effective. Why are we taught to pray for our enemies, who are plainly unwilling to lead a holy life, unless that God may produce willingness in them? And why are we ourselves taught to ask in order that may receive, unless that He who has created in us the wish, may Himself satisfy the wish? We pray, then, for our enemies, that the mercy of God may go before them, as it has gone before us; and we pray for ourselves that His mercy may follow us.

Enchiridion, 32

Grace creates a truly free will

Do we by grace destroy free will? God forbid! We *establish* free will. For even as the law is not destroyed but established by faith, so free will is not destroyed but established by grace. The law is fulfilled only by a free will. And yet the law brings the knowledge of sin; faith brings the acquisition of grace against sin; grace brings the healing of the soul from the disease of sin; the health of the soul brings freedom of will; free will brings the love of righteousness; and the love of righteousness fulfils the law. Thus the law is not destroyed but established through faith, since faith obtains grace by which the law is fulfilled. Likewise, free will is not destroyed through grace, but is established, since grace cures the will so that righteousness is freely loved. Now all the stages which I have here connected together in their successive links, are each spoken of individually in the sacred Scriptures. The law says: "You shall not covet" (Ex.20:17). Faith says: "Heal my soul, for I have sinned against You" (Ps.41:4). Grace says: "See, you have been made well: sin no more, in case a worse thing comes upon you" (Jn.5:14). Health says: "O Lord my God, I cried to You, and You have healed me" (Ps.30:2). Free will says: "I will freely sacrifice to You" (Ps.54:6). Love of righteousness says: "Transgressors told me pleasant tales, but not according to Your law, O Lord" (Ps. 119:85).

How is it then that miserable human beings dare to be proud, either of their free will, before they are set free, or of their own strength, if they have been set free? They do not observe that in the very mention of free will they pronounce the name of liberty. But "where the Spirit of the Lord is, there is liberty" (2 Cor.3:17). If, therefore, they are the slaves of sin, why do they boast of free will? For "by whatever a person is overcome, to that he is delivered as a slave" (2 Pet.2:19). But if they have been set free, why do they puff themselves up as if it were by their own doing? Why do they boast, as if their freedom were not a gift? Or are they so free that they will not have Him for their Lord Who says to them, "Without Me, you can do nothing" (Jn.15:5), and, "If the Son sets you free, you shall be truly free"? (Jn.8:36).

On the Spirit and the Letter, 52

Sovereign grace humbles human pride

God does not grant His mercy to some people *because* they know Him, but *in order that* they may know Him. Nor is it because they are upright in heart, but that they may become so, that He grants them His righteousness by which He justifies the ungodly. This thought does not inflate us with pride! The sin of pride arises when anyone has too much self-confidence, and makes himself the supreme reason for living. Driven by this conceited feeling, the proud person departs from the Fountain of life, from Whose streams alone we can drink the holiness which is itself the good life. Yes, the proud person departs from that unchanging Light, by sharing in which the rational soul is set on fire (so to speak) and becomes a created and reflected light.

On the Spirit and the Letter, 11

Spiritual desire comes from God

God does many good things in a human being that the human being does not do. But a human being does nothing good that God does not cause him to do. Accordingly, the Lord would not put a desire for something good in a person, if that thing were not indeed good; but if it is good, we derive it only from Him Who is supremely and incomparably good. For what is the desire for good but love? John the apostle speaks of this without any ambiguity, and says, "Love is from God" (1 Jn.4:7). Love does not begin from ourselves, and then get perfected by God. No, if love is from God, we have the whole of it from God. May God by all means turn us away from this folly of making ourselves first and Himself last in our reception of His gifts!

Against Two Letters of the Pelagians, 2:21

Love comes from God

It is no wonder that the light shines in the darkness, and the darkness does not comprehend it. In John's letter, the Light declares, "Behold what manner of love the Father has bestowed upon us, that we should be called the sons of God" (1 Jn.3:1). And in the Pelagian writings the darkness says, "Love comes to us from our own selves." Now, if the Pelagians only possessed true love, that is, Christian love, they would also know where they obtained possession of it. The apostle knew this when he said, "But we have received not the spirit of the world, but the Spirit Who is from God, so that we might know the things that are freely given to us by God" (1 Cor.2:12). And John says, "God is love" (1 Jn.4:16). So the Pelagians are saying that they actually have God Himself, not from God, but from their own selves! They admit that we have the knowledge of the law from

God, but they insist that love is from our own selves. They are not listening to the apostle when he says, "Knowledge puffs up, but love builds up" (1 Cor.8:21). Now what can be more absurd, what can be more insane and more alien to the very sacredness of love itself, than to maintain that God merely gives us the knowledge which (apart from love) puffs us up, while the love that prevents the possibility of this inflated knowledge springs from ourselves?!

On Grace and Free Will, 40

The difference between knowledge and love

Now even Pelagius should frankly confess that this grace is plainly set forth in the inspired Scriptures. He should not, with shameless insolence, hide the fact that he has too long opposed it. Let him admit it with healthy regret, so that the holy Church may cease to be troubled by his stubborn persistence, and rejoice instead in his sincere conversion. Let him distinguish between knowledge and love, as they ought to be distinguished. For "knowledge puffs up, but love builds up" (1 Cor.8:1). Knowledge no longer puffs up when love builds up. And since each is the gift of God (although one is less, and the other greater), Pelagius must not extol our righteousness above the praise which is due to God Who justifies us. Yet this is what he does, when he says that the lesser of these two gifts (knowledge) is assisted by divine grace, and claims that the greater gift (love) comes from the human will.

But if Pelagius agrees that we receive love from the grace of God, he must not think that any virtues of our own preceded our reception of the gift. For what virtues could we possibly have had, at the time when we did not love God? Indeed, so that we might receive the love that enables us to love, God loved us while as yet we had no love ourselves. This the apostle John most expressly declares: "Not that we loved God," says he, "but that He loved us" (1 Jn.4:10). And again, "We love Him, because He first loved us" (1 Jn.4:19). Most excellently and truly spoken! For we could not have any power to love Him, unless we received it from Him in His first loving us. And what good could we possibly do if we possessed no love? But how could we help doing good if we have love? God's command may appear sometimes to be kept by those who do not love Him, but only fear Him; but where there is no love, God does not reckon any work as good, nor is there any "good work" rightly so called. For "whatever is not from faith is sin" (Rom.14:23) and "faith works by love" (Gal.5:6).

On the Grace of Christ and Original Sin, 1:27

When we do good, God's will inspires ours

It is certain that we keep the commandments if we will. But because "the will is prepared by the Lord" (Prov.8:35, Septuagint), we must ask Him for such a force of will that is sufficient to make us act by willing. Again, it is certain that when we will, we are the ones who do the willing. But it is God Who causes us to will what is good, of whom it is said (as he has just now expressed it), "The will is prepared by the Lord." Of the same Lord it is said, "The steps of a man are ordered by the Lord, and He wills his way" (Ps.37:23). Of the same Lord it is also said, "It is God who works in you, even to will!" (Phil.2:13) Again, it is certain that when we act, we are the ones who act. But it is God who causes us to act, by applying efficacious powers to our will. As He has said, "I will make you to walk in my statutes, and to observe my judgments, and to do them" (Ezek.36:27). When he says, "I will make you ... to do them," what else does He say in fact than, "I will take away from you your heart of stone," from which used to arise your inability to act, "and I will give you a heart of flesh," in order that you may act (Ezek.36:26)? And what does this promise amount to but this: I will remove your hard heart, out of which you did not act, and I will give you an obedient heart, out of which you shall act?

On Grace and Free Will, 32

Called according to God's purpose, not ours

Why do the Pelagians say they believe that "grace assists the good resolution of everyone, but it does not instil the desire for virtue into a reluctant heart"? They say this as if a person from his own resources, without God's assistance, has a good resolution and a desire for virtue; and this preceding virtue is worthy of being assisted by the subsequent grace of God. For they think, perhaps, that when the apostle said, "For we know that He works all things for good to those who love God, to those who are called according to purpose" (Rom.8:28) — they think perhaps that Paul meant *human* purpose, so that this purpose, as a worthy quality, would secure the mercy of the God Who calls.

If that's what they think, they are ignorant of Paul's real meaning: "Who are called according to purpose," that is, not human purpose, but the purpose of God, by which before the world's creation He elected those whom He foreknew and predestined to be conformed to the image of His Son (Rom.8:29). For not all the called are "called according to purpose", since "many are called, few are chosen" (Matt.22:14). But those who are called according to purpose are the persons who were elected before the creation of the world. Of this purpose of God, it was also said (as I have already mentioned concerning the twins Esau and Jacob), "that the purpose of God might stand according to election, not by works, but by Him Who calls, it was said, that the elder shall serve the younger" (Rom.9:11-12). This purpose of God is also mentioned in that place where, writing to Timothy, he says, "Labour with the gospel according to the power of God, Who saves us and calls us with this holy calling, not according to our works, but according to His purpose and grace, which was given to us in Christ Jesus before eternal ages, but is now made manifest by the coming of our Saviour Jesus Christ" (2 Tim.1:8-10).

This, then, is the purpose of God, of which it is said, "He works together all things for good for those who are called according to purpose." Subsequent grace indeed assists a human good purpose, but the good purpose would not itself exist if grace did not work first.

Against Two Letters of the Pelagians, 2:22

Grace in operation and co-operation

"Love does no harm to a neighbour; therefore love is the fulfilling of the law" (Rom.13:10). This love the apostle Peter did not yet possess, when he denied the Lord three times out of fear. "There is no fear in love," says the gospel writer John in his first letter, "but perfect love casts out fear" (1 Jn.4:18). But still, however small and imperfect Peter's love was, it was not entirely lacking when he said to the Lord, "I will lay down my life for Your sake" (Jn.13:37). For he supposed he was able to carry out what he felt himself willing to do. And who was it that had begun to give Peter his love, however small? Who but God Who prepares the will, and perfects by His co-operation what He begins by His operation? For in beginning to work, He works *in us* to give us the will, and in perfecting this work, He works *with us* when we have the will. This is why the apostle says, "I am confident of this very thing, that He Who has begun a good work in you will complete it until the day of Jesus Christ" (Phil.1:6). He operates, therefore, without our help, in order that we may will; but when we will, and will so as to act, He co-operates with us. We can, however, ourselves do nothing to carry out good works of godliness, without God either working to give us the will, or co-working with us when we will.

On Grace and Free Will, 33

Give what You command, and command what You will

When we commit sin, we get no help from God; but we are not able to act justly, and to fulfil the law of righteousness in every part, unless we are helped by God. Light does not help our physical eyes to shut out light; rather, light helps our eyes to see, and the eye cannot see at all unless light helps it. Likewise God, Who is the light of the inner self, helps our mental sight, in order that we may do some good, not according to our own righteousness, but according to His. But if we turn away from God , it is our own act; then we are wise according to the flesh, and we consent to the lust of the flesh for unlawful deeds. When we turn to God, therefore, He helps us; when we turn away from Him, He forsakes us. But God even helps us to turn to Him; and this, certainly, is something that light does not do for the eyes of the body.

When, therefore, He commands us in the words, "Turn to Me, and I will turn to you" (Zech.1:3), and we say to Him, "Turn us, O God of our salvation" (Ps.85:4), and again, "Turn us, O God of hosts" (Ps.80:3) — what else do we say but, "Give what You command"? When He commands us, saying, "Understand now, O simple among the people" (Ps.94:8), and we say to Him, "Give me understanding, that I may learn your commandments" (Ps.119:73) — what else do we say but, "Give what You command"? When He commands us, saying, "Do not go after your lusts" (Ecclesiasticus 18:30), and we say to Him, "We know that no-one can be chaste, unless God gives it to him" (Wisdom 8:21) — what else do we say but, "Give what You command"?[4] When He commands us, saying, "Do justice" (Isa.56:1), and we say, "Teach me Your judgments, O Lord" (Ps.119:108) — what else do we say but, "Give what You command"? Likewise, when He says: "Blessed are those who hunger and thirst after righteousness; for they shall be filled" (Matt.5:6), from whom should we seek the meat and drink of righteousness, but from Him Who promises His fullness to those who hunger and thirst after it?

On the Merits and Forgiveness of Sins, 2:5

Is faith itself the gift of God?

We must still try to answer briefly this question: Is the will by which we believe itself the gift of God, or does it arise from that free will which is naturally implanted in us? If we say that faith is not the gift of God, we must then fear that we have discovered some answer to the apostle's reproachful appeal: "What do you have that you did not receive? Now, if you received it, why do you boast, as if you had not received it ?" (1 Cor.4:7) If the will to believe is not God's gift, we could reply: "See, we have the will to believe, which we did not receive. See what we boast about — even something we did not receive!" If, however, we were to say that this kind of will is entirely the gift of God, we would then have to fear that unbelieving and

---

[4] Augustine thought that the apocryphal books of Ecclesiasticus and Wisdom were part of the Old Testament canon. See Chapter 4, footnote 7.

ungodly people might unreasonably seem to have a fair excuse for
their unbelief, in the fact that God had refused to give them the will
to believe.

On the Spirit and the Letter, 57

Faith itself is God's gift

Paul's last statement here is, "I have kept the faith" (2 Tim.4:7). But
the man who says this is the same man who declares in another
passage, "I have obtained mercy that I might be faithful" (1 Cor.7:25).
He does not say, "I obtained mercy because I was faithful," but "in
order that I might be faithful." This shows that even faith itself
cannot be had without God's mercy, and that it is the gift of God.
Paul very expressly teaches us this when he says, "For by grace you
are saved through faith, and that not of yourselves; it is the gift of
God" (Eph.2:8). The Pelagians might possibly say, "We received
grace because we believed." as if they would attribute the faith to
themselves, and the grace to God. Therefore the apostle, having
said, "You are saved through faith," added, "And that not of
yourselves, but it is the gift of God." And again, in case they say
they deserved so great a gift by their works, he immediately added,
"Not of works, in case anyone should boast." Not that Paul denied
good works, or emptied them of their value, for he says that God
renders to everyone according to his works (Rom.2:6); but works
proceed from faith, not faith from works. Therefore it is from God
that we have works of righteousness, as it is from Him that we have
faith, concerning which it is written, "The just shall live by faith"
(Rom.1:17).

On Grace and Free Will, 17

Faith is part of our re-creation in Christ

And in case people should arrogate to themselves the merit at least
of their own faith, not understanding that this too is the gift of God,

this same apostle, who says in another place that he had "obtained mercy of the Lord to be faithful" (1 Cor.7:25), here also adds: "and that not of yourselves; it is the gift of God: not of works, in case anyone should boast" (Eph.2:8). And in case it should be thought that good works will be lacking in those who believe, he adds further: "For we are His workmanship, created in Christ Jesus for good works, which God has before ordained that we should walk in them" (Eph.2:10). We shall be made truly free, then, when God fashions us, that is, forms and creates us anew, not as human beings — for He has done that already — but as good people. His grace is now doing this, so that we may be a new creation in Christ Jesus, according as it is said: "Create in me a clean heart, O God" (Ps.51:10). For God had already created David's heart, so far as the physical structure of the human heart is concerned; but the psalmist prays for the renewal of the life which was still lingering in his heart.

Enchiridion, 31

If faith is not God's gift, salvation is no longer by grace

It follows, therefore, that without any virtue of our own, we receive the gift of faith, from which the rest of salvation flows — although according to the Pelagians, we obtain salvation because of our virtue. If, however, they insist on denying that faith is freely given to us, what is the meaning of the apostle's words: "According as God has dealt to everyone a measure of faith" (Rom.12:3)? And if they argue that faith is bestowed as a reward for virtue, not as a free gift, what then becomes of another saying of the apostle: "To you it is given on the behalf of Christ, not only to believe in Him, but also to suffer for His sake" (Phil.1:29)? The apostle's testimony makes each of these a gift — both that a person believes in Christ, and that he suffers for Christ's sake. These Pelagians, however, attribute faith to free will, in such a way as to make it seem that grace is given to faith not as a gratuitous gift, but as a debt. Thus grace ceases to be grace any longer. How can something be grace if it is not gratuitous?

On the Grace of Christ and Original Sin, 1:34

Giving thanks to God for faith proves that faith is His doing

The apostle gives thanks to God for those who have believed — not, clearly, because the gospel has been declared to them, but because they have believed. For he says, "in whom you also, having heard the word of the truth, the gospel of your salvation — in whom, having also believed, you were sealed with the Holy Spirit of promise, which is a pledge of our inheritance, for the redemption of God's own possession, for the praise of his glory. For this cause I also, having heard of the faith in the Lord Jesus and with reference to all the saints, cease not to give thanks for you" (Ephesians 1:13-16). Their faith was new and recent, following on the preaching of the gospel to them. When the apostle hears of this faith of theirs, he gives thanks to God for them. If he were to give thanks to someone for what he might think or know that person had not given, it would be called a flattery or a mockery, rather than a giving of thanks. "Do not be deceived, for God is not mocked" (Gal.6:7); for the beginning of faith is also His gift, unless we rightly judge the apostolic giving of thanks to be either mistaken or fallacious!

What then? Does that not stand forth as the beginning of the faith of the Thessalonians, for which the same apostle gives thanks to God when he says, "For this reason also we thank God without ceasing, because when you received the word of God which you heard from us, you received it not as the word of men, but as it is in truth, the word of God, which effectually works in you, and which you believed" (1 Thess.2:13)? What does Paul gives thanks to God for here? Surely it is a vain and idle thing if He to whom Paul gives thanks did not Himself do the thing! But, since this is not a vain and idle thing, certainly God, to whom Paul gave thanks for this work, Himself did it, so that when they had received the word of God which they heard, they received it not as the word of men, but as it is in truth, the word of God. God, therefore, works in human hearts with that "calling according to His purpose" (Rom.8:28), of which we have spoken a great deal, in order that people should not hear the gospel in vain, but when they hear it, should be converted and believe, receiving it not as the word of men, but as it is in truth, the word of God.

On the Predestination of the Saints, 39

The example of Lydia

For what is the meaning of, "praying also for us that God would open to us a door of the word" (Col.4:3), unless it is a most manifest demonstration that even the very beginning of faith is the gift of God? For faith would not be sought from God in prayer, unless it were believed to be given by Him. This gift of heavenly grace had descended to that seller of purple for whom, as Scripture says in the Acts of the Apostles, "The Lord opened her heart, and she gave heed to the things spoken by Paul" (Acts 16:14). For she was called so that she might believe. For God does what He wills in human hearts, either by His assistance or by His judgment, so that through their means may be fulfilled what His hand and counsel have predestined to be done.

On the Predestination of the Saints, 41

Why pray that God will give faith to unbelievers, if faith is not a gracious gift?

If God does not make people willing who were not willing, on what principle does the Church pray, according to the Lord's commandment, for her persecutors? ... For what do we pray on behalf of those who are unwilling to believe, except that God would work in them to make them willing? Certainly the apostle says, "Brethren, my heart's desire and my prayer to God for them is for their salvation" (Rom.10:1). He prays for those who do not believe — for what, except that they may believe? For they will obtain salvation in no other way. If, then, the faith of those praying precedes the grace of God [in converting unbelievers], what about the faith of those for whom prayer is offered that they may come to faith? Does *their* faith precede the grace of God? How can it, since this is the very thing we seek for them, that on those who do not believe — that is, who have no faith — faith itself may be bestowed?

On the Predestination of the Saints, 15

The same theme pursued

Now if faith comes simply from free will, and is not given by God, why do we pray for unbelievers that they may believe? This would be absolutely useless, unless we believe (quite correctly) that almighty God is able to take wills that are perverse and opposed to faith, and turn them to faith. Human free will is addressed when it is said, "Today, if you will hear His voice, do not harden your hearts" (Ps.95:7-8). But if God were not able to remove from the human heart even its obstinacy and hardness, He would not say, through the prophet, "I will take from them their heart of stone, and will give them a heart of flesh" (Ezek.11:19). All this was foretold in reference to the New Testament, as is shown clearly enough by the apostle when he says, "You are our epistle, written not with ink, but with the Spirit of the living God; not in tables of stone, but in fleshly tables of the heart" (2 Cor.3:2-3).

We must not, of course, suppose that this phrase is used as if those who ought to live spiritually might live in a fleshly way. But a stone, with which the hard human heart is compared, has no feeling. What was there left for God to compare the wise human heart with, but the flesh which possesses feeling? For this is what is said by the prophet Ezekiel: "I will give them another heart, and I will put a new spirit within you; and I will take the stony heart out of their flesh, and will give them a heart of flesh, so that they may walk in My statutes, and keep My ordinances, and do them: and they shall be My people, and I will be their God, says the Lord" (Ezek.11:19-20). Can we possibly, without utter absurdity, maintain that there first existed in anyone the good virtue of a good will, to entitle him to the removal of his heart of stone? How can we say this, when all the time this heart of stone itself signifies precisely a will of the hardest kind, a will that is absolutely inflexible against God? For if a good will comes first, there is obviously no longer a heart of stone.

On Grace and Free Will, 29

Repentance is the gift of God

The mercy of God is necessary not only when a person repents, but even to lead him to repent. How else can we explain what the apostle says of certain people: "if perhaps God may give them repentance" (2 Tim.2:25)? And before Peter wept bitterly, we are told by the gospel-writer, "The Lord turned, and looked upon him" (Lk.22:61).[5]

Enchiridion, 82

Grace is the death of pride

Beware, O Christian, beware of pride. Even though you are a disciple of the saints, ascribe it always and wholly to grace. It was not brought about by what you deserve, but by the grace of God, that there is any "remnant" in you. For the prophet Isaiah, having this remnant in view, had already said, "Unless the Lord of Hosts had left us a seed, we would have become like Sodom, and would have been like Gomorrah" (Isa.1:9, Rom.9:29). "So then," says the apostle, "at this present time also a remnant is saved through the election of grace. But if it is by grace," he says, "then it is no longer by works" (that is, "do not be puffed up any longer on what you deserve"); "otherwise grace is no longer grace" (Rom.11:5-6). For if you build on your own work, then a reward is rendered to you, rather than grace freely bestowed. But if it is grace, it is gratuitously given.

I ask you, then, O sinner, "Do you believe in Christ?" You say, "I do believe." What do you believe? Do you believe that all your sins can be forgiven freely through Him? Then you have what you have believed. O grace gratuitously given! And you, righteous soul, what do you believe? Do you believe that you cannot keep your righteousness without God? If you are righteous, then, impute it wholly to His mercy; but if you are a sinner, ascribe it to your own iniquity. Be your own accuser, and He will be your gracious Deliverer. For every crime, wickedness, or sin comes from our own negligence, but all virtue and holiness come from God's gracious goodness.

Sermons on the Gospels, 50:4

---

[5] In other words, Peter's repentance was caused by the Lord's gaze. It is the God-given knowledge of Christ and His love that begets repentance in the heart.

When God crowns our virtues, grace is crowning its own gifts

The Pelagians say that the only grace that is not given according to our virtues is the grace by which a person's sins are forgiven, but that the final grace of eternal life is given as a reward to our preceding virtues. They must not be allowed to go without an answer. If, indeed, they understand and acknowledge our virtues to be the gifts of God too, then their opinion would not deserve condemnation. But since they preach human virtues by declaring that a person has them from his own self, then most rightly the apostle replies: "Who makes you to differ from another? And what do you have that you did not receive? Now, if you received it, why do you boast as if you had not received it?" (1 Cor.4:7) To a person who holds such views, it is perfect truth to say: It is His own gifts that God crowns, not your virtues. If your virtues come from your own self, not from God, then they are evil, and God does not crown them. But if they are good, they are God's gifts, because, as the Apostle James says, "Every good gift and every perfect gift is from above, and comes down from the Father of lights" (Jam.1:17). In accordance with this John the Lord's forerunner also declares: "A man can receive nothing unless it is given to him from heaven" (Jn.3:27) — from heaven, of course, because from there came also the Holy Spirit, when Jesus ascended up on high, led captivity captive, and gave gifts to men. If, then, your good virtues are God's gifts, God does not crown them as your virtues, but as His own gifts.

On Grace and Free Will, 15

The same theme pursued

Finally, after the redemption from all corruption, what remains but the crown of righteousness? This at least remains, but even here, under the crown, do not let your head be swollen, in case it fails to receive the crown! Listen, mark well the psalm, how that crown will not rest on a swollen head. After the psalmist had said, "Who redeems your life from corruption," he says, "Who crowns you" (Ps.103:4). Here you were ready at once to say, "The phrase 'Crowns you' is an acknowledgment of my virtues; my own excellence has done it; it is the payment of a debt, not a gift." Listen rather to the psalm. For it is you again that say this; and "all men are liars" (Ps.116:11)!

Hear what God says: "Who crowns you with mercy and pity" (Ps.103:4). From His mercy He crowns you, from His pity He crowns you. For you had no worthiness that He should call you to Himself; or being called, no worthiness that He should justify you; or being justified, no worthiness that He should glorify you. "The remnant is saved by the election of grace. But if it is by grace, then it is no longer by works; otherwise grace is no more grace" (Rom.11:5-6). "For to him who works, the reward shall not be reckoned according to grace, but according to debt" (Rom.4:4). The apostle says, "Not according to grace, but according to debt." But "He crowns you with pity and mercy." If your own virtues have gone before, God says to you, "Examine well your virtues, and you shall see that they are My gifts."

This then is "the righteousness of God" (Rom.1:17). It is like the phrase, "the Lord's salvation" (Ex.14:13) — not that by which the Lord is saved, but which He gives to those whom He saves. So too the grace of God through Jesus Christ our Lord is called "the righteousness of God" — not that by which the Lord is righteous, but by which He justifies those ungodly people whom He makes righteous.

Sermons on the Gospels, 81:8-9

Chapter 6

Predestination and Election

I simply hold what I see the apostle has most plainly taught us: that owing to one man, all who are born of Adam pass into condemnation, unless they are born again in Christ; and that God has appointed to be regenerated, before they die in the body, those whom He predestined to everlasting life, as the most merciful bestower of grace; while to those whom He has predestined to eternal death, He is also the most righteous awarder of punishment, not only on account of the sins which they add in the indulgence of their own will, but also because of their original sin, even if, as in the case of infants, they add nothing to it.

*Augustine, **On the Soul and its Origin, 4:16***

Among those who today call themselves Evangelical, there is no doctrine more calculated to produce heated arguments and division than the doctrine of predestination and election. (The charismatic movement is equally divisive, but in the realm of worship and spirituality.) In a church where I was once a member, our newly inducted pastor preached a sermon on predestination in the opening weeks of his ministry. My heart warmed as I listened to his faithful and vivid exposition of Scripture's teaching that before the creation of the world, God had already chosen those who were to be saved — chosen us by unconditional grace, not because He foresaw we would believe and trust in Christ, but in order to liberate us from our hopeless bondage to unbelief and bestow upon us the sovereign gift of saving faith. The pastor himself was almost in tears as he preached, overwhelmed by such mercy from so just and holy a God to such appalling sinners. As I say, I listened with joy. But sitting a few feet away was one of our elders who, I knew, disbelieved very strongly in this doctrine of unconditional election. By the time the sermon was over, the poor man looked as if a death sentence had been passed on him. His face was a picture of grey misery. And yet he, no less than I, would have claimed to be an Evangelical Christian. The doctrine of predestination and election had divided us, in feeling if not in friendship. What was warm joy to me was cold death to him.

Once upon a time, this division among Evangelicals over predestination could not have happened. Let us go back in history to our forefathers who professed the name "Evangelical" five hundred years ago, at the time of the Protestant Reformation. The original Protestants called themselves *Evangelical* because they claimed they were recovering the fullness and purity of the *Evangel* (Greek for "gospel") — retrieving the Church's true treasure from out of the midst of various distortions and corruptions which, like some weed-infested overgrowth, had tragically concealed its beauty in later medieval Rome. And one of the doctrines that all the Reformers (with one exception) affirmed was the doctrine my pastor preached that fateful Sunday: the doctrine of predestination and election. At the time of the Reformation, to be Evangelical, to be a gospel believer, meant to confess predestination and election.

The one exception I mentioned was Martin Luther's right hand man, Philip Melanchthon. Even he started off believing in predestination, but changed his mind half way through his career. Many of his fellow Lutherans were outraged and accused

Melanchthon of betraying the original Reformation message. They were quite right. If there was one thing that united Martin Luther, Ulrich Zwingli, Martin Bucer, John Calvin, Peter Martyr, archbishop Cranmer and John Knox, it was their heartfelt belief that God, not sinful human beings, chose who would be saved. I do not choose myself for salvation; God chooses me. Or if I do choose God, it is only because He has first chosen me. Why has He chosen me? Not because He saw I was going to repent and believe; for I never would have repented or believed, if He had not chosen me first by pure grace. My faith, repentance and holiness are the fruits of His predestination, not its cause. So the Reformers believed; so even Melanchthon believed until he underwent his spectacular wobble half way round the track.

Timorous wobbling Melanchthon, seduced by Semi-Pelagian charms, was the only great Reformer who said a faithless farewell to predestination. Still, it did not take long for the other Reformers to discover that some of those who shared their critique of Rome were not really on the same wavelength. These were the "Anabaptists". Despite this nickname ("Rebaptisers"), their chief theological offence in the eyes of the Reformers was their rejection of predestination and election. Some were virtual Pelagians, denying original sin; others were more Semi-Pelagian. (Most of them also disbelieved in justification by faith alone). In England, the Reformer John Bradford, one of England's noble army of Protestant martyrs burnt by Mary Tudor, came across some of these Anabaptists who rejected predestination and election. His reaction was very interesting. Bradford was in prison at the time, awaiting his own execution for so-called heresy. But he took the time to write a treatise against these deniers of predestination. Bradford's verdict was strikingly robust: "The effects of salvation they so mingle with the cause, that if it be not seen to, more hurt will come by them than ever came by the papists" (**Defence of Election**, preface).

What has happened to the Evangelical world, when John Bradford's verdict on many Evangelicals today would have to be that they are worse than papists?

It is vital for us to grasp that the Reformers were not innovating in their proclamation of predestination and election. They were simply breathing fresh life into the mainstream theology of the Western Church throughout the Middle Ages. Almost all the famous Western theologians of the medieval period had believed in predestination:

Anselm of Canterbury, Peter Lombard, Bernard of Clairvaux, Thomas Aquinas, Duns Scotus, Gregory of Rimini, John Wyclif, John Huss. If we don't know who these men were, we are all the poorer in our ignorance. The last two, Wyclif and Huss, were the most outstanding examples of "Reformers before the Reformation"; and they were ardent believers in predestination. But behind them all, rising up from the sands of 5th century North Africa, stands the towering figure of Augustine of Hippo.

Augustine was the first great Church father who really scaled the heights and plumbed the depths of the apostle Paul's teaching on salvation by grace alone, as this teaching finds particular expression in the doctrine of election. It is not that before Augustine the Church rejected this doctrine. It is more the case that the Church, by and large, hadn't really thought about it. The energies of Christian thinkers were taken up with fighting other battles. In Augustine's words:

"What need is there to search into the works of those who lived before this heresy [Pelagianism] arose, when they were under no necessity of troubling themselves to solve this difficult question? Without doubt they would have done this, if they had been obliged to answer such things. Thus it is, that what they thought of the grace of God, they have briefly and hastily touched on in some places of their writings, whereas they dwelt at length on those things in which they disputed against the enemies of the Church, in exhortations to every virtue by which to serve the living and true God for the purpose of attaining eternal life and true happiness" (**On the Predestination of the Saints, 27**).

As I've already mentioned in Chapter 2, one of the early Church's chief struggles was against the pagan belief in fate and the Gnostic belief in a salvation that was available only to a spiritual elite. In such a setting, Christians naturally emphasised human freedom, dignity and responsibility. Some Church fathers, notably Origen, taught quite definitely that God predestined people to salvation on the basis of His foreknowledge of their own freely willed merits. (Then again, Origen taught many absurd things.) It was only when Pelagianism stepped into the arena that the Church was forced to face up squarely to the biblical teaching on divine predestination, as against the rampant Pelagian idolatry of human will-power. Augustine then emerged as the most brilliantly clear-thinking exponent of God's grace in election. But he was not the only one. We ought to bear in mind how the Catholics of North Africa were practically as one man in their "Augustinian" views of grace. A very conservative body, those North Africans; and they had no sense of adopting novelties when they reached for the sword of predestination to split the skull of Pelagian presumption. This lends some credence to the idea that predestination was "in the air" that Catholic theology breathed (at least in Africa). It needed only the heat of the Pelagian controversy to condense predestination into a distilled dew of explicit doctrine.

If Evangelicalism is ever to be restored to its true identity, so that it once more confesses the Evangel in its fullness and purity, it must recover its belief in God's gracious, unconditional predestination and election of His people in Christ. In a sense, there is a huge irony about this. The Reformers called the Roman Church of their day back to gospel purity, which involved a fresh confession of predestination. Today, it is Evangelicalism itself that needs to hear the same summons. One way the summons can be heard is to sit at Augustine's feet.

One last point. Those Evangelical readers who do believe in election may be confused by Augustine's insistence that no-one can know who the elect are in this present life — indeed, Augustine says, the individual believer cannot know whether he or she is among the elect. Only God knows. How can election be a joyful or encouraging doctrine in those circumstances?

Augustine's concern here was actually one that is shared by the Reformed heirs of the Reformation. It has to do with professing Christians who fall away. We meet these sad characters in Scripture (2 Tim.4:10, 1 Jn.2:19) and in experience. How do we account for the difference between the Christian who perseveres to the end and the Christian who makes shipwreck of his faith? Reformed thinking explains this by its doctrine of "temporary faith". The disciple who falls away had a temporary faith, but not the enduring faith of God's elect. So far, Augustine and Reformed theology agree. But of course, the pastoral question is then raised very sharply: how can I know whether *my* faith is temporary or persevering? Reformed theology insists that temporary faith is different *in character* from true persevering faith. That is, the temporary believer was never really regenerate; he did not have a genuine saving faith in Christ, only an intellectual belief in doctrine accompanied (perhaps) by some emotional experiences.

Augustine's position — at least, most of the time — was different. The bishop of Hippo was impressed by how *similar* temporary and persevering faith seem to be. Who can honestly tell the difference? he asked. The only absolutely sure way of telling them apart, according to Augustine, is that temporary faith falls away, and persevering faith perseveres! Augustine was ready to concede that a person might have a genuine experience of regeneration which does not prove enduring. (His belief in the baptismal regeneration of infants complicated matters at this point.) The distinctive thing about the elect, he argued, was not merely that God regenerates them, but that He also grants them the gift of perseverance. This gift guarantees that their faith will endure to the end. But I cannot know that I have this persevering faith of the elect unless — well, unless I persevere to the end!

Augustine's way of putting it, then, seems to rob the doctrine of election of any comfort for the believer. I, the Christian, am left suspended in doubt as to whether I am one of the elect. However, Augustine does not in fact leave me there, hanging in mid-air (always painful). He was a pastor and had a pastoral heart. And his pastoral heart carried him forward to a view that is very like the later Reformed understanding. If you the Christian are praying to God for the grace of perseverance, pastor Augustine said, you must trust that God will give it to you. You may not have in Scripture any infallible revealed statement that you personally are an elect soul; but you do have an infallible revealed statement that God answers the prayers of His people. So if you have reason to believe that you are among His people (*i.e.* a faithful Catholic Christian), and if you are sincerely praying for perseverance, then you must also surely believe and trust that God will answer your prayer. In Augustine's words:

"You, therefore, ought to hope that the gift of persevering in obedience will be given to you by the Father of Lights, from Whom comes down every excellent gift and every perfect gift; and you ought to ask for this gift in your daily prayers. And in doing this, you ought to trust that you are not aliens from the predestination of His people, because it is God Himself Who bestows even the power of praying for perseverance. Far be it from you to despair of yourselves!" (**On the Gift of Perseverance, 62**).

It might perhaps occur to us to say, "But why should I need to pray for the gift of perseverance? If I am a true Christian, God will give it to me anyway." But this would have made no sense to

Augustine. He would have said, "One of the marks of being a true Christian is that you *do* pray for perseverance. So how can you claim you are a true Christian if you are *not* praying for it?" To refuse to pray for the grace of perseverance would mean that we were not relying on God to preserve our faith. But faith, by its very nature, is reliance on God. *True faith will rely on God for its own continuance.* And it will express this reliance precisely by praying for the grace of perseverance. If Christ prayed for Peter that his faith should not fail (Lk.22:32), it must surely be right for us to pray that our own faith will not fail. Besides, the whole idea that we need not pray for things because "God will do them anyway" is the error that usually goes under the name of "hyper-Calvinism". If I am a true elect Christian, God will *sanctify* me; does that mean I should not *pray* for my sanctification? But if I do *not* pray for my sanctification, what right do I have to think I am a true elect Christian at all? The same reasoning applies to praying for perseverance.

Augustine, then, did after all have a doctrine of the personal assurance of salvation. The faith of God's elect is set apart from temporary faith by its constant prayerful reliance on God for the grace of perseverance. If I have all the other marks of being a Christian, and if I am sincerely praying for perseverance, I must hope and trust that God will indeed answer my prayer. "Far be it from you to despair of yourselves!" We may think that Augustine's view of assurance needs to be made somewhat richer and stronger. But he did have such a doctrine. Let us remember this, when we hear him saying that believers can have no certainty about their perseverance. Augustine did say this; but by a happy inconsistency, it wasn't all he said.

****

Predestination and Election

Our destiny lies not in the stars but in God's purpose

Those who believe in fate argue that actions, events, and even our very wills themselves depend on the position of the stars (which they call "constellations") at the time when we are conceived or born. But the grace of God stands above not only all stars and all heavens, but all angels too. In a word, believers in fate ascribe people's good and evil deeds and their fortunes to fate. In reality, when people suffer bad fortune, God is following up their vices with due retribution, while He bestows good fortunes by undeserved grace with a merciful will. He does both the one and the other, not according to a conjunction of the stars in time, but according to the eternal and high purpose of His severity and goodness. We see, then, that neither belongs to fate. But perhaps you will answer that this very benevolence of God, by which He does not deal with us according to our merits, but bestows undeserved benefits with free generosity – perhaps you will say that this should be called "fate". Well, the apostle calls it "grace", saying, "By grace you are saved through faith; and that not of yourselves, but it is the gift of God; not of works, in case anyone should boast" (Eph.2:8-9). If you think this is "fate", do you not understand, do you not perceive that we are not the ones who "teach fate under the name of grace"? No, you are the ones who call divine grace by the name of fate!

Against Two Letters of the Pelagians, 2:12

Election is an unsearchable mystery

What falsehood about free will are you setting before me? Your will is never going to be free to do righteousness unless you are one of the Lord's sheep. He Who makes His people into sheep liberates their wills for godly obedience. But why does God make some people into His sheep and not others, since there is no favouritism with Him? This is the very question the blessed apostle Paul answers to those who ask it more curiously than correctly: "Indeed, O man, who are you to reply against God? Will the thing formed say to Him Who formed it, 'Why have You made me like this?'" (Rom.9:20). This is the very question belonging to that "depth" which, in a sense, terrified the same apostle when he desired to look into it, causing him to exclaim, "O the depth of the riches both of the wisdom and knowledge of God! How unsearchable are His judgments, and His ways past finding out! For who has known the mind of the Lord? Or who has become His counsellor? Or who has first given to Him and it shall be repaid to him? For of Him, and through Him, and to Him, are all things, to Whom be glory for ever" (Rom.11:33-6). Let the Pelagians not dare to pry into that unsearchable question — these men who defend human goodness before grace, and therefore against grace, and want to give something first to God by their own free will so that it will be repaid to them as a reward. Let them wisely understand, or faithfully believe, that even what they think they have first given, they have actually received from Him from Whom all things exist, by Whom all things exist, in Whom all things exist.

But as to why this person should receive, and that person not receive, when neither of them deserves to receive, and whichever of them receives does so undeservingly — let the Pelagians measure their own strength and not search into things too strong for them. Let it be enough to know that there is no unrighteousness with God. For when Paul could find no worthy qualities in Jacob which could have made God prefer him over his twin brother, he said: "What shall we say, then? Is there unrighteousness with God? Certainly not! For He says to Moses, 'I will have mercy on whom I will have mercy, and I will have compassion on whom I will have compassion.' So then, it is not of him who wills, nor of him who runs, but of God Who shows mercy" (Rom.9:14-16). Therefore let us be thankful for His free compassion, even though we find no answer to this profound question.

Yet the same apostle does give an answer, as far as one can be given, when he says: "What if God, wanting to show His wrath and to make His power known, endured with much long-suffering the vessels of wrath prepared for destruction, that He might make known the riches of His glory on the vessels of mercy, which He had prepared beforehand for glory?" (Rom.9:22-23). Now, wrath is clearly not repaid unless it is deserved — otherwise there would indeed be "unrighteousness with God". But when undeserved mercy is bestowed, that cannot be called "unrighteousness with God". So let the vessels of mercy understand how freely mercy is provided for them, since they share a common reason for destruction with the vessels of wrath to whom righteous and deserved wrath is repaid. And with this, I have said enough in opposition to those who, by the freedom of the will, desire to destroy the freeness of grace.

Against Two Letters of the Pelagians, 4:15-16.

Election is the cause of faith

Let us, then, understand the calling by which the elect become elected — not those who are elected *because* they have believed, but elected *in order that* they may believe. For the Lord Himself also sufficiently explains this calling when He says, "You did not choose Me, but I chose you" (Jn.15:16). For if they had been elected because they had believed, they themselves would certainly have first chosen Him by believing in Him, so that they would deserve to be elected. But He takes away this notion altogether when He says, "You did not choose Me, but I chose you." And yet they themselves undoubtedly did choose Him when they believed in Him. Therefore the true reason that He says, "You did not choose Me, but I chose you," was because they did not first choose Him in order that He should then choose them, but He first chose them in order that they might then choose Him. For His mercy went before them according to grace, not according to debt. Therefore He chose them out of the world while He was wearing flesh, but as those who were already chosen in Himself before the creation of the world.

This is the changeless truth concerning predestination and grace. For what is it that the apostle says, "As He has chosen us in Himself before the creation of the world" (Eph.1:4)? And assuredly, if this was said because God *foreknew* that they would believe, not because He Himself would *make* them believers, the Son speaks against any such foreknowledge when He says, "You did not choose Me, but I chose you." For God should rather have foreknown this very thing, that they themselves would have chosen Him, so that they might then deserve to be chosen by Him. Therefore they were elected before the creation of the world with that predestination in which God foreknew what *He Himself* would do; but they were elected out of the world with that calling by which God fulfilled what He predestined. For whom He predestined, them He also called, with that calling which is according to purpose. Not others, therefore, but those whom He predestined, them He also called; not others, but those whom He called, them He also justified; not others, but those whom He predestined, called, and justified, them He also glorified, assuredly to that end which has no end.

On the Predestination of the Saints, 30

Chosen, not for good in me....

Therefore God chose us in Christ before the creation of the world,
and predestined us to be adopted as His children. He did this, not
because we were going to be holy and blameless by our own will,
but rather He chose and predestined us that we might *become* holy
and blameless. Moreover, He did this according to the good pleasure
of *His* will, so that nobody might glory in his own will, but in God's
will towards himself. He also did this according to the riches of His
grace, according to His good will, which He purposed in His beloved
Son. In Him we have obtained an inheritance, being predestined
according to the purpose (His, not ours) of the One Who works all
things to such an extent that He works even in our wills. Moreover,
He works according to the counsel of His will, so that we may be for
the praise of His glory.

This is the reason why we cry that no one should glory in anything
human, and thus not in himself; but whoever glories, let him glory in
the Lord, that he may be for the praise of the Lord's glory. For He
Himself works according to His purpose that we may be for the
praise of His glory, and, of course, holy and blameless, for which
purpose He called us, having predestined us before the creation of
the world (Eph.1:3-6). In all this, His purpose is the special calling
of the elect for whom He works all things together for good, because
they are called according to His purpose (Rom.8:28); and "the gifts
and calling of God are without repentance" (Rom.11:29).

On the Predestination of the Saints, 37

Chosen out of the world

He says to the apostles, "If you were of the world, the world would
love its own" (Jn. 15:19). But in case they arrogated more to
themselves than was appropriate, and — when He said that they
were not of the world — to prevent them imagining that this was by
nature, not by grace, He says, "But because you are not of the world,
but I have chosen you out of the world, therefore the world hates
you" (Jn.15:19). It follows that once they *were* of the world: for in
order that they might *not* be of the world, they were chosen *out* of
the world.

Now this election the apostle demonstrates to be, not from good qualities going before in good works, but an election by grace, saying thus: "And at this time a remnant is saved by the election of grace. But if it is by grace, then it is no longer by works, otherwise grace is no longer grace" (Rom.11:5-6). This is election by grace; that is, election in which, through the grace of God, people are elected. This, I say, is election by grace which goes before all good virtues of human beings. For if it is to any good virtues that it is given, then is it no longer given gratuitously, but is paid as a debt, and consequently is not truly called grace. For "reward," as the same apostle says, "is not imputed as grace, but as debt" (Rom.4:4). However, in order that it may be true grace, that is, gratuitous, it finds nothing in a person to which it is owed on the basis of his goodness. This is well understood in that saying, "You will save them for nothing" (Ps.56:7, Septuagint). Assuredly grace itself gives the good qualities, rather than being given to good qualities.

Consequently grace goes before even faith, from which all good works begin. "For the just," as is written, "shall live by faith" (Rom.1:17). Moreover, grace not only assists the just, but also justifies the ungodly. And therefore even when it does help the just man and seems to be rendered to his good qualities, not even then does it cease to be grace, because the very goodness it helps was bestowed by grace. With a view therefore to this grace, which precedes all good human virtues, Christ was put to death by the ungodly, and "died for the ungodly" (Rom.5:6). And before He died, He elected the apostles, who were not of course then just, in order that they might be justified. To them He says, "I have chosen you out of the world" (Jn.15:19). For He said, "You are not of the world," and then, in case they should reckon themselves never to have been of the world, He presently added, "But I have chosen you out of the world." Assuredly, the fact that they were not of the world was by His own election of them, conferred upon them.

Therefore, if it had been through their own righteousness, not through His grace, that they were elected, they would not have been chosen out of the world; for they would already not be of the world, if they were already just. And again, if the reason why they were elected was that they were already just, then they had already first chosen the Lord. For who can be righteous except by choosing righteousness? "But the end of the law is Christ, for righteousness is to everyone who believes" (Rom.10:4). "He is made to us wisdom from God, and righteousness, and sanctification, and redemption, so that, as it is written, He that glories, let him glory in the Lord" (1 Cor.1:30-31). Christ then is Himself our righteousness.

On Patience, 16-17

God chose us before we ever chose Him

Let no-one deceive you, my brothers. We would not love God unless He first loved us. John gives us the plainest proof of this when he says, "We love because He first loved us" (1 John 4:19). Grace makes us lovers of the law; but law without grace makes us into nothing but law-breakers. And this is exactly what our Lord's words show us, when He says to the disciples, "You did not choose Me, but I chose you" (John 15:16). For if we first loved Him, so that on account of this virtue He might then love us, then it follows that we first chose Him so that we might be worthy of being chosen by Him. But He Who is Truth says otherwise; He flatly contradicts this human conceit. "You did not choose Me," He says. So if you did not choose Me, clearly you did not love Me. How could they choose someone they did not love? "But," He says, "I chose you." And then how could they possibly help choosing Him, and preferring Him to all the blessings of this world? But it was because they were chosen that they chose Him; it was not because they chose Him that they were chosen. There could be no virtue in people's choice of Christ, if God's grace did not go beforehand in His choosing them.

On Grace and Free Will, 38

Christ chose us when we were incapable of choosing Him

"You did not choose Me," He says, "I chose you" (John 15:16). Such grace is beyond description. What were we, apart from Christ's choice of us, when we were empty of love?... What were we but sinful and lost? We did not lead Him to choose us by believing in Him; for if Christ chose people who already believed, then we chose Him before He chose us. How then could He say, "You did not choose Me," unless His mercy came before our faith? Here is the faulty reasoning of those who defend the foreknowledge of God in opposition to His grace. For they say that God chose us before the creation of the world, not in order to make us good, but because He foreknew we would be good. This was not the view of Him Who said, "You did not choose Me." For if He had chosen us because He foreknew we would be good, then He would also have foreknown that we would *not* first of all choose Him. There is no other possible way to be good, apart from choosing the good; so what was it that God chose in people who were not good? They were not chosen because of their goodness, for they could not be good without being chosen. Grace is no longer grace, if human goodness comes first. It is God's electing grace that comes first, as the apostle Paul says: "Even so at the present time, there is a remnant according to the election of grace" (Romans 11:5). To which he adds: "And if by grace, it is no longer of works; otherwise grace is no longer grace" (Romans 11:6).

Listen, you ungrateful person, listen! "You did not choose Me, but I chose you." Do not say, "I am chosen because I first believed." If you first believed, you had already chosen Him. But listen: "You did not choose Me." And do not say, "Before I believed, I was already chosen on account of my good works." What good work can come before faith, when the apostle Paul says, "Whatever is not from faith is sin" (Romans 14:23)? What then shall we say when we hear these words, "You did not choose Me"? We shall say this: We were evil, and we were chosen that we might become good by the grace of Him Who chose us. For salvation is not by grace if our goodness came first; but it is by grace — and therefore God's grace did not *find* us good but *makes* us good.

You see then, my beloved, how it is that Jesus does not choose good people, but chooses people in order to make them good. "I chose you," He says, "and appointed you that you should go and bear fruit, and that your fruit should remain." Our fruit is what He has already spoken about when He said, "Without Me you can do nothing" (John 15:5). So He has chosen us and appointed us to go and bear fruit. It follows that we had no fruit which could have made Him choose us. "That you should go and bear fruit": we go to bear fruit, and He is Himself the way along which we go and has appointed us to go. And so His mercy comes first in everything we do.

Sermons on John, 86:2-3

The Lord knows who His elect are, even when we cannot tell

I say then, "The Lord knows those who are His" (2 Tim.2:19). He knows those who were foreknown, He knows those who were predestined; because it is said of Him, "For those whom He foreknew, He also predestined to be conformed to the image of His Son, that He might be the firstborn among many brothers. Moreover, those whom He predestined, He also called; those whom He called, He also justified; those whom He justified, He also glorified. If God is for us, who can be against us?" (Rom.8:29-31). Add to this: "He that spared not His own Son, but delivered Him up for us all, how has He not with Him also freely given us all things?" (Rom.8:32) But who are the "us"? Those who are foreknown, predestined, justified, glorified — those of whom he then says, "Who shall lay anything to the charge of God's elect?" Therefore "the Lord knows those who are His." They are the sheep. Such sometimes do not know themselves to be sheep, but the Shepherd knows them, according to this predestination, this foreknowledge of God, this election of the sheep before the foundation of the world. For the apostle also says, "According as He has chosen us in Him before the foundation of the world" (Eph.1:4).

According, then, to this divine foreknowledge and predestination, how many sheep are outside [the Church], how many wolves within! And how many sheep are within, how many wolves outside! How many are now living in immorality who will one day be chaste! How many are blaspheming Christ who will one day believe in Him! How many are giving themselves to drunkenness who will one day be sober! How many are preying on other people's property who will one day freely give of their own! But at present they are hearing the voice of another, they are following strangers. Likewise, how many are praising within [the Church] who will one day blaspheme; how many are chaste who will one day be fornicators; how many are sober who will afterwards wallow in drink; how many are standing who will one day fall! These are not the sheep. For we speak of those who were predestined, whom the Lord knows that they are His. And yet these latter people [the non-elect with a temporary faith] do listen to the voice of Christ, so long as they keep right. Indeed, they hear Him, while the others [the unconverted elect] do not; and yet, according to predestination, these [the non-elect with a temporary faith] are not His sheep, while the others [the unconverted elect] are.

Sermons on John, 45:12

Mercy and judgment revealed in people's response to the gospel

"Many hear the word of truth; but some believe, while others contradict. Therefore, the former will to believe; the latter do not will." Who does not know this? Who can deny this? But since in some the will is prepared by the Lord, while in others it is not prepared, we must certainly be able to distinguish what comes from God's mercy, and what comes from His judgment. "What Israel sought for," says the apostle, "it has not obtained, but the elect have obtained it; and the rest were blinded, as it is written, God gave to them the spirit of stupor — eyes that they should not see, and ears that they should not hear, even to this day. And David said, Let their table be made a snare, a retribution, and a stumbling block to them; let their eyes be darkened, that they may not see; and bow down their back always" (Rom.11:7-10). Here is mercy and judgment — mercy towards the elect, who have obtained the righteousness of God, but judgment to the rest who have been blinded. And yet the former, because they willed, believed; the latter, because they did not will, did not believe. Therefore mercy and judgment were manifested in their actual wills.

Certainly such an election is of grace, and not at all of human virtues. For Paul had previously said, "So, therefore, even at this present time, the remnant has been saved by the election of grace. And if it is by grace, it is no longer by works; otherwise grace is no longer grace" (Rom.11:5-6). Therefore the elect obtained what they obtained gratuitously; none of those things preceded which they might first give to God so that He might reward them. God saved them without any contribution from them. But to the rest who were blinded, as the verse plainly declares, this was indeed done to pay them back. "All the paths of the Lord are mercy and truth' (Ps.25:10). Yet His ways are unsearchable. Therefore the mercy by which He freely saves, and the truth by which He righteously judges, are equally unsearchable.

On the Predestination of the Saints, 11

Election is not favouritism because no injustice is involved

We rightly call it "favouritism" where a judge ignores the merits of the case he is judging, and favours one person against the other, because he finds something in him which is worthy of honour or pity. But if anyone has two debtors, and he chooses to cancel the debt of the one, but to insist on payment from the other, he is generous to whom he pleases and is defrauding nobody. This is not to be called "favouritism," since there is no injustice. Those with small understanding may think it favouritism where the owner of the vineyard gave to those labourers who had worked there for one hour as much as he gave to those who had born the burden and heat of the day, paying them equal wages when there had been such a difference in their labour. But what did he reply to those who complained against the good landowner concerning this alleged favouritism? "Friend," he said, "I do you no wrong. Did you not agree with me for a denarius? Take what is yours, and go; but I choose to give to this last man the same as to you. Is it not lawful to me to do what I will with my own things? Is your eye evil because I am good?" (Matthew 20:13-15).

Here, truly, is the entire justice of the case: "I choose this. To you I have paid what I owe you; on him I have bestowed a gift. I have not taken anything away from you to bestow it on him; nor have I either diminished or denied what I owed to you. May I not do what I will? Is your eye evil because I am good?" So there is no favouritism here, because one is honoured freely in such a way that the other is not defrauded of what is due to him.

Likewise, when one person is called according to the purpose of God, and another is not called, a free blessing is bestowed on the one that is called — indeed, the calling itself is the beginning of the blessing. By contrast, evil is repaid to the one that is not called, since all are guilty from the fact that sin entered into the world through one man. And in that parable of the labourers, indeed, where those who laboured for one hour received one denarius, as well as those who laboured twelve times as long, the latter ought by human reckoning (vain though it is) to have received twelve denarii in proportion to the amount of their labour. Still, both were put on an equality of benefit, not some delivered and others condemned. For even those who laboured longer owed it to the good landowner himself that they were effectually called into his vineyard, and that they

were so fed as to lack nothing. But where it is said, "Therefore, He
has mercy on whom He will, and whom He will He hardens" (Romans
9:18), Who "makes one vessel for honour and another for dishonour"
(Romans 9:20), grace is given freely to the undeserving, who belong
to the same mass [of condemned humanity] as those to whom it is
not given. But evil is deservedly repaid as a matter of debt, since
evil is justly repaid to the evil in the condemned mass. And to the
person to whom it is repaid, it is an evil to him, because it is his
punishment; but it is good in God to repay the evil with punishment,
because it is God's right to do so.

Against Two Letters of the Pelagians, 2:13

God's sovereignty in relation to evil

These are "the great works of the Lord, sought out according to all
His pleasure" (Psalm 111:2). They are so wisely sought out, that
when his intelligent creation, both angelic and human, sinned —
doing not God's will but their own — He used the very will of the
creature, which was working in opposition to the Creator's will, as
an instrument for carrying out His own will. The supremely Good
thus turns to good account even what is evil: for the condemnation
of those whom in His justice He has predestined to punishment, and
for the salvation of those whom in His mercy He has predestined to
grace. For, as far as it relates to their own intention, these beings did
what God wished not to be done. But in view of God's omnipotence,
they could in no way achieve their purpose. For in the very fact that
they acted in opposition to His will, His will concerning them was
fulfilled!

So it is that "the works of the Lord are great, sought out according
to all His pleasure," because in a way unspeakably strange and
wonderful, even what is done in opposition to God's will does not
defeat His will. For it would not be done if He did not permit it —
and of course, God permits things willingly, not unwillingly. Nor
would a Good Being permit evil to be done, except that in His
omnipotence He can turn evil into good.

Sometimes, however, a human being in the goodness of his will
desires something that God does not desire, even though God's will
is also good, indeed, much more fully and more surely good than

ours (for His will never can be evil). For example, a good son may be anxious that his father should live, when it is God's good will that he should die. Again, it is possible for a person with an evil will to desire what God wills in His goodness. For example, a bad son may wish his father to die, when this is also the will of God. It is plain that the good son wishes what God does not wish, and that the bad son wishes what God does wish. And yet the filial love of the good son is more in harmony with the good will of God, though its desire is different from God's, than the lack of filial affection in the bad son, though its desire is the same as God's.

This shows how necessary it is, in determining whether a human being's desire should be approved or disapproved, to consider what it is proper for human beings to desire, and what it is proper for God to desire, and what is in each case the real motive of the will. For God accomplishes some of His purposes, which of course are all good purposes, through the evil desires of wicked men. For example, it was through the wicked designs of the Jews, working out the good purpose of the Father, that Christ was put to death; and this event was so truly good, that when the apostle Peter expressed his unwillingness that it should take place, he was called "Satan" by the One Who had come to be put to death. How good seemed the intentions of the godly believers who were unwilling that Paul should go up to Jerusalem, in case the evils which Agabus had foretold should there befall him! And yet it was God's purpose that Paul should suffer these evils for preaching the faith of Christ, and thereby become a witness for Christ. And this divine purpose, which was good, God did not fulfil through the good counsels of the Christians, but through the evil counsels of the Jews. Thus those who opposed His purpose were more truly His servants than those who were the willing instruments of its accomplishment!

Still, however strong may be the purposes either of angels or of humans, whether good or bad, whether these purposes harmonise with the will of God or run counter to it, the will of the Almighty is never defeated. And His will can never be evil, because even when it inflicts evil, God's will is just; and what is just is certainly not evil. The omnipotent God, then, whether in mercy He pities whom He will, or in judgment hardens whom He will, is never unjust in what He does — never does anything except of His own free will — and never wills anything that He does not perform.

Enchiridion, 100-102

In what sense does God will all human beings to be saved?

Hence we must inquire in what sense the apostle most truly says of God, "Who will have all men to be saved" (1 Timothy 2:4). For, as a matter of fact, not all, nor even a majority, are saved! So it would seem that what God wills is not done, because the human will interferes with the will of God and hinders it. When we ask the reason why all are not saved, the ordinary answer is: "Because people themselves are not willing." This, indeed, cannot be said of infants, for it is not in their power either to will or not to will. But if we could ascribe to their will the childish movements they make at baptism, when they make all the resistance they can, we should say that even they are not willing to be saved!

In the gospel, however, our Lord says plainly, when denouncing the ungodly city: "How often would I have gathered your children together, even as a hen gathers her chickens under her wings, and you were not willing!" (Matt.23:37) It seems as if the will of God had been overcome by the will of human beings, and when the weakest stood in the way with their lack of will, the will of the strongest [God] could not be carried out. Where now is that omnipotence which has done all that it pleased on earth and in heaven, if God willed to gather together the children of Jerusalem, and did not accomplish it? Or rather, Jerusalem was not willing that her children should be gathered together; but even though she was unwilling, God gathered together as many of her children as He wished. For He does not will some things and do them, and will others and fail to do them; no, "He has done all that He pleased in heaven and in earth" (Ps.135:6).

And, moreover, who will be so foolish and blasphemous as to say that God *cannot* change evil human wills, whichever, whenever, and wherever He chooses, and direct them to what is good? But when He does this, He does it out of mercy; when He does not do it, it is out of justice that He does not do it, for "He has mercy on whom He will have mercy, and whom He will He hardens" (Rom.9:18). And when the apostle said this, he was illustrating the grace of God, in connection with which he had just spoken of the twins in the womb of Rebecca, "who being not yet born, neither having done any good or evil, that the purpose of God according to election might stand, not by works, but by Him Who calls, it was said to her, The elder shall serve the younger' (Rom.9:11-12).

In reference to this matter, he quotes another prophetic testimony: "Jacob have I loved, but Esau have I hated" (Rom.9:13). But perceiving how what he had said might disturb those who could not penetrate by their understanding the depth of this grace, Paul adds: "What shall we say then? Is there unrighteousness with God? God forbid" (Rom.9:14). For it seems unjust that, in the absence of any merit or demerit arising from good or evil works, God should love the one and hate the other. Now, if the apostle had wished us to understand that there were *future* good works of Jacob, and evil works of Esau, which of course God foreknew, he would never have said, "not of works," but, "of future works," and in that way he would have solved the difficulty — or rather, there would then have been no difficulty to solve!

As it is, however, after answering, "God forbid" (that is, God forbid that there should be unrighteousness with God), he goes on to prove that there is no unrighteousness in God's doing this, and says: "For He says to Moses, I will have mercy on whom I will have mercy, and I will have compassion on whom I will have compassion" (Rom.9:15). Now, who but a fool would think that God was unrighteous, either in inflicting penal justice on those who had earned it, or in extending mercy to the unworthy? Then he draws his conclusion: "So then it is not of him that wills, nor of him that runs, but of God that shows mercy" (Rom.9:16). Thus both the twins were born children of wrath, not on account of any works of their own, but because they were bound in the fetters of that original condemnation which came through Adam. But He who said, "I will have mercy on whom I will have mercy," loved Jacob by His undeserved grace, and hated Esau by His deserved judgment. And because this judgment was due to both, Jacob learnt from Esau that the fact that the same punishment had not fallen on himself gave him no room to glory in any merit of his own, but only in the riches of the divine grace. For "it is not of him that wills, nor of him that runs, but of God that shows mercy." And indeed the whole face, and (if I may use the expression) every contour of the aspect of Scripture, conveys by a very profound analogy this wholesome warning to every one who looks carefully into it, that he who glories should glory in the Lord (1 Cor.1:31).

After commending the mercy of God, saying, "So it is not of him that wills, nor of him that runs, but of God that shows mercy," that he might commend His justice also (for the sinner who does not obtain mercy finds, not injustice, but justice — there being no injustice with God), Paul immediately adds: "For the Scripture says to Pharaoh, Even for this same purpose have I raised you up, that I might show My power in you, and that My name might be declared throughout all the earth" (Rom.9:17). And then he draws a conclusion that applies to both, that is, both to God's mercy and His justice: "Therefore has He mercy on whom He will have mercy, and whom He will He hardens" (Rom.9:18). God has mercy out of His great goodness; He hardens without any injustice. Thus the one who is pardoned cannot glory in any merit of his own, nor can the one who is condemned complain of anything but his own demerit. For it is grace alone that separates the redeemed from the lost, since all are involved in one common ruin through their common origin [Adam].

Now suppose that someone, on hearing this, should say, "Why does He still find fault? For who has resisted His will?" (Rom.9:19), as if a person should not be blamed for being bad, because God has mercy on whom He will have mercy, and whom He will He hardens. God forbid that we should be ashamed to answer in the same way the apostle answered: "No, but O man, who are you that answer back against God? Shall the thing formed say to Him that formed it, Why have You made me like this? Has not the potter power over the clay, from the same lump to make one vessel for honour, and another for dishonour?" (Rom.9:20-21)

Some foolish people think that in this verse, the apostle had no answer to give, and for lack of an explanation to offer, merely rebuked the presumption of his interrogator. But there is great weight in this saying: "No, but O man, who are you?" In such a matter as this, it suggests to a human being in a single word the limits of his human ability, and at the same time it does in fact convey an important explanation. For if a human being does not understand these matters, who is he that he should answer back against God? And if he does understand these things, he finds no further reason to answer back. For then he would perceive that the whole human race was condemned in its rebellious head by a divine judgment so just, that if not a single member of the race had been redeemed, no one could justly have questioned the justice of God. He would also perceive how right it was that those who are redeemed should be redeemed in such a way as to show, by the greater number who are unredeemed and left in their just condemnation, what the whole human race deserved, and where the deserved judgment of God would lead even the redeemed, if His undeserved mercy did not intervene. Thus every mouth is stopped of those who wish to glory in their own merits, so that he who glories might glory in the Lord ...

Accordingly, when we hear and read in Scripture that God "will have all men to be saved," although we know well enough that all are not saved, we are not on that account to restrict the omnipotence of God. Rather we should understand the Scripture, "Who will have all men to be saved," as meaning that no-one is saved unless God wills his salvation. Not that there is no-one whose salvation He does not will, but that no-one is saved apart from His will. Therefore, we should ask God to will *our* salvation, because if He wills it, it must necessarily be accomplished. And it was concerning prayer to God that the apostle was speaking when he used this expression. On the same principle, we interpret the expression in the gospel: "The true light which enlightens every man that comes into the world" (Jn.1:9). Not that everyone is enlightened, but that no-one is enlightened except by Christ.

Thus it is said, "Who will have all men to be saved." It is not that He wills everyone's salvation, for how then do we explain the fact that He was not willing to work miracles in the presence of some who, He said, would have repented if He had worked them (Matt.11:20-24)? No, we are to understand by "all men" *the human race in all its varieties of rank and circumstances* — kings, subjects, noble, commoner, high, low, learned, unlearned, the healthy in body, the sick, the clever, the dull, the foolish, the rich, the poor, and those of middling circumstances; males, females, infants, boys, youths; young, middle-aged, and old men; of every tongue, of every fashion, of all arts, of all professions, with all the innumerable differences of will and conscience, and whatever else there is that makes a distinction among human beings. For which is there of all these classes from which God does not will that people should be saved in all nations, through His Only-begotten Son, our Lord? And therefore He *does* save them; for whatever He may will, the Almighty cannot will in vain.

Now the apostle had commanded that prayers should be made for all men, and had especially added, "For kings, and for all that are in authority" (1 Tim.2:2), who might be supposed, in the pride and pomp of their worldly rank, to shrink from the humility of the Christian faith. Then Paul says, "For this is good and acceptable in the sight of God our Saviour" (1 Tim.2:3) — that is, that prayers should be made for such as these. Then he immediately adds, as if to remove any ground of despair, "Who will have all men to be saved, and to come to the knowledge of the truth." God, then, in His great graciousness, has judged it good to grant to the prayers of the lowly the salvation of the exalted.

Assuredly we have many examples of this way of speaking. Our Lord, too, makes use of the same mode of speech in the gospel, when He says to the Pharisees: "You tithe mint, and rue, and *every herb*" (Lk.11:42). The Pharisees did not actually tithe what belonged to others, nor all the herbs of all the inhabitants of other lands. So in this place we must understand "every herb" to mean every *kind* of herb. Likewise in the former passage, we may understand "all men" to mean every kind of man. And we may interpret it in any other way we please, so long as we are not compelled to believe that the omnipotent God has willed anything to be done which was not done. For setting aside all ambiguities, if "He has done all that He pleased in heaven and in earth" (Ps.135:6), as the psalmist sings of Him, He certainly did not will to do anything that He has not done.

Enchiridion, 97-99, 103

"All" does not always mean all!

And what is written, that "He wills all men to be saved" (1 Tim.2:4), while yet all men are not saved, may be understood in many ways, some of which I have mentioned in other writings of mine. Here I will say one thing: "He wills all men to be saved" is said so that all the predestined may be understood by it, because every kind of person is found among them. Just as it was said to the Pharisees, "You tithe every herb" (Lk.11:42), where the expression is only to be understood of every herb that *they* had; for they did not tithe every herb which was found throughout the whole earth. According to the same manner of speaking, it was said, "Even as I also please all men in all things" (1 Cor.10:33). For did he who said this please the multitude of his persecutors? But he pleased every kind of person that assembled in the Church of Christ, whether they were already established in it, or were yet to be introduced into it.

On Rebuke and Grace, 44

230 The Triumph of Grace

Why preach to all if only some are elect?

Because we do not know who belongs to the number of the
predestined, we ought to be influenced by the affection of love so as
to will all people to be saved. For this is the case when we endeavour
to lead all individuals to that point where they may meet with those
agencies by which we may prevail to accomplish this result, that
being justified by faith they may have peace with God. This peace,
moreover, the apostle announced when he said, "Therefore, we are
ambassadors for Christ, as though God were exhorting through us,
we beg you on Christ's behalf to be reconciled to God" (2 Cor.5:20).
For what is "to be reconciled" to Him but to have peace with Him?

For the sake of this peace, moreover, the Lord Jesus Christ Himself
said to His disciples, "Into whatever house you enter first, say, Peace
be to this house; and if a son of peace is there, your peace shall rest
upon it; but if not, it shall return to you again" (Lk.10:5-6). When
they preach the gospel of this peace of whom it is predicted, "How
beautiful are the feet of those that publish peace, that announce
good things!" (Isa.52:7, Rom.10:15), then indeed *to us* everyone
begins to be a son of peace who obeys and believes this gospel, and
who, being justified by faith, has begun to have peace towards God.
But according to God's predestination, he was already a son of peace.
For it was not said, "Upon whomever your peace shall rest, he shall
become a son of peace"; but Christ says, "If a son of peace is there,
your peace shall rest upon that house." Already, therefore, and before
the announcement of that peace to him, a son of peace was there, as
he had been known and foreknown, not by the evangelist, but by
God.

For we need not fear that we will lose the peace, if in our ignorance
he to whom we preach is not a son of peace, for it will return to us
again. That is, the preaching will profit us, and not him; but if the
peace proclaimed rests upon him, it will profit both us and him. So
then, in our ignorance of who will be saved, God commands us to
will that all to whom we preach this peace may be saved, and He
Himself works this in us by diffusing love in our hearts by the Holy
Spirit Who is given to us.

On Rebuke and Grace, 46-47

Paul and Christ taught predestination and preached the gospel

But they say that the "definition of predestination is opposed to the benefit of preaching" — as if, indeed, it were opposed to the preaching of the apostle Paul! Did not that teacher of the pagans so often, in faith and truth, both commend predestination, and not cease to preach the word of God? For he who said, "It is God that works in you both to will and to do for His good pleasure" (Phil.2:13), did he not also exhort that we should both will and do what is pleasing to God? Or because he said, "He who has begun a good work in you will carry it on even until the day of Christ Jesus" (Phil.1:6), did he on that account cease to persuade people to begin and to persevere to the end? Doubtless, our Lord Himself commanded people to believe, and said, "Believe in God, believe also in me" (Jn.14:1). And yet His opinion is not therefore false, nor is His definition idle when He says, "No-one comes to Me" — that is, no-one believes in Me — "unless it has been granted to him by My Father" (Jn.6:65). Christ's first precept does not become empty because this latter definition is true. Why, therefore, do we think the definition of predestination useless to preaching, to precept, to exhortation, to rebuke? All these things the divine Scripture repeats frequently; and the same Scripture commends this doctrine!

On the Gift of Perseverance, 34

God uses means in saving and sanctifying the elect — and the means include preaching and exhortation

Hence, as far we are concerned, we are not able to distinguish those who are predestined from those who are not; and we ought for this very reason to desire all to be saved. Severe rebuke should be applied as medicine to all so that they do not perish themselves, or that they may not be the means of destroying others. It belongs to God, however, to make that rebuke useful to those Whom He Himself has foreknown and predestined to be conformed to the image of His Son. For, if at any time we abstain from rebuking, fearing that by our rebuke a person might perish, why do we not also rebuke, fearing that a person might perish by our withholding it?

For we do not have a greater heart of love than the blessed apostle who says, "Rebuke those that are unruly; comfort the feeble-minded; support the weak; be patient towards all men. See that none renders to anyone evil for evil" (1 Thess.5:14). Here it is to be understood that evil is rendered for evil when one who ought to be rebuked is not rebuked, but by a wicked cheat is neglected. He says, moreover, "Those who sin, rebuke before all, that others also may fear" (1 Tim.5:20). This must be taken as referring to those sins which are not concealed, in case Paul is thought to have spoken in opposition to the word of the Lord. For the Lord says, "If your brother sins against you, rebuke him between yourself and him" (Matt.18:15). Even so, the Lord Himself carries out the severity of rebuke to the extent of saying, "If he will not hear the Church, let him be to you as a pagan and a tax collector" (Matt.18:17). And who has more loved the weak than He Who became weak for us all, and in that very weakness was crucified for us all?

And since these things are so, grace does not hinder rebuke, nor does rebuke hinder grace. On this account, righteousness is to be prescribed, so that we may ask in faithful prayer that what is prescribed may be done by God's grace; and both of these things are to be done in such a way that righteous rebuke may not be neglected. But let all these things be done with love, since love does not sin, and covers the multitude of sins.

On Rebuke and Grace, 49

The preaching of the gospel and of predestination are two parts of one undivided message

Therefore, by the preaching of predestination, the preaching of a persevering and progressive faith is not to be hindered. In this way, those who are granted obedience may hear what is necessary. For how shall they hear without a preacher? Again, the preaching of a progressive faith which continues even to the end does not hinder the preaching of predestination, so that he who is living faithfully and obediently may not be puffed up by his own obedience, as if by a benefit of his own which he had not received. No, he who glories must glory in the Lord. For "we must boast in nothing, since nothing is our own." This truth Cyprian[1] most faithfully saw and most fearlessly explained, and thus he pronounced predestination to be most assured. For if we must boast in nothing, seeing that nothing is our own, certainly we must not boast of the most persevering obedience. It must not be called our own, as if it were not given to us from above. And, therefore, persevering obedience is God's gift, which, by the confession of all Christians, God foreknew that He would give to His people, those who were called by that calling of which it was said, "The gifts and calling of God are without repentance" (Rom.11:29). This, then, is the predestination which we faithfully and humbly preach.

Nor yet did the same teacher and doer [Cyprian], who both believed on Christ and most perseveringly lived in holy obedience, even to suffering for Christ, cease on that account to preach the gospel, to exhort to faith, and to godly living, and to that very perseverance to the end. For he said, "We must boast in nothing, since nothing is our own." And here he declared without ambiguity the true grace of God, that is, the grace which is not given in respect of our merits. Since God foreknew that He would give His grace, predestination was announced beyond a doubt by these words of Cyprian; and if this did not prevent Cyprian from preaching obedience, it certainly ought not to prevent us.

On the Gift of Perseverance, 36

To preach predestination makes people hope not in themselves, but in God

But it is said, "It is by his own fault that anyone deserts the faith, when he yields and consents to the temptation which is the cause of his desertion of the faith." Who denies that? But we must not on that account say that perseverance in the faith is not a gift of God. For this is what a person daily asks for when he says, "Lead us not into temptation." And if God hears him, perseverance is what he receives.

---

[1] Cyprian of Carthage (200-258) was North Africa's most famous and influential bishop, theologian and martyr. In some ways, particularly in his doctrine of perseverance, he anticipated the more lucid and systematic teaching of Augustine. The quotation given by Augustine, "We must boast in nothing, since nothing is our own," is from Cyprian.

And thus as he daily asks for perseverance, he assuredly places the hope of his perseverance not in himself, but in God. I, however, am reluctant to exaggerate the case with my words, but I rather leave it to them to consider, and see the thing which they have persuaded themselves is true — namely, "that the preaching of predestination impresses more of despair than of exhortation upon the hearers." For this is to say that a person despairs of his salvation when he has learned to place his hope not in himself, but in God! But the prophet cries, "Cursed is he who has his hope in man" (Jer.17:5).

On the Gift of Perseverance, 46

Predestination must be preached!

Therefore, if both the apostles and the teachers of the Church who came after them and imitated them did both of these things — that is, they both truly preached the grace of God which is not given according to our good qualities, and instilled by wholesome precepts a godly obedience — why do these people of our time think themselves rightly bound by the invincible force of truth to say, "Even if what is said about the predestination of God's benefits is true, yet it must not be preached to the people"? It must absolutely be preached, so that he who has ears to hear may hear. And who has these ears, unless he has received them from Him Who says, "I will give them a heart to know me, and ears to hear" (Baruch 2:31)?[2] Certainly, he who has not received [spiritual ears] may reject [the truth]. But he who receives [spiritual ears] may take and drink, may drink and live. For godliness must be preached, so that God may be rightly worshipped by him who has ears to hear. Modesty must be preached, so that no lustful act may be perpetrated by his fleshly nature by him who has ears to hear. Charity must be preached, so that God and his neighbours may be loved by him who has ears to hear. And likewise, predestination of God's benefits must be preached, so that he who has ears to hear may glory, not in himself, but in the Lord.

On the Gift of Perseverance, 51

---

[2] Augustine thought that the apocryphal book of Baruch was part of the Old Testament canon. See Chapter 4, footnote 7.

Objections against predestination can just as easily be made against God's foreknowledge

But according to you, they [the Semi-Pelagians] say: "No-one can be aroused by the incentives of rebuke, if we say in the assembly of the Church to the multitude of hearers: The definite meaning of God's will concerning predestination is such that some of you will receive the will to obey and will come out of unbelief to faith, or will receive perseverance and abide in the faith; but others of you who are lingering in the delight of sins have not yet arisen, because the help of merciful grace has not yet raised you up. However, if there are any whom by His grace God has predestined to be chosen, who are not yet called, you will receive that grace by which you may will and be chosen; but if any of you obey, and you are predestined to be rejected, the strength to obey will be withdrawn from you, so that you will cease to obey."

Well, although someone might say these things, that should not deter us from confessing the true grace of God — that is, the grace which is not given to us in respect of our virtues — and from accordingly confessing the predestination of the saints. After all, we are not deterred from confessing God's foreknowledge, even though someone might speak to the people about it like this: "Whether you are now living righteously or unrighteously, you will be one or the other at some point, since the Lord has foreknown that you will be. You will either be good, if He has foreknown you as good, or bad, if He has foreknown you as bad." For if on hearing this, some should lapse into sluggishness and sloth, cease from striving, and rush headlong to lust after their own desires, is it therefore to be reckoned that what was said about the foreknowledge of God is false? If God has foreknown that they will be good, they will indeed be good, whatever may be the depth of evil in which they are now engaged. And if He has foreknown them as evil, they will indeed be evil, whatever goodness may now be discerned in them.

There was a man in our monastery, who, when the brethren rebuked him for doing some things that ought not to be done, and for not doing some things that ought to be done, replied, "Whatever I may now be, I will be what God has foreknown that I will be." And this man certainly said what was true, although he was not profited by this truth for good, but progressed in evil — in fact, he deserted the society of the monastery, and became a dog who returned to his vomit. Nevertheless, it is uncertain what this man is yet to become. For the sake of souls of this kind, then, is the truth about God's foreknowledge either to be denied or to be kept back — even at such times when, if it is not spoken, other errors are incurred?

On the Gift of Perseverance, 38

Why does God not save all human beings?

Why, then, does God not teach all that they may come to Christ? Because all whom He teaches, He teaches in mercy, while those whom He does not teach, in judgment He does not teach them. For "He has mercy on whom He will, and whom He will He hardens" (Rom.9:18). But He has mercy when He gives good things; He hardens when He pays back what is deserved ...

And yet in a certain sense, the Father teaches "all" to come to His Son. For it was not in vain that it was written in the prophets, "And they shall all be taught by God" (Jn.6:45). And when Christ too had premised this testimony, He added, "Everyone, therefore, who has heard and learned from the Father comes to Me." We speak rightly when we say of any teacher of literature who is the only one in a city, "He teaches literature here to everybody" — not that absolutely everyone learns, but that there is no-one who learns literature in that place who does not learn it from him. So we rightly say, God teaches all to come to Christ — not because absolutely all come, but because no-one comes in any other way. And why He does not teach all absolutely, the apostle explained, as far as he judged that it was to be explained: it was because, "willing to show His wrath, and to exhibit His power, He endured with much patience the vessels of wrath that were prepared for destruction, that He might make known the riches of His glory on the vessels of mercy which He has prepared for glory" (Rom.9:22-3).

Thus it is that the "word of the cross is foolishness to those who perish; but to those who are saved, it is the power of God" (1 Cor.1:18). God teaches all such to come to Christ, for He wills all such to be saved, and to come to the knowledge of the truth. And if He had willed to teach even those to whom the word of the cross is foolishness to come to Christ, beyond all doubt these too would have come. For Christ neither deceives nor is deceived when He says, "Everyone who has heard and learned from the Father comes to Me." Away, then, with the thought that anyone who has heard and learned from the Father fails to come!

On the Predestination of the Saints, 14

God displays His mercy in the elect, His justice in the rest

Eternal punishment seems hard and unjust to human perceptions, because in the weakness of our mortal condition there is lacking that highest and purest wisdom by which it can be perceived how great a wickedness was committed in that first transgression. The more enjoyment humanity found in God, the greater was its wickedness in abandoning Him; and the human race, by destroying in itself a good which might have been eternal, became worthy of eternal evil. Hence the whole mass of the human race is condemned; for he who at first gave entrance to sin has been punished with all his offspring who were in him as in a root.

Thus no one is exempt from this just and due punishment, unless delivered by mercy and undeserved grace; and the human race is so distributed that in some is displayed the efficacy of merciful grace, in the rest the efficacy of just retribution. For both could not be displayed in all; for if all had remained under the punishment of just condemnation, there would have been seen in no-one the mercy of redeeming grace. But, on the other hand, if all had been transferred from darkness to light, the severity of retribution would have been manifested in none. Yet many more are left under punishment than are delivered from it, in order that it may thus be shown what was due to all.[3] And if it had actually been inflicted on all, no one could

---

[3] Augustine's belief that the elect are comparatively few has been rejected by many Augustinian theologians. Many Augustinians in the Reformed tradition have held that the elect outnumber the non-elect, often arguing that many or all infants dying in infancy are elect. Augustus Toplady, the great 18th century Calvinist preacher and hymnwriter, even spoke of the "few reprobate" compared to the countless hosts of the elect. These optimistic Augustinians argue from the contrast between Adam and Christ in Romans 5, that the second Adam must save more than are ultimately lost in the first Adam, because grace abounds over sin. As John Calvin says on Rom.5:15, "there is a greater measure of grace procured by Christ, than of condemnation introduced by the first man ... It may indeed be

justly have found fault with the justice of Him who takes vengeance; whereas, in the deliverance of so many from that just retribution, there is cause to render the most hearty thanks to the free bounty of Him who delivers.

City of God, 21:12

The two worlds: one predestined to condemnation, the other to life

"O righteous Father," He says, "the world has not known You" (Jn.17:25). Just because You are righteous it has not known You. In its character as that world which has been predestined to a well-deserved condemnation, it has not known Him. However, the world which He has reconciled to Himself through Christ has known Him, not from its merit, but by grace. For what else is knowing God, but eternal life? While He undoubtedly withheld this from the condemned world, He bestowed it on the reconciled world. On that very account, therefore, the world has not known You, because You are righteous, and have rendered to it according what it deserves, that it should not know You. Yet on the same account, the reconciled world has known You, because You are merciful; and, not for any merit of its own, but by grace, You have supplied it with the needed help to know You. And then follows, "But I have known You." Jesus is the Fountain of grace, Who is by nature God; and, by grace ineffable, He is also man, born of the Holy Spirit and the Virgin. And then on His own behalf, because the grace of God is through Jesus Christ our Lord, He adds, "And these have known that You have sent Me." Such is the reconciled world. But it is because You have sent Me that they have known; by grace, therefore, they have known.

Sermons on John, 111:5

([3] cont) justly inferred, that since the fall of Adam had such an effect as to produce the ruin of many, much more efficacious is the grace of God to the benefit of many; inasmuch as it is admitted, that Christ is much more powerful to save, than Adam was to destroy.'

The comfort of predestination when we see so many deceivers at work in the Church

We should not think that what the same teacher [Paul] says can at any time fail: "Whoever desires to live a godly life in Christ shall suffer persecution" (2 Tim.3:12). Sometimes those outside [unbelievers] do not rage, and thus there seems to be, and really is, tranquillity, which brings a great deal of consolation, especially to the weak. Yet even then, there are still not lacking within the Catholic Church (indeed, there are many) who by their morally abandoned lives torment the hearts of those who live in a godly way, since by these loose-livers the Christian and Catholic name is blasphemed. The dearer that name is to those who will live godly in Christ, the more they grieve that through the wicked, who have a place within the Church, Christ's name comes to be less loved than godly minds desire. The heretics too, since they are thought to have the Christian name and sacraments, Scriptures and profession, cause great grief in the hearts of the godly. For many who wish to be Christians are compelled to hesitate by the dissensions of the heretics, and many evil-speakers also find in the heretics cause for blaspheming the Christian name, because the heretics too are at any rate *called* Christians.

By these and similar corrupt human manners and errors, those who will live godly in Christ suffer persecution, even when no one molests or disturbs their bodies; for they suffer this persecution, not in their bodies, but in their hearts. This is the meaning of that word, "According to the multitude of my griefs in my heart" (Ps.94:19); for he does not say, "in my body". Yet, on the other hand, none of the godly can perish. For we must consider the unchangeable promises of God; and the apostle says, "The Lord knows those who are His" (2 Tim.2:19); for "those whom He foreknew, He also predestined to be conformed to the image of His Son" (Rom.8:29), which means that none of them can perish. Therefore it follows in that psalm, "Your consolations have delighted my soul" (Ps.94:19).

City of God, 18:51

No-one in this life can know with certainty that he is among the elect....

Seeing that such things as these are spoken to saints who will persevere, as if it were reckoned uncertain whether they will persevere, this is a reason why they ought to hear these things in this spirit, since it is good for them "not to be high-minded, but to fear" (Rom.11:20). For who of the multitude of believers can presume, so long as he is living in this mortal state, that he is in the number of the predestined? It is necessary that in this earthly condition, predestination should be kept hidden. Here we have to beware so much of pride, that even so great an apostle as Paul was buffeted by a messenger of Satan, in case he should be puffed up. Thus it was said to the apostles, "If you abide in Me" (Jn.15:7); yet He said this knowing for a certainty that they would abide. Through the prophet God says, "If you are willing, and will hear Me" (Isa.1:19), although He knew in whom He would produce this willingness also. And many similar things are said.

This secret nature of predestination is very useful in preventing anyone being puffed up, so that all, even although they are running well, should fear, because it is not known who will attain the prize. On account of the usefulness of this secrecy, we must believe that some of the children of destruction, who have not received the gift of perseverance to the end, begin to live in the faith which works by love, and live for a time faithfully and righteously, and afterwards fall away, and are taken away from this life after their apostasy. If this had not happened to any of these non-elect, those who had attained to Christ's grace by which to live a godly life would not possess that very wholesome fear, by which the sin of presumption is kept down. For as soon as they attained to grace, they would for the future feel carnally secure that they would never fall away from Christ. And such presumption in this earthly condition of trials is not fitting, where there is such great weakness that security may easily engender pride.

On Rebuke and Grace, 40

Predestination and Election   241

But if we are casting ourselves on God for the gift of perseverance, we should hope and trust that we are indeed among the elect!

What I have said about the way that predestination should be preached will not be adequate for him who speaks to a congregation, unless he adds this, or something like it: "You, therefore, ought to hope that the gift of persevering in obedience will be given to you by the Father of Lights, from Whom comes down every excellent gift and every perfect gift (Jam.1:17); and you ought to ask for this gift in your daily prayers. And in doing this, *you ought to trust that you are not aliens from the predestination of His people,* because it is God Himself Who bestows even the power of praying for perseverance. Far be it from you to despair of yourselves! For you are bidden to put your hope in God, not in yourselves. Indeed, cursed is everyone who puts his hope in man (Jer.17:5). It is better to trust in the Lord than to trust in man, for blessed are all those who put their trust in the Lord. Holding this hope, serve the Lord in fear, and rejoice before Him with trembling. No-one can securely enjoy the eternal life which God, Who does not lie, has promised from eternity to the children of promise — no-one, until that life of his, which is a state of trial upon the earth, is completed. *But He will make us persevere in Himself to the end of this life,* since we daily say to Him, 'Lead us not into temptation.'"

When these and similar things are said, whether to few Christians or to the multitude of the Church, why do we fear to preach the predestination of the saints and the true grace of God — that is, the grace which is not given according to our virtues — as the Holy Scripture declares it? Or must it be feared that a person should despair of himself, when his hope is shown to be placed in God? Should he not rather despair of himself if, in his excess of pride and unhappiness, he places his hope in himself?

On the Gift of Perseverance, 62

Chapter 7

Sinless perfection?

Where is the human being who is altogether without sin? Where is the person who is without any vice, without the fuel or root (as it were) of sin, when even he who reclined on the breast of the Lord says, 'If we say that we have no sin, we deceive ourselves, and the truth is not in us'?

Augustine, **Letter 167:10**

Charles Spurgeon, the great Augustinian Baptist preacher of the 19th century, once said: "He who boasts of being perfect is perfect in folly. I never saw a perfect man. Every rose has its thorns, and every day its night. Even the sun shows spots, and the skies are darkened with clouds. And faults of some kind nestle in every bosom."

The Augustinian tradition has always stood out for its robust denial that the Christian will ever be sinlessly perfect this side of heaven. In a way, this is the wildest of paradoxes; for Augustine's doctrine of grace provides the only real basis on which the wayfaring Christian *could* become perfect. Just as grace sovereignly rescues the sinner's will from the bondage of sin, the same grace could (in theory) sovereignly make the liberated will completely sinless even now, on earth. A handful of renegade Augustinians (such as Jean de Labadie in the 17th century) have taken this extreme position; but they are such an insignificant minority, and so seriously isolated from the wide-flowing Augustinian mainstream, that we can safely neglect these few eccentrics. By the wise permission of God, Christians still sin, even as Christians still die. Immaculate souls, like immortal bodies, will have to wait for another world. Augustine's bracingly frank vision of persisting sin in the life of the regenerate has been fully shared by all the great theologians and saints, Catholic and Protestant, Jansenists and Calvinists, who have followed in his footsteps.

Two broad reasons stand behind the Augustinian view. First is a deep-rooted conviction of what constitutes *the normal Christian life*. Augustinians are convinced that Scripture presents this as a ferocious warfare with the world, the flesh and the devil, which rages on through every spiritual valley and mountaintop of our lives until death alone brings blessed release. Here on earth, Christian souls are not raptured up to some cloudy plane of serenity, high above the sordid conflict; like our Old Testament ancestors at the exodus, we are warrior-pilgrims marching through hostile deserts to a land of future promise. The company of God's redeemed but not yet glorified people is always the Church Pilgrim and the Church Militant. Rest and triumph come later. And among our virulent foes on this journey is "the flesh": the residue of indwelling sin in our own hearts. "For the flesh lusts against the Spirit, and the Spirit against the flesh, and these are contrary to one another, so that you do not do the things you wish" (Gal.5:17). Although I am now a new creation in Christ, the person I used to be lingers on in the shadows, ceaselessly calling to me to slink out of the purity of the light for the pleasures of the dark. Augustine passionately prayed, "Lord, deliver me from that wicked man — myself!" Such is the Christian pilgrim's lifelong prayer.

This is crucial for our moral and spiritual sanity. Very simply, it saves us from the devastating blight of false expectations. The Christian life is not a soft fragrant bed of thornless roses, either physically (health and wealth) or spiritually (freedom from all sin). Our fellowship with Christ is not rooted in *our* glory or perfection, but in *His*. If we do not grasp this, we will destroy our assurance, and lapse into "righteousness by good works" as we seek to earn our right to the Saviour's mercy. As that great Augustinian, Martin Luther, put it:

"Beware of aspiring to such purity that you do not wish to be regarded as a sinner, or to be one. For Christ dwells only in sinners. For this reason He descended from heaven, where He dwelt among the righteous, in order that He might dwell among sinners. Meditate on this love of His, and you will see His sweet encouragement. Why did He have to die, if we could obtain a good conscience by our own works and sufferings? Thus you will find peace only in Christ, only when you despair of yourself and your own works. Further, you will learn from Him that even as He has received you, so He has made your sins His own, and has made His righteousness yours."[1]

This is not a recipe for being complacent about our sanctification; but it is the sweet balm of Gilead for bleeding twice-born hearts, crushed by their repeated sins, scarcely able to believe that Christ could want anything more to do with them.

This realistic Augustinian view of the Christian life also saves us from going off into fantasies about "second blessing" baptisms/ anointings of the Spirit which will free us from all sin. Such fantasies are deeply divisive; they create first and second class Christians. In an extreme form, they may even conjure up the spectacle of as many as six classes of Christian: washed in the blood, perfectly sanctified, baptised in the Spirit and fire, and then baptised with dynamite, lyddite and oxidite (I jest not: this was the "dynamite heresy" of Benjamin Irwin, one of the formative influences on Pentecostalism). All such divisive quackeries are rendered null and void by the

---

[1] Letter to George Spenlein, April 8th, 1516 – written 18 months before the 95 theses.

Augustinian recognition that every single Christian without exception, even the most spiritually mature, is still beset by indwelling sin, by insidious inward temptations to pride, covetousness, lust, envy, gluttony, anger and sloth. The answer is not an elitist initiation into some second blessing. It is to keep on fighting "the good fight of faith" (1 Tim.6:12) — the self-same faith in Jesus Christ, the virgin-born, crucified and risen God-man, by which we were saved at first, and which will save us at last, if we stand in it and hold fast to it (1 Cor.15:1-4). In what J.I.Packer once called "the God-given confidence of self-despair", we keep casting ourselves on Christ, always on Christ, for daily mercy, daily wisdom, daily strength. It may not be as stimulating to the nerves as a dose of "dynamite baptism", but it is a more sure, sober, safe and Scriptural path to heaven.

The second broad reason behind the Augustinian view lies in its perception of *the radical seriousness of sin*. Sin is not, as Pelagius imagined, merely bad deeds, nor even just deliberate wrong choices. We have to probe deeper, far deeper, below the tip of the psychological iceberg, into the heart's underlying motives. In these motives, which are often semi-conscious or unconscious, we find jagged masses of sin. It might take me a long time to realise that it is actually envy that is motivating me to be so critical of a colleague. Or it might need a crisis to wake me up fully to how much I love a friend. It is here, Augustine argued, in this hugely profound and subtle realm of motive, that sin most truly lurks. For it is my heart's motives that inspire my choices and issue in deeds. "Guard your heart with all diligence, for out of it spring the issues of life" (Prov.4:23). "Who can say, I have made my heart clean, I am pure from sin?" (Prov.20:9). "Every way of a man is right in his own eyes, but the Lord weighs hearts" (Prov.21:2). "Truly the hearts of the sons of men are full of evil; madness is in their hearts while they live" (Ecc.9:3). "The heart is deceitful above all things and desperately sick; who can know it?" (Jer.17:9). "I am He Who searches the minds and the hearts, and I will give to each of you according to your works" (Rev.2:23).

The clearer our vision of the dark sin-tangled forest of our hearts, the harder it becomes to ascribe sinless perfection to ourselves. That is why the Pelagian or neo-Pelagian advocates of perfection are usually quite liberal in watering down the definition of sin. For them, freedom from sin means freedom from overt acts of sin, or from deliberate sinful choices, or from transgression committed against the full light of knowledge. So John Wesley, the archetypal Evangelical perfectionist, thought it meant freedom from all "willing and witting sin". To all such unbiblical dilutions, however, we must resolutely pose the piercing retort of Anselm of Canterbury: "You have not sufficiently considered the seriousness of sin." Augustine had considered it — known and felt sin's depth in his own Christian heart. Therefore he could have no truck with the romantic sinless perfectionism of Pelagius and his ilk. By pretending to *exalt* God's law with their message that it could be perfectly obeyed, these superficial idealists were in reality *debasing* God's law by restricting its scope to blatant deed and explicit decision.

But the bishop of Hippo knew that the empire of God's holy and spiritual law extended much further, to our innermost thoughts, feelings and desires — "You shall not covet" — and even to all the secret motives of our hearts. Once acknowledge this, and perfectionism is dead; and its place is taken by the true Christian doctrine of sanctification — a lifelong process, with many defiling temptations, many agonising conflicts, many grievous falls, much to be forgiven every day. The Christian is "always a sinner, always repenting, always justified" (Luther). For the glory of God's grace is not only that it heals us of sin, but forgives us for sin's foul residue, and goes on forgiving, until in grace's crowning moment we see our Redeemer as He is, and truly become like Him at last, presented without fault before His throne of grace in the everlasting beauty of heaven's holiness.

****

Sinless Perfection?

The four states of human nature

Plunged in the darkest depths of ignorance, a human being lives according to the flesh, untroubled by any conflict of reason or conscience: this is his *first* state. Afterwards, when the law has brought the knowledge of sin, but the Spirit of God has not yet intervened with His aid, a human being strives to live according to the law, but is frustrated in his efforts and falls into conscious sin; and so, being overcome by sin, he becomes its slave ("for by whom a man is overcome, to him he is enslaved", 2 Pet.2:19). Thus the effect produced by the knowledge of the commandment is this, that sin produces in a person all manner of evil desire, and he is involved in the additional guilt of wilful transgression. So is fulfilled what is written: "The law entered that the transgression might abound" (Rom.5:20). This is a human being's *second* state.

But if God has pity on him, and inspires him with faith in God's help, and the Spirit of God begins to work in him, then the mightier power of love strives against the power of the flesh. Although there is still in the person's own nature a power that fights against him (for his disease is not completely healed), yet he lives the life of the righteous by faith; he lives in righteousness to the extent that he does not surrender to his evil desire, but conquers it by the love of holiness. This is the *third* state of a person of good hope. Whoever by steadfast piety advances in this course will attain at last to peace — that peace which, when this life is over, will be perfected in the repose of the spirit, and finally in the resurrection of the body. Of these four different stages, the first is before the law, the second is under the law, the third is under grace, and the fourth is in full and perfect peace.

Enchiridion, 118

Is it *possible* for a human being to be sinless on earth? Is anyone *actually* sinless?

We must not with careless rashness immediately oppose those who claim that a human being can exist in this life without sin. For if we denied the very possibility, we would detract both from the free will of the person who desires it, and from the power or mercy of God, Who by His help brings it about. But it is one question, whether a sinless human being *could* exist; and another question, whether he actually *does* exist....

Now, concerning this fourfold set of questions: suppose you ask me first, whether it is possible for a human being in this life to be without sin? I would allow the possibility, through the grace of God and the person's own free will. I do not doubt that the free will itself comes from God's grace, in other words, it is a gift of God — not only regarding its existence, but also its goodness, that is, its conversion to obeying the commandments of God. So it is that God's grace both reveals what ought to be done, and also brings the possibility of doing what it reveals. "What indeed have we that we have not received?" (1 Cor.4:7) Thus also Jeremiah says: "I know, O Lord, that the way of man is not in himself; it is not in man to walk and direct his steps" (Jer.10:23). Accordingly, when in the Psalms the speaker says to God, "You have commanded me to keep Your precepts diligently" (Ps.119:4), he instantly adds not a word of confidence in himself, but a wish to be able to keep these precepts: "O that my ways," he says, "were directed to keep Your statutes! Then I would not be ashamed, when I have respect to all Your commandments" (Ps.119:5-6). Now who wishes for what he already has in his own power, so that he needs no further help to attain it? To whom, then, does he direct his wish? Not to fortune, or to fate, but only to God. This he shows with sufficient clarity in the following words, where he says: "Order my steps in Your word; do not let any iniquity have dominion over me" (Ps.119:133). From the bondage of this accursed dominion, those people are liberated to whom the Lord Jesus gives the power to become the sons of God. From this horrible tyranny they were to be freed, to whom He says, "If the Son shall make you free, then you will be truly free" (Jn.8:36). From these and many other testimonies, I cannot doubt that God has laid no impossible command on mankind. For by God's aid and help, nothing is impossible, since He works in us what He commands. In this way a person may, if he wishes, be without sin by the assistance of God.

If, however, you ask me the second question which I have suggested — whether a sinless human being *actually* exists — I believe there is no such person. For I believe the Scripture, which says: "Enter not into judgment with Your servant; for in Your sight no living man will be justified" (Ps.143:2). We therefore need the mercy of God, which "triumphs over judgment" (Jam.2:13), and which no-one will obtain unless he shows mercy himself. And whereas the prophet says, "I said, I will confess my transgressions to the Lord, and You forgave the iniquity of my heart," he then immediately adds, "For this shall every saint pray to You in an acceptable time" (Ps.32:5-6). Not indeed every sinner, but "every saint"; for it is the voice of the saints that says, "If we say that we have no sin, we deceive ourselves, and the truth is not in us" (1 Jn.1:8).

On the Merits and Forgiveness of Sins, 2:7-8

The moral frailty of the Christian to the end of life

This sickness — that is to say, that disobedience of which we spoke in the fourteenth book — is the punishment of the first disobedience. It is therefore not our nature, but a fault in our nature; and therefore it is said to the good who are growing in grace, and living in this pilgrimage by faith, "Bear one another's burdens, and so fulfil the law of Christ" (Gal.6:2). Likewise it is said elsewhere, "Warn the unruly, comfort the feeble-minded, support the weak, be patient toward all. See that none render evil for evil to anyone" (1 Thess.5:14-15). And in another place, "If anyone is overtaken in a fault, you who are spiritual should restore such a person in the spirit of meekness; considering yourself, in case you also are tempted" (Gal.6:1). And elsewhere, "Let not the sun go down upon your wrath" (Eph.4:26). And in the gospel, "If your brother sins against you, go and tell him his fault between you and him alone" (Matt.18:15). So too of sins which may create scandal the apostle says, "Those who sin rebuke before all, that others also may fear" (1 Tim.5:20). For this purpose, and that we may keep that peace without which no man can see the Lord, many precepts are given which carefully inculcate mutual forgiveness; among which we may number that terrible word in which the servant is ordered to pay his formerly remitted debt of ten thousand talents, because he did not remit to his fellow-servant his debt of two hundred pence. To which parable the Lord Jesus added the words, "In the same way my Heavenly Father will deal with you, if you do not all of you forgive one another from your hearts" (Matt.18:35).

It is thus the citizens of the city of God are healed while still they dwell as pilgrims in this earth, sighing for the peace of their heavenly country. The Holy Spirit, too, works within, that the medicine externally applied may have some good result. Otherwise, even though God Himself made use of the created things that are subject to Him — even if in some human form He addressed our human senses, whether we received those impressions in sleep or in some external appearance — still, if He does not by His own inward grace sway and act upon the mind, no preaching of the truth is of any avail. But God does act inwardly on the mind, distinguishing between the vessels of wrath and the vessels of mercy, by His own very secret but very just providence. He Himself aids the soul in His own hidden and wonderful ways. Then the sin which dwells in our members, and which is itself, as the apostle teaches, the punishment of sin, does not *reign* in our mortal body to obey its lusts. Then we no longer yield our members as instruments of unrighteousness (Rom.6:12-13). When all this happens, the soul is converted from its own evil and selfish desires; God possesses it, and it possesses itself in peace even in this life. Afterwards, with perfected health and endowed with immortality, it will reign without sin in everlasting peace.

City of God, 15:6

A graphic portrait of the Christian's earthly pilgrimage

In this perishable body, which burdens the soul, we live a miserable life. But we who are now redeemed by the Mediator, and have received the pledge of the Holy Spirit, have a blessed life in prospect, although we do not possess it as yet in reality. "But a hope that is seen is not hope; for why does anyone hope for what he sees? But if we hope for what we do not see, then with patience we wait for it" (Rom.8:24-5). And it is in the evils that every one suffers, not in the good things that he enjoys, that he has need of patience. The present life, therefore — of which it is written, "Is not the life of man a season of trial upon earth?" (Job 7:1), and in which we are daily crying to the Lord, "Deliver us from evil" (Matt.6:13) — this life a person is compelled to endure, even when his sins are forgiven him, although it was the first sin that caused our falling into such misery. For the penalty lasts longer than the fault, in case the fault should be accounted small, if the penalty were to end with the fault. This is why a person is kept amid the penalty through the time of life, even when he is no longer held by his sin as liable to everlasting condemnation. It is either to demonstrate our debt of misery, or to correct our passing life, or to exercise us in necessary patience.

This is the truly deplorable yet righteous condition of the present evil days we pass in this mortal state, even while we look with longing eyes for the days that are good. It comes from the righteous anger of God, of which the Scriptures say, "Man, that is born of woman, is of few days and full of anger" (Job 14:1). For God's anger is not like human anger, the disturbance of an agitated man, but the calm assigning of righteous punishment. In this anger of His, God does not restrain His tender mercies, as Scripture says (Ps.77:9). There are many consolations to the miserable, which He never ceases to bestow on the human race. Then, in the fullness of time, when He knew that it must be done, He sent His Only-begotten Son, through Whom He created all things, so that He might become human while remaining God, and so be "the Mediator between God and men, the man Christ Jesus" (1 Tim.2:5).

God did this so that those who believe in Christ might be absolved by the washing of regeneration from the guilt of all their sins — both the original sin they have inherited by birth, to counter which, in particular, rebirth was instituted, and all other sins incurred by evil conduct — and might be delivered from perpetual condemnation. They are then to live in faith and hope and love while journeying through this world, and be walking onward to God's visible presence amid the world's burdensome and dangerous temptations on the one hand, but amid the comforts of God, both bodily and spiritual, on the other, ever keeping to the Way which Christ has become to them. And because, even while walking in Christ, they are not exempt from sins, which creep in through the weaknesses of this life, the Lord has given them the healthy remedy of giving to others in charity, by which their prayers might be helped; for He taught them to say, "Forgive us our debts, as we also forgive our debtors." So does the Church act in blessed hope through this troublesome life ...

Sermons on John, 124:5

Saints may live without crime, but not without sin

But the angels even now are at peace with us when our sins are pardoned. Hence, in the order of the Creed,[2] after the mention of the

---

[2] The Apostles' Creed. After 'I believe in the holy Catholic Church', the next item is 'the forgiveness of sins'.

Holy Church is placed the forgiveness of sins. For it is by forgiveness that the Church on earth stands: it is through forgiveness that what had been lost, and was found, is saved from being lost again. For, setting aside the grace of baptism,[3] which is given as an antidote to original sin, so that what our birth imposes upon us, our new birth relieves us from (this grace, however, also takes away all the actual sins that have been committed in thought, word, and deed): setting aside, then, this great act of favour, from which humanity's restoration begins, and in which all our guilt (both original and actual) is washed away, the rest of our life from the time that we have the use of reason provides constant occasion for the forgiveness of sins, however great may be our advance in righteousness. For the children of God, as long as they live in this body of death, are in conflict with death. And although it is truly said of them, "As many as are led by the Spirit of God, they are the children of God" (Rom.8:14), yet they are led by the Spirit of God, and advance towards God as His children, under this drawback — that they are led also by their own spirit, which is weighed down by the corruptible body; and that, as the children of humanity, under the influence of human affections, they fall back to their old level, and so commit sin. There is a difference, however. For although every crime is a sin, not every sin is a crime. And so we say that the life of holy people, as long as they remain in this mortal body, may be found without *crime*; but, as the Apostle John says, "If we say that we have no *sin*, we deceive ourselves, and the truth is not in us" (1 Jn.1:8).

Enchiridion, 64

Faith is the true Christian's perfection

Our faith — that is, the Catholic faith — distinguishes the righteous from the unrighteous, not by the law of works, but by that of faith, because "the righteous lives by faith" (Rom.1:17). By this distinction,

---

[3] Augustine's high view of the spiritual effect of baptism comes out here very clearly. See Chapter 1, footnote 1. Most Evangelicals today will not want to follow Augustine on this particular point. At least Augustine took baptism very seriously as the proper God-ordained beginning of Christian life and discipleship and Church membership, even if we may think he exaggerated its effects.

the following consequence comes about. Imagine a man who leads his life without murder, without theft, without false-witness, without coveting other people's goods, giving due honour to his parents, chaste and pure from all carnal intercourse whatever, even within marriage, most generous in giving to charity, most patient in injuries. This man not only does not deprive another of his goods, but does not even ask again for what has been taken away from himself; or perhaps he has even sold all his own property and given it to the poor, and possesses nothing that belongs to him as his own. This man's character seems praiseworthy. Yet if he does not have a true and Catholic faith in God, he must depart from this life to condemnation.

But imagine another man, who does good works from a right faith that works by love. This man maintains his purity within the honesty of marriage, although he does not, like the other, refrain from sex altogether, but pays and repays the debt of carnal union, and has intercourse not only for the sake of offspring, but also for the sake of pleasure, although only with his wife, which the apostle allows to those that are married as pardonable.[4] He does not receive injuries with so much patience as the other man, but is provoked into anger with the desire for revenge; but, in order that he may say, "as we also forgive our debtors" (Matt.6:12), he forgives when he is asked. He possesses personal property, giving some of it to charity, but not so generously as the first man. He does not take away what belongs to another, but contends for his own, although by ecclesiastical, not by civil judgment.

Certainly this second man seems very inferior in morals to the first. Yet he has the right faith which he puts in God; by this faith he lives; and according to this faith, in all his sins he accuses himself, and in all his good works praises God, counts himself a disgrace

---

[4] This shows the high estimate that most of the early Church fathers put on complete abstinence from sex. They usually saw celibacy as (potentially, at least) more profitable than marriage, a sort of 'bloodless martyrdom' of the passions, and an anticipation by grace of the heavenly life. Even within marriage, husband and wife ought to have sexual relations for the noble purpose of begetting children, rather than merely for physical pleasure. Augustine followed this outlook whole-heartedly. In part, it was an understandable reaction against the sex-saturated culture of a decadent and dying Roman Empire. Most Evangelicals will think that the early Christians tilted rather too far towards the glories of celibacy than Scripture really warrants. But have we tilted too far the other way?

and gives to God the glory, and receives from Him both the forgiveness of sins and a love of doing what is right. On account of his faith, this man will be saved in this life, and depart to be received into the company of those who shall reign with Christ. Why, if not on account of faith? This faith, although without works it saves no-one (it is not a reprobate faith, since it works by love), yet sins are remitted on its account, because the righteous live by faith. But without this faith, even those things which seem to be good works are turned into sins: "For everything which is not from faith is sin" (Rom.14:23).

Against Two Letters of the Pelagians, 3:14

No Christian on earth dare compare himself with Christ

The Christian martyr is far inferior to Christ Himself. But if anyone compares himself, not with the power but with the *innocence* of Christ, and (I would not say) in thinking that he is healing the sins of others, but at least that he has no sins of his own, even here his zeal is overstepping the requirements of the method of salvation…. For in asserting his own sinlessness, he cannot prove, but only pretend, that he is righteous. And so it is said, "For such have a deceiving life" (Proverbs 23:3, Old Latin version). There is only One Who could at the same time have human flesh and be free from sin.

Sermons on John, 84:2

Cyprian's exposition of the Lord's Prayer refutes the Pelagians

In the fifth sentence of the prayer we say, "Forgive us our debts, as we also forgive our debtors" (Matt.6:12), the only petition where we find perseverance is not asked for. For the sins which we ask to be forgiven us are past. Perseverance, however, which saves us for eternity, is indeed necessary for the time of this life, but not for the time that is past — rather for the time that remains, even to its end. Yet it is worth the labour to consider for a little, how even already in this petition the heretics who were to arise long after were transfixed by the tongue of Cyprian, as if by the most invincible dart of truth.

For the Pelagians dare to say even this: that the righteous person in this life has no sin at all, and that in such people there is even at the present time a Church not having spot or wrinkle or any such thing, which is the one and only bride of Christ. As if she were not His bride who, throughout the whole earth, says what she has learnt from Him: "Forgive us our debts."

But observe how the most glorious Cyprian destroys these heretics. For when he was expounding that very clause of the Lord's Prayer, he says among other things: "And how necessarily, how providently and beneficially are we admonished that we are sinners, since we are compelled to beseech God for our sins. And while pardon is asked from God, the soul recalls its own consciousness. In case anyone should flatter himself that he is innocent, and by exalting himself should more deeply perish, he is instructed and taught that he sins every day, for he is exhorted every day to beseech God for his sins. Thus, moreover, John also in his Letter warns us, and says, 'If we say that we have no sin, we deceive ourselves, and the truth is not in us.'" (1 Jn.1:8). And so Cyprian continues; it would be too long to insert in this place.

On the Gift of Perseverance, 8

The perfection of apostles and prophets

So then, all the righteous, both the more ancient and the apostles, lived from a right faith which is in Christ Jesus our Lord. Along with their faith they also had a moral life that was so holy that, although they might not be of such perfect virtue in this life as they would attain to after this life, yet whatever of sin might creep in from human weakness was constantly done away by the godliness of their faith itself. Consequently, in comparison with the wicked whom God will condemn, it must be said that these were "righteous," since by their godly faith they were so far removed into the opposite camp from the wicked that the apostle cries out, "What part has a believer with an unbeliever?" (2 Cor.6:15)

But it is plain that the Pelagians, these modern heretics, seem to themselves to have a religious love of the saints, praising them. For the Pelagians do not dare to say that the saints had an imperfect virtue. This is despite the fact that the elect vessel Paul confesses this! For when considering the state he was still in, the corrupted body dragging down the soul, he says, "Not that I have already attained or am yet perfect; brothers, I do not count myself to have apprehended" (Phil.3:12-13). And yet, a little later, he who had denied that he was perfect says, "Let us therefore, as many as are perfect, be thus minded" (Phil.3:15). He says this in order to show that, according to the standard of this present life, there is a certain kind of perfection, but that when this perfection is ascribed, it should be allied with the knowledge that we are not yet perfect. For what is more perfect, or what was more excellent, than the holy priests among the ancient people? And yet God prescribed to them to offer sacrifice first of all for their own sins. And what is more holy among the new people than the apostles? And yet the Lord prescribed to them to say in their prayer, "Forgive us our debts." For all the godly, therefore, who lie under this burden of a corruptible flesh, and groan in the weakness of this life of theirs, there is only one hope: "We have an advocate with the Father, Jesus Christ the righteous: and He is the propitiation for our sins" (1 Jn.2:2).

Against Two Letters of the Pelagians, 3:15

Even the righteous are sinful in this life

Do the righteous, while living by faith, not need to say: "Forgive us our debts, as we forgive our debtors" (Matt.6:12)? And do they prove the Scripture wrong that says, "In Your sight no-one living shall be justified" (Ps.143:2)? And this: "If we say that we have no sin, we deceive ourselves, and the truth is not in us" (1 Jn.1:8)? Again, "There is no-one who does not sin" (1 Kings 8:46)? And again, "There is not on the earth a righteous man who does good and does not sin" (Eccles.7:20)? For these statements are expressed in a general future sense — "does not sin," "will not sin" — not in the past tense, "has not sinned". And there are all the other places contained in the Holy Scripture that teach the same. Since, however, these passages cannot possibly be false, it plainly follows (to my mind) that whatever the quality or extent of the righteousness we may definitely ascribe to the present life, there is not a human being living in it who is absolutely free from all sin. It is necessary for everyone to give, that it may be given to him, and to forgive that it may be forgiven him. Whatever righteousness a person has, he must not presume that he has it from himself, but from the grace of God, Who justifies him. He must still go on hungering and thirsting for righteousness from Him Who is the living bread, and with Whom is the fountain of life. God makes His saints righteous as they toil amid temptation in this life, in such a way that He still has something to give them generously when they ask, and something to forgive them mercifully when they confess.

On the Spirit and the Letter, 65

Noah, Daniel and Job

Now, I suppose it is difficult to find in God's Scripture so impressive a testimony of holiness given about anyone as that which is written of His three servants, Noah, Daniel, and Job. The prophet Ezekiel describes them as the only men able to be delivered from God's impending wrath (Ezek.14:14,20). In these three men, he no doubt prefigures three classes of mankind to be delivered: in my view, Noah represents righteous leaders of nations, by reason of his government of the ark as a type of the Church; Daniel represents people who are righteous in celibacy; Job represents those who are righteous in marriage — to say nothing of any other view of the passage, which it is unnecessary to consider just now. It is, at any rate, clear from this testimony of the prophet, and from other inspired statements, how eminent these worthy men were in righteousness. Yet no-one must be led by their history to say, for instance, that drunkenness is not sin, although so good a man as Noah was overtaken by it (Gen.9:21); for we read that Noah was once drunk (although God forbid that we should think he was a habitual drunkard!)

As for Daniel, after the prayer which he poured out before God, he actually says of himself, "While I was praying and confessing my sins, and the sins of my people, before the Lord my God" (Dan.9:20). This is the reason, if I am not mistaken, why in the previously mentioned prophet Ezekiel, a certain very haughty person is asked, "Are you then wiser than Daniel?"[5] Nor can we possibly

---

[5] That is, "Do you think you are without sin when Daniel did not think he was?"

say about Daniel's prayer what some argue for in opposition to the Lord's Prayer. "For although," they say, "that prayer was offered by the apostles, after they became holy and perfect, and had no sin whatever, yet they did not pray it on behalf of their own selves, but it was for imperfect and still sinful people that they said, 'Forgive us our debts, as we also forgive our debtors' (Matt.6:12). They used the word *our* in order to show that in one body are contained both those who still have sins, and the apostles who were already quite free from sin."

Now this certainly cannot be said in the case of Daniel, who (I suppose) foresaw as a prophet this presumptuous opinion. For he said so often in his prayer, "We have sinned" (verses 5,8,11,15). He then explained to us why he said this, so that we would not take him to mean, "While I was praying and confessing *the sins of my people* to the Lord, my God." Nor should we blur the distinction between Daniel and Israel, as if he might have prayed this way on account of his fellowship in one body with sinners — "While I was confessing *our* sins to the Lord my God." No, he expresses himself in language so distinct and precise, as if he were overflowing with the distinction himself, and wanted above all things to commend it to our notice: "*My sins*," he says, "*and the sins of my people.*" Who can argue against evidence like this, except someone who is more intent on defending his own opinion than on finding out what his opinion ought to be?

Now let us see what Job has to say of himself, after God's great testimony of his righteousness. "Truly I know," he says, "that it is so; for how shall a mortal man be righteous before the Lord? For if He should enter into judgment with a man, no man would be able to obey Him" (Job 9:2-3) ... In another of his speeches he says: "For You have written evil things against me, and have compassed me with the sins of my youth. You have placed my feet in the stocks. You have watched all my works, and inspected the soles of my feet, which decay like a rotten thing, or like a moth-eaten garment. For man that is born of a woman has but a short time to live, and is full of trouble. Like a flower that has bloomed, so he falls; he is gone like a shadow, and does not continue. Have You not taken account even of him, and caused him to enter into judgment with You? For who is pure from uncleanness? Not even one, even if his life lasted but a day" (Job 13:26-14:4) ... See how Job, too, confesses his sins, and says how sure he is that there is none righteous before the Lord.

So Job is sure of this also, that "if we say we have no sin, the truth is not in us" (1 Jn.1:8).

On the Merits and Forgiveness of Sins, 2:12-14

Was Job sinlessly perfect?

That illustrious testimony of God, therefore, in which Job is commended, is not contrary to the passage in which it is said, "In Your sight no man living shall be justified" (Ps.143:2). For it does not lead us to suppose that there was nothing at all in Job which could rightly be blamed, either by himself truly or by the Lord God, even though at the same time he might truly be said to be a righteous man, a sincere worshipper of God, and one who keeps himself from every evil work. For these are God's words concerning him: "Have you diligently considered my servant Job? For there is no-one like him on the earth, blameless, righteous, a true worshipper of God, who keeps himself from every evil work" (Job 1:8).

First, Job is here praised for his excellence in comparison with all persons on earth. He therefore excelled all who were at that time able to be righteous upon earth; and yet he was not wholly without sin, on account of this superiority over others in righteousness. He is next said to be "blameless" — no one could fairly bring an accusation against him in respect of his life; "righteous" — he had advanced so greatly in moral probity, that no-one could be mentioned on a level with him; "a true worshipper of God" — because he was a sincere and humble confessor of his own sins; "who keeps himself from every evil work" — but it would have been amazing if this had extended to every evil *word* and *thought*!

How great a man indeed Job was, we are not told; but we know that he was a righteous man. We know, too, that in the endurance of terrible afflictions and trials he was great; and we know that it was not on account of his sins, but for the purpose of demonstrating his righteousness, that he had to bear so much suffering. But the language in which the Lord commends Job might also be applied to him who "delights in the law of God after the inner man, whilst he sees another law in his members warring against the law of his mind" (Rom.7:22-23). Especially when he says: "The good that I would, I do not do: but the evil which I would not do, that I do. Now, if I do what I would not, it is no longer I that do it, but sin that dwells in me" (Rom.7:19-20). Observe how Paul too is separate from every evil work in his inward self, because he does not himself bring about such work, but the evil which dwells in his flesh does it. And yet, even his ability to delight in the law of God comes from the grace of God; and so, still in need of deliverance, he exclaims, "O wretched man that I am! Who shall deliver me from the body of this death? God's grace, through Jesus Christ our Lord!" (Rom.7:24-25)

There are then on earth righteous people, great people, brave, prudent, chaste, patient, godly, merciful, who endure all kinds of earthly trials with a calm mind for righteousness' sake. If, however, there is truth — or rather, because there is truth — in these words, "If we say we have no sin, we deceive ourselves" (1 Jn.1:8), and in these, "In Your sight no man living shall be justified" (Ps.143:2), these people are not without sin. Nor is there one among them so proud and foolish as not to think that the Lord's Prayer is needful to him, by reason of his manifold sins.

On the Merits and Forgiveness of Sins, 2:17-18

Was Zacharias sinlessly perfect?

Now what shall we say of Zacharias and Elisabeth, who are often alleged against us in discussions on this question? Well, there is clear evidence in the Scripture that Zacharias was a man of eminent righteousness among the chief priests, whose duty it was to offer up the sacrifices of the Old Testament (Lk.1:6-9). We also read, however, in the Epistle to the Hebrews, in a passage which I have already quoted in my previous book, that Christ was the only High Priest who had no need (as the other high priests did) to offer daily a sacrifice for his own sins first, and then for the people. "For such a High Priest," it says, "was fitting for us, holy, innocent, undefiled, separate from sinners, and made higher than the heavens, Who does not need daily, as those high priests, to offer up sacrifice, first for his own sins" (Heb.7:26-7). Among the priests here referred to was Zacharias, among them was Phinehas, yes, Aaron himself, from whom this priesthood had its beginning, and whatever others there were who lived praiseworthy and righteous lives in this priesthood. And yet all these were under the necessity, first of all, to offer sacrifice for their own sins! Christ, of whose future coming they were a type, was the only one Who had no such necessity, since He was a priest incapable of defilement.

On the Merits and Forgiveness of Sins, 2:19

Struggling with sin on earth, freedom in the resurrection

Quite intolerably the Pelagians object to our teaching that after the resurrection we will be so spiritually advanced, people will then be able to start fulfilling the commands of God, which they fail to do on earth. For we say that there will then be no sin at all, no struggle with any desire for sin. Will the Pelagians dare to deny this? Wisdom and the knowledge of God will then be perfected in us, and there will be such rejoicing in the Lord as to amount to a full and a true security. Who will deny this, unless he is so hostile to the truth that on this very account he cannot attain to it?

However, heaven will not be about obeying precepts, but an experience of reward for keeping those precepts here on earth – and the neglect of these precepts here does not lead to the reward there. But here the grace of God gives the desire to keep His commandments; and if we do not perfectly observe anything in these commandments, He forgives us on account of what we say in prayer. For we say both "Your will be done" (Matt.6:10) and "Forgive us our debts" (Matt.6:12). Here, then, God commands us not to sin; there, the reward is that we cannot sin. Here, the precept is that we must not obey the desires of sin; there, the reward is that we have no desires for sin. Here, the precept is, "Understand, you senseless among the people; and you fools, be wise at last" (Ps.94:8); there, the reward is full wisdom and perfect knowledge. "For we see now through a glass in an enigma," says the apostle, "but then face to face: now I know in part; but then I shall know even as also I am known" (1 Cor.13:12). Here, the precept is, "Exult in the Lord, our helper" (Ps.81:1), and, "Rejoice, you righteous, in the Lord" (Ps.33:1); there, the reward is to rejoice with a perfect and unspeakable joy. Lastly, the precept says, "Blessed are those who hunger and thirst after righteousness"; but the reward says, "Because they shall be filled" (Matt.5:6). I ask you, what shall they be filled with, except with what they hunger and thirst after? Who, then, is so alienated, not only from divine perception but even from human perception, as to say that a human being can have this righteousness while he is still hungering and thirsting for it, to the same degree that he will have it when he is filled with it?

Against Two Letters of the Pelagians, 3:17

The sense in which we can be "perfect" on earth

The virtue of the righteous person is called "perfect" to this extent, that its perfection involves both the true knowledge and humble confession of imperfection itself. For in respect of our weakness, the little righteousness of a human being is "perfect" according to its measure, when it understands even what it lacks. And therefore the apostle calls himself both perfect and imperfect — imperfect, in the thought of how much he lacks of the full righteousness for which he is still hungering and thirsting; but perfect, in that he does not blush to confess his own imperfection, and presses forward in goodness in order to attain perfection. Likewise we can say that the wayfarer is travelling "perfectly" when he is following the correct route, although his purpose is not fulfilled unless he actually arrives.

Against Two Letters of the Pelagians, 3:19

Our moral and spiritual renewal is perfected only at death

Certainly this renewal does not take place in the single moment of conversion itself. It is unlike the renewal that occurs in baptism, which takes place in a single moment by the forgiveness of all sins; for not even the smallest sin remains unforgiven.[6] But it is one thing to be free from fever, and another to grow strong again from the weakness which the fever produced. Likewise it is one thing to pull out of the body a weapon that has been thrust into it, and another to heal the wound by a successful cure. Our first cure is to remove the cause of weakness, and this is effected by the forgiving of all sins; but the second cure is to heal the weakness itself, and this takes

---

[6] See footnote 3.

place gradually by making progress in the renewal of the divine image.

These two things are clearly shown in the Psalm, where we read, "Who forgives all your iniquities" (Ps.103:3), which takes place in baptism; and then follows, "and heals all your infirmities" (Ps.103:3), which takes place by daily additions, while this image is being renewed. And the apostle has spoken of this most expressly, saying, "And though our outward self perishes, yet the inner self is being renewed day by day" (2 Cor.4:16). And "it is renewed in the knowledge of God, *i.e.* in righteousness and true holiness," according to the testimonies of the apostle cited earlier (Eph.4:24).

He, then, who is day by day renewed by making progress in the knowledge of God, and in righteousness and true holiness, transfers his love from things temporal to things eternal, from things seen with the eyes to things seen with the soul, from things carnal to things spiritual, and he laboriously perseveres in curbing and lessening his desire for the former, and in binding himself by love to the latter. And he does this in proportion as he is helped by God. For it is the verdict of God Himself, "Without me you can do nothing" (Jn.15:5).

So when the last day of life finds anyone holding fast to faith in the Mediator in such progress and growth as this, he will be welcomed by the holy angels, and be led to God Whom he has worshipped, to be made perfect by Him. And thus he will receive at the end of the world an incorruptible body, not for punishment, but for glory. For the likeness of God will then be perfected in this image, when the vision of God will be brought to perfection. And of this the apostle Paul speaks: "Now we see through a glass, in an enigma, but then face to face" (1 Cor.13:12). And again: "But we with open face, beholding as in a glass the glory of the Lord, are changed into the same image, from glory to glory, even as by the Spirit of the Lord" (2 Cor.3:18). And this is what happens from day to day in those that make good progress.

On the Trinity, 14:23

The man of Romans 7:14-25

[It has always been a classic hallmark of the Augustinian tradition that the "wretched man" of Romans 7:14-25 has been seen as the Christian, the regenerate soul struggling with the fierce residue of indwelling sin. Our old self has been, not tamed, but crucified with Christ; but the ghost of that old crucified self haunts us till our dying hour. A person's Augustinian convictions about sin and grace are undergoing serious disintegration if he begins to think that Paul is not describing the Christian in Romans 7, since that must mean the "wretched man" is some kind of noble unbeliever. Who but a Christian could undertake the heroic warfare with sin portrayed in these verses, loving God's law inwardly and torn apart by conflict with all that opposes God's law? Our view of sin must be somewhat superficial if we believe that the unregenerate are capable of such exploits. Either that, or we end up with two kinds of Christian, the second-class defeated Christian of Romans 7, and the first-class victorious Christian of Romans 8. And then the problem is twofold: an elitism of the super-spiritual, quite unknown to Scripture, allied to a superficial view of sin in the believer, as if we could fundamentally leave it behind this side of death and glory. Here is Augustine's exposition of this key passage:]

The Pelagians contend that what the apostle said, "I know that in me, that is, in my flesh, dwells no good thing, for to will is present with me, but how to perform what is good I do not find" (Rom.7:18), and other such things, Paul was speaking not of himself, but of somebody else. I do not know who this "somebody else" was who was suffering these things. Therefore this passage in his epistle must be carefully considered and investigated, so that their error may not lurk in any obscurity of Paul's. Although, therefore, the apostle is here arguing broadly, and with great and enduring conflict maintaining grace against those who were boasting in the law, yet we do come upon a few matters that relate to the specific topic in hand.

On this topic Paul says: "Because by the law no flesh will be justified in His sight. For by the law is the knowledge of sin. But now the righteousness of God apart from the law is revealed, being witnessed to by the law and the prophets, even the righteousness of God by faith in Jesus Christ to all those who believe. For there is no difference. For all have sinned and come short of the glory of God, being justified freely by His grace through the redemption that is in Christ Jesus" (Rom.3:20-24). And again: "Where is boasting? It is excluded. By what law? Of works? No; but by the law of faith. Therefore we conclude that a man is justified by faith without the works of the law" (Rom.3:27-8). And again: "For the promise that he should be the heir of the world was not to Abraham or to his seed through the law, but by the righteousness of faith. For if those who are of the law be heirs, faith is made void, and the promise made of no effect. The law brings wrath, for where there is no law, there is no transgression" (Rom.4:13-15).

And in another place: "Moreover, the law entered that the offence might abound. But where sin abounded, grace much more abounded" (Rom.5:20). In still another place: "For sin shall not have dominion over you, for you are not under law, but under grace" (Rom.6:14). And again in another place: "Do you not know, brothers (for I speak to those who know the law), that the law has dominion over a man so long as he lives? For the woman who is under a husband is joined to her husband by the law so long as he lives; but if her husband is dead, she is freed from the law of her husband." And a little after: "Therefore, my brothers, you also have become dead to the law by the body of Christ, that you should belong to another, who has risen from the dead that we should bring forth fruit for God. For when we were in the flesh the passions of sins which are aroused by the law worked in our members to bring forth fruit for death, but now we are delivered from the law of death in which we were held, so that we may serve in newness of spirit, and not in the oldness of the letter" (Rom.7:1-6).

With these and other similar testimonies, the teacher of the Gentiles showed with sufficient evidence that the law could not take away sin, but rather increased it, and that grace is what takes sin away. The law knew how to command, but weakness collapses under the command; grace knows to assist, by which love is poured into us. And in case anyone, on account of these testimonies, should reproach the law, and contend that the law is evil, the apostle, seeing what might occur to those who understand the law wrongly, proposed to himself the same question. "What shall we say, then? Is the law sin? Far from it. But I did not know sin except through the law" (Rom.7:7). He had already said before, "For through the law is the knowledge of sin" (Rom.3:20). Law does not bring about the *removal* of sin, but the *knowledge* of sin. And from this point Paul now begins — and it was on this account that I undertook to consider these things — to introduce his own person, and to speak as if it were about himself. But the Pelagians will not have it that the apostle himself is to be understood as speaking here. They say that he has transfigured another person into himself — that is, a man who was still placed under the law, and not yet freed by grace....

But it is not so clear how what follows can be understood concerning Paul. "For we know," says he, "that the law is spiritual, but I am fleshly" (Rom.7:14). He does not say, "I was," but, "I am." Was the apostle fleshly, then, when he wrote this? Or does he say this with respect to his body? For he was still in the body of this death, which had not yet been made into what he speaks of elsewhere: "It is sown a natural body, it shall be raised a spiritual body" (1 Cor.15:44). For then the whole of Paul, that is, his body and his soul, will be a spiritual man; for even the body will then be spiritual. It is not absurd that in the future life even the flesh will be spiritual, if in this life even the spirit itself may be fleshly, in those who still love earthly things. Thus then, Paul said, "But I am fleshly," because the apostle had not yet a spiritual body. It is as if he were saying, "But I am mortal," which certainly he could only have said in respect of his body, which had not yet been clothed with immortality.

What about what he added, "sold under sin"? In case anyone thought that he was not yet redeemed by the blood of Christ, this expression too may be understood as referring to those words of the apostle: "And we ourselves, having the first-fruits of the Spirit, even we ourselves groan within ourselves, waiting for the adoption, the redemption of our body" (Rom.8:23). For he says that he is sold under sin in this respect, that his body has not yet been redeemed from corruption. Or perhaps it means that he was sold once, in the first transgression of the commandment, reaping a corruptible body which drags the soul down. So why should we not understand the apostle here to be saying this about himself in such a way that we may understand all who know themselves to be experiencing a reluctant struggle between spiritual delight and the emotions of the flesh? And we should take this as including Paul himself, even if by speaking in his person he does not wish himself alone to be signified.

Or do we perhaps fear what follows? "For I do not understand what I do, for what I will I do not do, but what I hate I do" (Rom.7:15). Perhaps from these words someone will suspect that the apostle is positively consenting to the evil works of the lustful desires of the flesh. But we must consider what he adds: "But if I do what I do not will, I consent to the law that it is good" (Rom.7:16). For he says that he consents to the law rather than to the lustful desire of the flesh. Consenting to lustful desire he calls by the name of sin. Therefore he said that he acted and laboured, not with the intention of consenting to sinful desire and fulfilling it, but from the impulse of sinful desire itself. That is why he says, "I consent to the law that it is good." I consent to the law, because I do not will what it does not will. Afterwards he says, "Now, then, it is no longer I that do it, but sin that dwells in me" (Rom.7:17). What does he mean by "now then"? Surely he means now at length, under the grace which has delivered the delight of my will from consent to sinful desire. For, "it is not I that do it," is best understood as meaning that Paul does not positively consent to offer his members as instruments of unrighteousness for sin. For if he lusts, and then he consents, and then he acts, how can he be said not to do the thing himself, even although he may grieve that he does it, and deeply groan at being overcome? ...

And he declares both more plainly in what follows: "For I delight in the law of God after the inward man; but I see another law in my members, warring against the law of my mind, and bringing me into captivity to the law of sin which is in my members" (Rom.7:22-3). But since he said, "bringing me into captivity," he can feel emotion without consenting to it. Thus, we have three things, two of which we have already considered. When Paul says, "But I am carnal," and "Sold under sin," and this third, "Bringing me into captivity in the law of sin, which is in my members," the apostle seems to be describing a man who is still living under the law, and is not yet under grace. But as I have expounded the first two sayings as referring to the still corruptible flesh, so the third too may be understood as if he had said, "bringing me into captivity" in the flesh, not in the mind — in emotion, not in positive consent. Therefore he says "bringing me into captivity" — "me" because even in the flesh there is not an alien nature, but our own. So then, as therefore he himself expounded what he had said, "For I know that in me, *that is, in my flesh,* dwells no good thing," so also now from this exposition we ought to learn the meaning of this passage, as if he had said, 'Bringing me into captivity,' that is, "my flesh," "to the law of sin, which is in my members" ...

It had once appeared to me also that the apostle was, in this argument of his, describing a man under the law. But afterwards I was compelled to give up that idea by those words where he says, "Now, then, it is no longer I that do it." For to this belongs what he says subsequently: "There is, therefore, now no condemnation for those who are in Christ Jesus" (Rom.8:1). And I do not see how a man under the law should say, "I delight in the law of God after the inward man". For this very delight in good, by which he does not consent to evil, not from fear of punishment, but from love of righteousness (for this is meant by "delighting") — this can be attributed only to grace.

Against Two Letters of the Pelagians, 1:13-14, 17-18, 20, 22

Chapter 8

The Perseverance of the Saints

I do not wonder to see the minds of believers disturbed by Satan. Resist him, continuing in the hope which rests on the promises of God, Who cannot lie. He has not only graciously chosen to promise eternal rewards to us who believe and hope in Him, and who persevere in love to the end, but has also foretold that offences shall not be lacking by which our faith must be tried and proved on earth; for He said, "Because iniquity will abound, the love of many will wax cold"; but He added immediately, "and whoever endures to the end shall be saved."

*Augustine, **Letter 77:1***

I suppose most Christians are interested in whether they can lose their salvation and end up back in sin's bondage and Satan's domain, heading for hell. It is not necessarily a self-centred question. If I delight in God's holiness and want to glorify Him, I may well want to know whether He will indeed be glorified in me, and go on being glorified in me for eternity. Will Father, Son and Holy Spirit accomplish their sanctifying purposes in my existence? Or can I frustrate and defeat them by the erratic and unstable treachery of my sin-tainted will?

One of the distinguishing features of the Augustinian tradition has always been its strong doctrine of the "perseverance of the saints" — that is, that the elect are predestined to eternal salvation, and therefore cannot lose that salvation. Sometimes this is called the doctrine of "eternal security". This phrase, however, tends to put a somewhat man-centred spin on what Augustine actually taught. He was not concerned to make Christians feel "secure" in a complacent sort of way. His basic concern was to spotlight perseverance to the end as the true mark of the faith of God's elect. If I am chosen by God, my election will show itself in the persevering quality of my faith and my faith-inspired obedience. However many times I may be defeated by the world, the flesh and the devil, I always return to the attack; and death finds me a battle-scarred warrior, still struggling, still refusing to give up the "good fight" (1 Tim.6:12). Yes, it is comforting to believe that my faith will persevere *to the end*; but it will *persevere* to the end — obstinately persist in the pursuit of holiness, obedience, sanctification, without which no-one will see the Lord (Heb.12:14). There is no ground here for a lazy security. As a Puritan quaintly put it, "The inspiration of the Spirit does not negate the perspiration of the saints."

One of the weirder paradoxes of Christian life is that the doctrine of perseverance is often the only aspect of Augustinian theology that Evangelicals take on board. For original sin, the bondage of the will, predestination, particular redemption, and sovereign grace in regeneration, they have little or no time. But perseverance (or "eternal security", as they are more likely to say) is a different matter! "Once saved, always saved." Yes, that's a comforting thought: we can go along with that. And so modern Evangelical theology demonstrates its tendency to believe things because they are comforting, meeting a "felt need", rather than because they are objectively true.

Yet in the bright cleansing light of reality, we simply cannot believe in perseverance alone, divorced from the rich totality of Augustinian doctrine. If the rest of our theology makes us idolise human free-will, and play down the corrupting effects of sin and the radically transforming power of God's grace in regeneration, we are left with no basis for our "comforting" belief in perseverance. If my salvation was ultimately a matter of my freely willing myself to accept Christ, what is to stop me freely willing to reject Him again? If God did not actually *bring* me to Christ by sovereign efficacious grace, why should I think He will *keep* me in Christ by sovereign efficacious grace? The costly price of affirming that our salvation is grasped by a decision springing ultimately from our own wills, is that we must be able to lose that salvation by another decision that springs ultimately from those same wills. Freely and autonomously I came in, freely and autonomously I can go out again.

The Augustinian (and of course Biblical) doctrine of persever-ance is massively underpinned by the truth that we did not in fact come to Christ by some ultimately self-generated choice of our own. God the Father drew us to Christ, gave us to Christ, and bound us to Christ, by His own unconditional, omnipotent, sin-conquering, will-transforming grace. If He had left us to ourselves, we would never have come. Our slavery to sin was too deep, too ruinous. But having brought His elect to Christ, God keeps them in Christ. Having be-gun the good work of spiritual renovation, He carries it on until it reaches perfection on the day of Christ Jesus. By grace the elect believed; by grace they go on believing; by grace their faith issues in love, and goes on issuing in love; by faith-begotten love they strive to obey God's law, and go on striving to obey it; and he who by grace endures to the end shall be saved. Perseverance is the holy and beautiful flower that blooms from the stem of sovereign grace in regeneration, itself rooted deep in the eternal soil of divine predesti-nation and election.

There are many Christians who do not believe in perseverance. As to how edifying or spiritually enriching their disbelief is to them, their own souls must bear witness. Since it throws them in the last analysis on their own resources — will I carry on cooperating with God? — it seems to put impossible strains on the notorious fickleness and unreliability of the human will. However that may be, the deniers of perseverance often take their stand on the exhortations and warnings that Scripture addresses to believers. We are exhorted to persevere in the faith (Jn.8:31, Col.1:23, Heb.3:12-4:11); we are warned of eternal consequences if we fail (Matt.10:22, Jn.15:6, Heb.6:4-8). How are these exhortations and warnings consistent with a belief in the impossibility of the elect losing their salvation?

This is a question that Augustinians must not duck. Nor have they. The classical Augustinian response is as follows: Yes, Scripture exhorts us to persevere in the faith, and warns us that there will be eternal consequences if we fail. *It is precisely by means of these exhortations and warnings that the Holy Spirit moves and inspires us to persevere.* Through the exhortations, He galvanises our wills to be active in "keeping ourselves in the love of God" (Jude 21); through the warnings, He redoubles our commitment, by making us realise that our eternal future is at stake.

It may seem a paradox that threats of hell as the consequence of apostasy are the very means that keep us from apostasy. But is it not a principle found in ordinary life? Consider: why are danger signs posted? Not in order to spark off a philosophical discussion about whether any given individual will fall into the danger and be killed. Danger signs are posted in order to *prevent* people falling into the danger and being killed. The purpose is intensely practical. So it is with Scripture's exhortations and warnings. Yes, he who commits apostasy from Christ will be eternally lost. By placarding this terrifying danger sign across the path of drifting, *God prevents His elect from going down that path.* If this is so, it is perfectly appropriate to threaten even true Christians with hell as the end-result of drifting from Christ. In the Spirit's hand, this harsh warning may be the very instrument that saves us and begets perseverance within us.

In other words, it is the same with God's exhortations and warnings as with His other commands. Why should God give me Ten Commandments about a holy life, if He is going to produce that holiness in me anyway through the Spirit's indwelling? Because it is by means of those Ten Commandments that the Spirit produces my holiness. He inscribes the commandments on my mind, and makes me love them with my affections; and so these very commandments become the tool in the master craftsman's hand to shape and fashion me into holiness. His mighty energy works *through* the commandments, not without them or despite them. As Augustine says about the apostle Paul's dealings with the Corinthians, "he was in the habit of speaking to them, and doing all those things which I have mentioned — he admonished, he taught, he exhorted, he rebuked. But he knew that all these things which he was openly doing in the way of planting and watering were of no avail, unless He Who secretly gives the increase answered his prayer on the Corinthians' behalf. For as the same teacher of the Gentiles says, 'Neither he who plants is anything, nor he who waters, but God Who gives the increase' (1 Cor.3:7)" (**On Rebuke and Grace, 3**).

In brief, this is the great pervasive principle that *the Spirit works through the Word*. And so it is with the exhortations to persevere and warnings against apostasy. Through this stern and bracing aspect of the Word, the Spirit works in the elect to keep them — "kept by the power of God through faith for salvation ready to be revealed in the last time" (1 Pet.1:5). Thanks be to God for His Word, for all of His Word: for the rousing exhortations and the grim warnings, as well as the warm encouragements and sweet promises. For the refreshing new wine and the keen pruning knife are equally needful in the salvation of a sinner.[1]

****

The Perseverance of the Saints

The Shepherd preserves the sheep

"And they shall never perish" (Jn.10:28). You may hear the undertone, as if Jesus had said to them [unbelieving Jews], You shall perish for ever, because you are not of My sheep. "No one shall pluck them out of My hand" (Jn.10:28). Pay still greater attention to this: "That which my Father gave Me is greater than all" (Jn.10:29). What can the wolf do? What can the thief and the robber do? They destroy none but those predestined to destruction. But of those sheep

---

[1] In my introduction to Chapter 6, I have already looked at Augustine's understanding of whether a Christian has any warrant to believe that he in particular will persevere, given Augustine's view that the non-elect can have a real but temporary faith.

concerning whom the apostle says, "The Lord knows those who are His" (2 Tim.2:19), and "those whom He foreknew, He also predestined; and those He predestined, He also called; and those whom He called, He also justified; and those whom He justified, He also glorified" (Rom.8:29-30) — there are none of these sheep that the wolf seizes, or the thief steals, or the robber slays. He Who knows what He gave for them is sure of their number. And it is this that He says: "No-one shall pluck them out of My hand."

Sermons on John, 48:6

Perseverance is God's gift, not a human achievement

We cannot deny that perseverance in good, progressing even to the end, is also a great gift of God. It does not exist unless it comes from Him of Whom it is written, "Every best gift and every perfect gift is from above, coming down from the Father of lights" (Jam.1:17). But we must not on that account fail to rebuke the one who has not persevered, "if God perhaps may give him repentance, and he recovers from the snares of the devil" (2 Tim.2:25). For to the usefulness of rebuke the apostle has added this decision, saying, as I have above mentioned, "rebuking with moderation those that think differently, if perhaps God may give them repentance." For if we said that such a perseverance, so praiseworthy and so blessed, belongs to human power, in such a way that a person does not derive it from God, we first of all make empty what the Lord says to Peter: "I have prayed for you that your faith may not fail" (Lk.22:32). For what did He ask for Peter, but perseverance to the end? And assuredly, if a human being could gain this from another human being, it would not have been asked from God.

Then when the apostle says, "Now we pray to God that you do no evil" (2 Cor.13:7), beyond doubt he prays to God on their behalf for perseverance. For certainly a person does not "do no evil" who forsakes the good, fails to persevere in it, and turns to the evil from which he ought to turn away. In that place, moreover, where he says, "I thank my God in every remembrance of you, always in every prayer of mine for you all, making request with joy for your fellowship in the gospel from the first day until now, being confident of this very thing, that He who has begun a good work in you will perform it until the day of Jesus Christ" (Phil.1:3-6) — what else does he promise to them from God's mercy other than perseverance in good to the end?

And again, where he says, "Epaphras salutes you, who is one of you, a servant of Christ Jesus, always striving for you in prayer, that you may stand perfect and fulfilled in all the will of God" (Col.4:12) — what does "that you may stand" mean but "that you may persevere"? This is why it was said of the devil, "He stood not in the truth" (Jn.8:44): because he was once there, but he did not continue there. For assuredly those [for whom Epaphras prayed] were already standing in the faith. And when we pray that he who stands may continue to stand, we do not pray for anything else than that he may persevere. Jude the apostle, again, when he says, "Now to Him Who is able to keep you without offence, and to establish you before the presence of His glory, blameless in joy" (Jude 24), does he not most manifestly show that perseverance to the end in goodness is God's gift? For what else but a good perseverance does He give Who preserves souls without offence, that He may place them before the presence of His glory blameless in joy?

Moreover, we read in the Acts of the Apostles: "And when the Gentiles heard, they rejoiced and received the word of the Lord; and as many as were ordained to eternal life believed" (Acts 13:48). Who could be ordained to eternal life except by the gift of perseverance? And when we read, "He who perseveres to the end will be saved" (Matt.10:22), what salvation is this but eternal salvation? And when, in the Lord's Prayer, we say to God the Father, "Hallowed be Your name" (Matt.6:9), what do we ask but that His name may be hallowed *in us*? And since this has already been accomplished by means of the washing of regeneration, why do believers ask for it every day, except that we may persevere in what is already done in us? For the blessed Cyprian also understands it in this manner, since in his exposition of the same prayer, he says: "We say, 'Hallowed be Your name,' not that we wish that God may be hallowed by our prayers, but rather that we ask God that His name may be hallowed *in us*. But by whom is God hallowed, since He Himself hallows? Well, because He said, 'Be holy, since I also am holy' (1 Pet.1:16), we ask and entreat that we who have been hallowed in baptism may persevere in what we have begun to be." Behold the most glorious martyr [Cyprian] is of this opinion, that in these words Christ's faithful people are daily asking that they may persevere in what they have begun to be. And no-one need doubt, that whoever prays to the Lord for perseverance in the good, confesses thereby that such perseverance is God's gift.

On Rebuke and Grace, 10

Christ's prayer the guarantee of Peter's faith

You say that it pertains to human free will — which you defend, not in accordance with God's grace, but in opposition to it — that anyone perseveres in good, or fails to persevere, and it is not by the gift of God if he perseveres, but by the performance of the human will. Why will you strive against the words of Him who says, "I have prayed for you, Peter, that your faith may not fail" (Lk.22:32)? Will you dare to say that even when Christ prayed that Peter's faith might not fail, it would still have failed if Peter had willed it to fail — that is, if Peter had been unwilling that his faith should continue to the end? As if Peter's will could in any measure be otherwise than Christ had asked for Peter that his will might be! For who does not know that Peter's *faith* would have perished, if Peter's faithful *will* failed, but that his faith would have continued if that same will remained? But "the will is prepared by the Lord" (Prov.8:35, Septuagint). Therefore Christ's petition on Peter's behalf could not be a vain petition.

So when Christ prayed that Peter's faith should not fail, He asked that in his faith Peter should have a most free, strong, invincible, persevering will! Behold to what an extent the freedom of the will is defended in accordance with the grace of God, not in opposition to it. For the human will does not attain to grace by freedom, but rather attains to freedom by grace, and to a delightful constancy, and to an indomitable firmness, that it may persevere.

On Rebuke and Grace, 17

Christ's prayer the guarantee of our perseverance

"I do not pray," He adds, "that You should take them out of the world, but that You should keep them from the evil one" (Jn.17:15).

For they still accounted it necessary to be in the world, although they were no longer of it. Then He repeats the same statement: "They are not of the world, even as I am not of the world. Sanctify them in the truth" (Jn.17:16-17). For in this way they are kept from the evil one, as He had previously prayed that they might be. But it may be asked how they were no more of the world, if they were not yet sanctified in the truth; or, if they already were, why He prays that they should be sanctified. Surely it is because even those who are sanctified still continue to make progress in the same sanctification, and grow in holiness; and they do so only with the help of God's grace, by His sanctifying their progress, even as He sanctified their beginning. And thus the apostle likewise says: "He who has begun a good work in you, will perform it until the day of Jesus Christ" (Phil.1:6).

Sermons on John, 108:2

Love for God gives us security and makes us bold to face the day of judgment

Now concerning this same boldness, let us see what he says. From what source do we understand that love is perfect? "There is no fear in love" (1 Jn.4:18). Then what do we say of him that has begun to fear the day of judgment? If love were perfect in him, he would not fear. For perfect love would make perfect righteousness, and he would have nothing to fear. Indeed, he would have something to desire: that iniquity may pass away, and God's kingdom come. So then, "there is no fear in love." But in what love? Not in love begun: in what then? "But perfect love," he says, "casts out fear" (1 Jn.4:18). Then let fear make the beginning, because "the fear of the Lord is the beginning of wisdom" (Prov.1:7). Fear, so to speak, prepares a place for love. But when once love has begun to dwell there, the fear which prepared the place for it is cast out. For in proportion as this love increases, the fear decreases; and the more this love comes to be within, the fear is cast out. Greater love, less fear: less love, greater fear.

But if there is no fear, there is no way for love to come in. As we see in sewing, the thread is introduced by means of the needle; the needle first enters, but unless it comes out, the thread does not come into its place. Likewise, fear first occupies the mind, but the fear does not remain there, because it enters only in order to introduce love. When once there is the sense of security in the mind, what joy we have, both in this world and in the world to come! Even in this world, who shall hurt us, being full of love? See how the apostle exults over this very love: "Who shall separate us from the love of Christ? Shall tribulation, or distress, or persecution, or famine, or nakedness, or peril, or sword?" (Rom.8:35). And Peter says: "And who will harm you, if you are followers of what is good?" (1 Pet.3:13). "There is no fear in love; but perfect love casts out fear, because fear has torment."

Sermons on the First Letter of John, 9:4

None of the elect can perish

Of such says the apostle, "We know that to those who love God He works together all things for good, to those who are called according to His purpose; because those whom He foreknew, He also predestined to be conformed to the image of His Son, that He might be the first-born among many brothers. Moreover, those whom He predestined, He also called; and those whom He called, He also justified; and those whom He justified, He also glorified" (Rom.8:28-30). Of these not one perishes, because all are elected. And they are elected because they were called according to the purpose — not their own purpose, but God's. Of this purpose, Paul elsewhere says, "That the purpose of God according to election might stand, not by works, but by Him Who calls, it was said to her that the elder shall serve the younger" (Rom.9:11-12). And in another place he says, "Not according to our works, but according to His own purpose and grace" (2 Tim.1:9).

When, therefore, we hear, "Moreover, those whom He predestined, He also called," we ought to acknowledge that they were called according to God's purpose. For Paul began by saying, "He works together all things for good to those who are called according to His purpose," and then added, "Because those whom He foreknew, He also predestined to be conformed to the image of His Son, that He might be the first-born among many brothers." And to these promises He added, "Moreover, those whom He predestined, He also called."

So then, Paul wishes these to be understood as those whom God called according to His purpose, in case any among them should be thought to be called but not chosen, on account of that sentence of the Lord's: "Many are called but few are chosen" (Matt.20:16). For whoever are chosen are without doubt also called; but whoever are called are not necessarily chosen. Those, then, are elected, as I have often said, who are called according to God's purpose, who also are predestined and foreknown. If any one of these perishes, God is mistaken; but none of them perishes, because God is not mistaken. If any one of these perishes, God is overcome by human sin; but none of them perishes, because God is overcome by nothing.

On Rebuke and Grace, 14

None of Christ's little ones, known by humility, can perish

"And this," He says, "is the will of the Father that sent Me, that of all that He has given Me I should lose nothing" (Jn.6:39). Whoever continues in humility was given to Christ; Christ receives such a person. Whoever fails to keep humility is far from the Master of humility. "That of all He has given Me, I should lose nothing." "So it is not the will of your Father that one of these little ones should perish" (Matt.18:14). The proud may perish; but of the little ones, none perish. For "if you will not become as this little one, you shall not enter into the kingdom of heaven" (Matt.18:3). "Of all that the Father has given me, I shall lose nothing, but I will raise it up again on the last day."

Sermons on John, 25:19

The saints cannot help persevering!

Food does not necessarily cause a person to live, and yet without food he cannot live. Therefore the first man [Adam], in that goodness in which he had been created upright, received the ability not to sin, the ability not to die, the ability not to forsake that goodness. He was also was given the aid of perseverance — not the perseverance by which it would be brought about that he would *actually* persevere, but the perseverance *without* which he could not persevere by free will alone.

But now, to the saints predestined to the kingdom of God by God's grace, the help of perseverance that is given is not like the help given to Adam. To the saints, perseverance itself is bestowed. They are not only given the gift by means of which they *can* persevere; more than that, they are given the gift by means of which they cannot *help* persevering. For not only did Christ say, "Without me you can do nothing" (Jn.15:5), but He also said, "You have not chosen me, but I have chosen you, and appointed you to go and bring forth fruit, and that your fruit should remain" (Jn.15:16). By these words, He showed that He had given them not only righteousness, but perseverance in righteousness. For when Christ appointed them to go and bring forth fruit, and that their fruit should remain, who would dare to say, It shall not remain? Who would dare even to say, Perhaps it will not remain? "For the gifts and calling of God are without repentance" (Rom.11:29). But the calling is of those who are called according to God's purpose. When Christ intercedes, therefore, on behalf of these, that their faith should not fail, doubtless it will not fail, even to the end. And thus their faith shall persevere even to the end; and the end of this life will find their faith continuing.

On Rebuke and Grace, 34

We commend ourselves to God that He may preserve our faith

[Pelagius says] "What, then, is the meaning of what the same apostle says: 'I have fought a good fight, I have finished my course, I have kept the faith; henceforth there is laid up for me a crown of righteousness, which the Lord, the righteous judge, shall give me at that day' (1 Tim.4:7-8)? Surely these are rewards paid to the worthy, not gifts bestowed on the unworthy!"

Pelagius does not consider that the crown could not have been given to the man who is worthy of it, unless grace had been first bestowed on him while he was unworthy of it. Paul says indeed: "I have fought a good fight," but he also says: "Thanks be to God, Who gives us the victory through Jesus Christ our Lord" (1 Cor.15:57). He says too: "I have finished my course," but he says again: "It is not of him that wills, nor of him that runs, but of God that shows mercy" (Rom.9:16). He says, moreover: "I have kept the faith," but then Paul is also the one who says: "I know whom I have believed, and am persuaded that He is able to keep my deposit against that day" (2 Tim.1:12) — that is, "my commendation", for some copies do not have the word deposit, but commendation, which gives a clearer sense. Now, what do we commend to God's keeping, except the things which we pray Him to preserve for us, and among these our very faith? For what else did the Lord procure for the apostle Peter by His prayer for him, of which He said, "I have prayed for you, Peter, that your faith may not fail" (Lk.22:32)? Surely the Lord here procured that God would preserve Peter's faith, that it should not fail by giving way to temptation.

Therefore, blessed Paul, great preacher of grace, I will say it without fear of any man (for who will be less angry with me for saying so than yourself, who have told us what to say, and taught us what to teach?) — I will, I repeat, say it, and fear no man for the assertion: Your crown is a reward for your virtues; but your virtues are the gifts of God!

On the Proceedings of Pelagius, 35

If the elect fall, God restores them

Paul signified such persons to Timothy, where he said that Hymenaeus and Philetus had subverted the faith of some, but then added, "Nevertheless the foundation of God stands sure, having this seal, The Lord has known those who are His" (2 Tim.2:19). The faith of these, which works by love, actually does not fail at all; or if there are any of them whose faith fails, it is restored before their life is ended, and the iniquity which had intervened is done away, and perseverance even to the end is granted to them.

But then there are those who are not destined to persevere, and who will fall away from Christian faith and conduct, so that the end of this life shall find them in that fallen state. Beyond all doubt, such are not to be reckoned in the number of these [whom the Lord knows as His], even during that time when they are living rightly and piously. For they are not made to differ from the mass of destruction by the foreknowledge and predestination of God, and therefore they are not called according to God's purpose (Rom.8:28-30), and thus they are not elected. No, they are "called" among those of whom it was said, "Many are called," but not among those of whom it was said, "few are chosen" (Matt.20:16).

And yet who can deny that they are elect, since they believe and are baptised, and live according to God? Manifestly, they are called elect by those who are ignorant of what they *will* be, but not by God Who knew that they would not have the perseverance which leads the elect forward into the blessed life, and knows that they "stand" only in the context of His foreknowledge that one day they will fall.

On Rebuke and Grace, 16

Election is demonstrated by continuing with Christ

"The words that I have spoken to you are spirit and life. But there are some of you who do not believe. For Jesus knew from the beginning who were the believing ones, and who would betray Him; and He said, Therefore I said to you, that no-one comes to Me unless it has been granted by my Father. From this time many of His disciples went away from Him, and no longer walked with Him" (Jn.6:63-6). Are not even these people in the words of the gospel called disciples? And yet they were not truly disciples, because they did not continue in His word, according to what He says: "If you continue in My word, then you are indeed My disciples" (Jn.8:31).

So then, because they did not possess the gift of perseverance, they were not truly disciples of Christ; and so they were not truly children of God even when they appeared to be so, and were called such. *We* call people "elect", and "Christ's disciples", and "God's children", because we see them living a godly life as regenerate people — and this is proper. But they are only *truly* what they are called if they *abide* in that life on account of which we call them God's children. However, if they do not have the gift of perseverance — that is, if they do not continue in what they have begun to be — then *we* may *call* them God's children, but they are not truly such. For they are not God's children in the sight of Him to Whom it is known what they are going to be — that is to say, Who sees that from being good people, they will become bad people.

On Rebuke and Grace, 22

Only the predestined are truly God's children

John says, "They went out from us, but they were not of us, because if they had been of us, they would, no doubt, have continued with us" (1 Jn.2:19). He does not say, "They went out from us, but because they did not abide with us they are no longer now of us." Rather he says, "They went out from us, but they were not of us" — that is to say, even when they appeared among us, they were not of us. And as if it were said to him, "How do you prove this?" he says, "Because if they had been of us, they would assuredly have continued with us".… It is not, therefore, to His own predestined children that God has failed to give perseverance; for they [who fell away] would have had perseverance, if they were among that number of children. And what would they have which they had not received, according to the apostolic and true judgment?

And thus such children would be given to Christ the Son just as He Himself says to the Father, "That all whom You have given Me may not perish, but have eternal life" (Jn.17:12). Those, therefore, are understood to be given to Christ who are ordained to eternal life. These are the ones who are predestined and called according to God's purpose, of whom not one perishes. And therefore if any of them changes from good to evil, he will not die in that state; for he is ordained, and for that purpose given to Christ, that he may not perish, but may have eternal life. And again, those whom we call His enemies, or the infant children of His enemies, whichever of them He will regenerate so that they may leave this life in the faith which works by love — these, even before they are regenerated, are already God's children according to predestination. And they are given to Christ His Son, that they may not perish, but have everlasting life.

On Rebuke and Grace, 20-21

Only those called according to God's purpose are God's children and cannot perish

For this reason the apostle, after he had said, "We know that to those who love God, He works all things together for good" (Rom.8:28) — knowing that some people love God, but do not continue in that good way to the end, he immediately added, "to those who are the called according to His purpose." For these called ones continue in their love for God even to the end. And if they wander from the way for a season, they return, so that they may continue to the end what they had begun to be in goodness. To show, however, what it means to be "called according to God's purpose", he immediately added what I have already quoted above, "Because those whom He foreknew, He also predestined to be conformed to the image of His Son, that He might be the first-born among many brothers. Moreover, those whom He predestined, He also called" — namely, according to His purpose — "and those whom He called, He also justified; and those whom He justified, He also glorified" (Rom.8:29-30).

All those things are already done: He foreknew, He predestined, He called, He justified. For all [the elect] are already foreknown and predestined, and many are already called and justified; but what he placed at the end, "He also glorified" (if, indeed, we are to understand by "glory" here the attribute of which the same apostle says, "When Christ your life shall appear, then you will also appear with Him in glory," Col.3:4), this is not yet accomplished. However, even those two things — that is, He called and He justified — have not been accomplished in all of those about whom it is said; for still, even until the end of the world, there remain many to be called and justified. Nevertheless, Paul used verbs of the past tense, even concerning things future, as if God had already arranged from eternity that they should come to pass ...

Whoever, therefore, in God's most providential ordering, are foreknown, predestined, called, justified, glorified — these, although they are not yet born again, and even although they are not yet born at all, are already children of God, and absolutely cannot perish. These truly come to Christ, because they come in such a way as He Himself says, "All that the Father gives Me will come to Me, and him that comes to Me I will not cast out" (Jn.6:37). And a little later, He says, "This is the will of the Father Who sent Me, that of all that He has given Me I shall lose nothing" (Jn.6:39). From Him, therefore, also comes the gift of perseverance in good even to the end; for it is given only to those who shall not perish, since those who do not persevere shall perish.

On Rebuke and Grace, 23

Only the gift of perseverance lifts us out of the condemned mass of humanity in Adam

Consequently, those who have not heard the gospel — and those who, having heard the gospel and been changed by it for the better, have not received the gift of perseverance — and those who, having heard the gospel, have refused to come to Christ, that is, to believe in Him (since He Himself says, "No-one comes to Me, unless it has been granted to him by my Father," Jn.6:65) — and those who by their tender age were unable to believe, but could be absolved from original sin by the sole washing of regeneration, and yet have not received this washing, and have perished in death: none of these [four categories] are made to differ from that mass of mankind which clearly is condemned. For they all go from one [sinful state] into condemnation.

Some are made to differ, however, not by their own merits, but by the grace of the Mediator. That is to say, they are justified freely in the blood of the second Adam. We hear, "For who makes you to differ? What do you have which you have not received? Now, if you have received it, why do you boast as if you had not received it?" (1 Cor.4:7). From this we ought to understand that from that mass of destruction which originated through the first Adam, no-one can be made to differ except he who has this gift [of perseverance]. And whoever has it, has received it by the grace of the Saviour. And this apostolic testimony is so great, that the blessed Cyprian writing to Quirinus put it down as a chapter heading, when he says, "That we must boast in nothing, since nothing is our own."

On Rebuke and Grace, 12

The millennial binding of Satan: he cannot harm the elect

"And he cast him into the abyss" (Rev.20:3) — *i.e.*, cast the devil into the abyss. By the abyss is meant the countless multitude of the wicked whose hearts are unfathomably deep in their hostility against the Church of God. Not that the devil was not in the abyss previously, but he is said to be cast there, because he is prevented from harming believers, and thus takes more complete possession of the ungodly.

For that person is more fully possessed by the devil who is not only alienated from God, but also unwarrantably hates those who serve God. "And he shut him up, and set a seal upon him, that he should deceive the nations no more till the thousand years should be fulfilled" (Rev.20:3). "Shut him up" — *i.e.*, prohibited him from going out, from doing what was forbidden.

The addition of "set a seal upon him" seems to me to mean that it was designed to keep it a secret who belonged to the devil's party and who did not. For in this world this is a secret. We cannot tell whether even the person who seems to stand shall fall, or whether he who seems to be fallen shall rise again. Still, by the chain and prison-house of this interdict, the devil is prohibited and restrained from seducing those nations which belong to Christ, but which he formerly seduced or held in subjection. For before the creation of the world, God chose to rescue these nations from the power of darkness, and to transfer them into the kingdom of His beloved Son, as the apostle says. For what Christian is not aware that the devil seduces nations even now, and draws them with himself to eternal punishment? But he does not harm those predestined to eternal life.

And let no-one be dismayed by the fact that the devil often seduces even those who have been regenerated in Christ, and begun to walk in God's way. For "the Lord knows those who are His" (2 Tim.2:19); and of these, the devil seduces none to eternal damnation. For it is in His nature as God that the Lord knows them — God, from Whom nothing is hidden even of future things. The Lord does not know them as a human being does. For one human being sees another in his present condition (if he can be said to see one whose heart he does not see); but he does not see even himself so far as to be able to know what kind of person he will in future be.

City of God, 20:7

How greatly we need the gift of perseverance!

Certainly a greater liberty is necessary in the face of so many and so great temptations, which had no existence in Paradise. We need a liberty fortified and confirmed by the gift of perseverance, so that we may overcome this world, with all its loves, its fears, and its errors. The martyrdoms of the saints have taught this. In short, Adam had nobody to make him afraid, and yet in spite of the authority of God's fear, he used his free will to fall from such a state of happiness, such an ability of not sinning. But the martyrs, I say, not under the fear of the world, but in spite of the rage of the world aimed at making them fall, stood firm in the faith. Adam could see the good things present which he was going to forsake; the martyrs could not see the good things future which they were going to receive. How did this come about, save by the gift of Him from whom they obtained mercy to be faithful? From Him they received the spirit, not of fear, by which to yield to the persecutors, but the spirit of power, and of love, and of self-control, in which they could overcome all threats, all seductions, all torments.

To Adam, then, without any sin, was given the free will with which he was created; and Adam used it to serve sin. But although the will of the saints had once been the servant of sin, their will was delivered by Him who said, "If the Son shall make you free, you shall be free indeed" (Jn. 8:36). And by that grace they receive a great freedom. For although as long as they live on earth, they are fighting against sinful lusts, and some sins creep upon them unawares, on account of which they daily say, "Forgive us our debts" (Matt.6:12), yet they do not any more obey the sin which is unto death. Of this the apostle John says, "There is a sin unto death: I do not say that he should pray for that" (1 Jn.5:16). Concerning this sin (since it is not expressed) many and different notions may be entertained. I, however, say that this sin is to forsake even unto death the faith which works by love. This sin the saints no longer serve. They are not in the first condition, as Adam was, the condition of being *free*; rather, they are *set free* by the grace of God through the second Adam. By that deliverance they have the free will which enables them to serve God, and not that by which they may be made captive by the devil. By being set free from sin, they have become the servants of righteousness, in which they will stand till the end, by the gift of perseverance given to them by Him who foreknew them, predestined them, called them according to His purpose, justified them, and glorified them, since He has even already formed those things that are to come which He promised concerning them.

On Rebuke and Grace, 35

Our weakness must glory in the Lord when we persevere

God willed that His saints should not — even concerning perseverance in goodness itself— glory in their own strength, but in Himself. For He not only gives them such help as He gave to the first man, without which they cannot persevere even if they will; but He also causes in them also the will to persevere. Since they will not persevere unless they both can and will, both the capability and the will to persevere are bestowed on them by the generosity of divine grace. By the Holy Spirit, their will is so much enkindled that they can persevere, because they will to persevere; and they so will because God works in them to will.

For let us suppose in the great weakness of this life (in which weakness, however, for the sake of checking pride, strength is to be perfected), their own will were left to themselves, that they might, if they willed, continue in the help of God, without which they could not persevere. Let us suppose that God did not work in them the will to persevere, in the midst of so many and so great weaknesses. In that case, their will itself would give way, and they would not be able to persevere. Why? Because failing from infirmity, they would not will to persevere; or in the weakness of will, they would not will to persevere in such a way that they would be able to do it. Therefore help is brought to the infirmity of the human will, so that it might be unchangeably and invincibly influenced by divine grace; and thus, although weak, it still will not fail, nor be overcome by any adversity.

Thus it happens that the human will, weak and incapable, immature in goodness, perseveres by God's strength. By contrast, the will of the first man was strong and healthy, and enjoyed the power of free choice, and yet did not persevere in a greater good. For although God's help was not lacking, without which Adam's will could not persevere even if it would, yet this grace was not so great a help as that by which God would actually work perseverance in the human will. To the strongest will of Adam, He yielded and permitted it to do what Adam willed [sin]; but to those who were weak, He has reserved it that by His own gift they should most invincibly will what is good, and most invincibly refuse to forsake this good. Therefore when Christ says, "I have prayed for you that your faith may not fail" (Lk.22:32), we may understand that it was said to him who is built upon the rock. And thus if the man of God glories, he must glory in the Lord, not only because he has obtained mercy to be faithful (1 Cor.7:25), but also because his faith itself does not fail.

On Rebuke and Grace, 38

The mysterious nature of God's grace in perseverance

Of two godly men, why one should be given perseverance to the end, but it should not be given to the other — here God's judgments are even more unsearchable. Yet to believers it ought to be a most certain fact that the former [who perseveres] is among the predestined, and the latter is not. "For if they had been of us," says one of the predestined, who had drunk this secret from the breast of the Lord, "certainly they would have continued with us" (1 Jn.2:19). What, I ask, is the meaning of, "They were not of us; for if they had been of us, they would certainly have continued with us"? Were not both created by God — both born of Adam — both made from the earth, and given souls of one and the same nature by Him who said, "I have created all breath"(Isa.57:16, Septuagint)? Lastly, had not both been called, and followed Him that called them? And had not both, having been wicked men, become justified men, and both been renewed by the washing of regeneration?

But if John were to hear this (and beyond all doubt, he knew what he was saying), he might answer: These things are true. In respect of all these things, they were of us. Nevertheless, in respect of a certain other distinction, they were not of us, for if they had been of us, they certainly would have continued with us. What then is this distinction? God's books lie open, let us not turn away our view; the divine Scripture cries aloud, let us give it a hearing. They were not of them, because they had not been "called according to the purpose" (Rom.8:28); they had not been chosen in Christ before the creation of the world (Eph.1:4); they had not gained a destiny in Him; they had not been predestined according to His purpose who works all things (Eph.1:11). For if they *had* been this, they would have been "of them", and without doubt they would have continued with them.

On the Gift of Perseverance, 21

Lifelong Church membership is not the same as persevering in Christ!

People who lead an abandoned and depraved life must not be confident of salvation, even though they persevere to the end in the communion of the Catholic Church, and comfort themselves with the words, "He that endures to the end shall be saved." By the iniquity of their life, they abandon the righteousness of life that Christ offers to them, whether by fornication, or by perpetrating in their body the other unclean acts which the apostle would not so much as mention, or by a corrupt luxury, or by doing any of those things of which he says, "Those who do such things shall not inherit the kingdom of God" (Gal.5:21).

Consequently, those who do such things will not exist anywhere but in eternal punishment, since they cannot be in the kingdom of God. For while they continue in such sinful things to the very end of life, they cannot be said to abide in Christ to the end. To abide in Christ is to abide in the faith of Christ. And this faith, according to the apostle's definition of it, "works by love" (Gal.5:6). And "love," as he elsewhere says, "works no evil" (Rom.13:10).

Neither can these people be said to eat the body of Christ, for they cannot even be reckoned among His members. Not to mention other reasons, they cannot be at once the members of Christ and the members of a prostitute. In short, Christ Himself, when He says, "He who eats My flesh and drinks My blood dwells in me, and I in him" (Jn.6:56), shows what it is in reality, and not sacramentally, to eat His body and drink His blood. It means to dwell in Christ, that He also may dwell in us. It is as if He said, "He who does not dwell in Me, and in whom I do not dwell, let him not say or think that he eats My body or drinks My blood." Accordingly, those who are not Christ's members do not dwell in Him. And those who unite themselves with a prostitute are not members of Christ unless they have penitently abandoned that evil, and have returned to the good in order to be reconciled to it.

City of God, 21:25

[Let us end on a positive note with Augustine's words of reassurance to those Christians who fear they may not be true disciples and thus lack the gift of perseverance. I have already quoted these words at the end of the chapter on predestination and election, but they are worth hearing again:]

What I have said about the way that predestination should be preached will not be adequate for him who speaks to a congregation, unless he adds this, or something like it: "You, therefore, ought to hope that the gift of persevering in obedience will be given to you by the Father of Lights, from Whom comes down every excellent gift and every perfect gift (Jam.1:17); and you ought to ask for this gift in your daily prayers. And in doing this, *you ought to trust that you are not aliens from the predestination of His people,* because it is God Himself Who bestows even the power of praying for perseverance. Far be it from you to despair of yourselves! For you are bidden to put your hope in God, not in yourselves. Indeed, cursed is everyone who puts his hope in man (Jer.17:5). It is better to trust in the Lord than to trust in man, for blessed are all those who put their trust in the Lord. Holding this hope, serve the Lord in fear, and rejoice before Him with trembling. No-one can securely enjoy the eternal life which God, Who does not lie, has promised from eternity to the children of promise — no-one, until that life of his, which is a state of trial upon the earth, is completed. *But He will make us persevere in Himself to the end of this life,* since we daily say to Him, 'Lead us not into temptation.'"

When these and similar things are said, whether to few Christians or to the multitude of the Church, why do we fear to preach the predestination of the saints and the true grace of God — that is, the grace which is not given according to our virtues — as the Holy Scripture declares it? Or must it be feared that a person should despair of himself, when his hope is shown to be placed in God? Should he not rather despair of himself if, in his excess of pride and unhappiness, he places his hope in himself?

On the Gift of Perseverance, 62

Appendix 1

The anti-Pelagian canons of the council of Carthage, 418 AD

1. If anyone says that Adam, the first man, was created mortal, so that whether or not he sinned, he would have died from natural causes, and not as the wages of sin: let him be anathema.

2. If anyone says that new-born children do not need to be baptised, or that they are baptised "for the forgiveness of sins" even though no original sin is derived from Adam to be washed away in the washing of regeneration, so that in their case the baptismal formula "for the forgiveness of sins" is to be understood in a fictitious sense and not in its true sense: let him be anathema.[1]

3. If anyone says that there is in the kingdom of heaven, or in any other place, a middle zone where children who depart this life unbaptised live in bliss: let him be anathema.

4. If anyone says that the grace of God, by which humanity is justified through Jesus Christ our Lord, avails only for the forgiveness of sins already committed, and not for assistance to prevent the further commission of sins: let him be anathema.

5. If anyone says that this same grace of God through our Lord Jesus Christ helps us not to sin merely because it reveals and opens to us an understanding of the commandments, so that we may know what to seek and what to avoid, but that it does not give us the love and strength to do what we have recognised to be our duty: let him be anathema. For since the apostle says, "Love builds up, but

---

[1] For Augustine's views on infant baptism, see the introduction to Chapter 1.

knowledge puffs up" (1 Cor.8:1), it would be very wrong to believe that we have the grace of Christ for the knowledge which puffs up, but not for the love which builds up. For both are gifts of God — both the knowledge of what we ought to do and the love to do it, so that built up by love we may not be puffed up by knowledge. Just as it is written of God: "He teaches people knowledge" (Ps.94:10), so too it is written: "Love is from God" (1 Jn.4:7).

6. If anyone says that the grace of justification is given to us so that we may do more easily with grace what we are commanded to do by means of our free will, as if even without grace we were able (though not easily) to fulfil the divine commands: let him be anathema. For when the Lord spoke of the fruits of the commands, He did not say that without Him we could do these things only with difficulty, but rather, "Without Me, you can do nothing" (Jn.15:5).

7. When St John the apostle says, "If we say we have no sin we deceive ourselves, and the truth is not in us" (1 Jn.1:8), whoever understands this to mean that we must say "We have no sin" out of humility, not because it is true: let him be anathema. For the apostle continues, "If we confess our sins, He is faithful and righteous to forgive us our sins and cleanse us from all unrighteousness" (1 Jn.1:9). From this passage it is quite clear that this is not said only out of humility, but also in truth. For the apostle could have said, "If we say we have no sin, we are boasting and humility is not in us." But since he says, "We deceive ourselves and the truth is not in us," he clearly shows that anyone who says he has no sin is speaking not truly but falsely.

8. If any says that the reason why the saints say in the Lord's prayer, "forgive us our debts," is not that they are saying it for themselves, because this petition is no longer necessary for them, but for others among their people who are sinners, and that this is why the saints do not say "forgive me my debts" but "forgive us our debts," so that the righteous person is understood to pray for others, not for himself: let him be anathema. For the apostle James was a holy and righteous man when he said, "We all stumble in many things" (Jam.3:2). Why was the word "all" added, if not to bring the expression into harmony with the psalm where we read, "Do not enter into judgment with Your servant, for no living person is righteous before You"

(Ps.143:2)? And in the prayer of Solomon, the wise man: "There is no-one who does not sin" (1 Kings 8:46). And in the book of the holy man Job: "He seals up the hand of every man, so that every man may know his weakness" (Job 37:7).[2] Even the holy and righteous Daniel used the plural in his prayer when he said: "We have sinned, we have done wickedly" (Dan.9:5,15), and other things which he truly and humbly confesses. And in case anyone thinks, as some do, that he was not speaking of his own sins, but of the sins of his people, he also said: "While I was praying and confessing my sin and the sin of my people to the Lord my God" (Dan.9:20). He would not say "our sins", but spoke of the sins of his people *and his own sins*; for as a prophet, he foresaw that in the future there would be some who would badly misunderstand him.

9. If anyone says that the words of the Lord's prayer where we say, "forgive us our debts," are said by the saints out of humility but not truthfully: let him be anathema. Who could tolerate that a man who prays should lie not to men but to the Lord Himself, by saying that he wishes to be forgiven, while in his heart denying that he has any debts to be forgiven?

The "Indiculus" (between 435 and 442 AD)

1. In the sin of Adam, all human beings lost their natural power for good and their innocence. No-one can by his own free will rise up out of the depth of this fall, unless he is lifted up by the grace of the merciful God. This is the pronouncement of pope Innocent of blessed memory in his letter to the council of Carthage: He [Adam] acted by his own free will when he used his gifts recklessly; he fell into the chasm of sin, sank, and found no means to rise again. Betrayed for ever by his freedom, he would have remained weighed down by his fall unless the future coming of Christ had not raised him up again by His grace, when through the cleansing of a new regeneration all previous guilt was washed away in the bath of His baptism.

---

[2] This is an ancient mistranslation from the Hebrew.

2. No-one is good from himself, unless God alone Who is good makes him to participate in Himself. This is what the same pope declares in the same letter where he says: "Can we now expect anything good from those who think they can attribute to themselves the fact that they are good, without considering Him Whose grace they receive every day, and who trust that apart from Him they can achieve so much?"

3. Nobody — not even the one who has been renewed by the grace of baptism — is capable of overcoming the pitfalls of the devil and vanquishing the lust of the flesh, unless he receives perseverance in good conduct through God's help every day. This truth is confirmed by the teaching of the same pope in the above-quoted letter: "For although He redeemed humanity from its past sins, knowing that humanity could sin again, He kept many means by which He could restore people and set them right afterwards, offering us those daily remedies on which we must always rely with confidence and trust. For by no other means will we ever be able to overcome our human errors. For it is unavoidable that without His help we are vanquished, even as with His help we vanquish ... All the efforts and all the works and merits of the saints must be referred to the praise and glory of God, for no-one can please Him except by means of what He Himself has given" ...

5. God works in human hearts and in the free will itself, so that a holy thought, a good purpose, and every movement of a good will, come from God, since it is through Him that we are able to do any good, and without Him we can do nothing. The same teacher [pope] Zosimus instructed us to profess this doctrine when he addressed the bishops of the whole world concerning the assistance of divine grace, saying, "Is there ever a time when we do not need God's help? In all our actions and affairs, in all our thoughts and inclinations, we must pray to Him as our Helper and Protector. For it is the pride of our human nature to claim things for itself, whereas the apostle declares, 'We are not struggling with flesh and blood, but with the principalities, the powers, the world rulers of this present darkness, the spiritual hosts of wickedness in the heavenly places' (Eph.6:12). As he also says: 'Wretched man that I am! Who will rescue me from this body of death? The grace of God, through Jesus Christ our Lord!' (Rom.7:24, Vulgate). Again: 'By the grace of God

I am what I am. And His grace towards me was not in vain. On the contrary, I worked harder than any of them — yet not I, but the grace of God which is in me'" (1 Cor.15:10) ...

9. Therefore with the Lord's help we are strengthened by these standards of the Church and these documents derived from divine authority, so that we confess God as the author of all good desires and deeds, of all efforts and virtues by which a person moves towards God, from the very beginning of faith. We do not doubt that all human merits are preceded by the grace of Him through Whom we begin to will and to do any good work. By this help and gift of God, free will is surely not destroyed but set free, so that it is brought into light out of darkness, to uprightness out of evil, to health out of sickness, to wisdom out of folly. For such is God's goodness to all, He wishes His own gifts to be our merits, and He will give us an eternal reward for what He has Himself bestowed on us. In fact, God works in us so that we will and do what He wills. He does not allow to lie idle in us what He gave us for the purpose of being employed, not neglected, so that we may cooperate with the grace of God. And if we perceive that something is growing slack in us because of our negligence, we should turn seriously to Him Who heals all our diseases and redeems our life from destruction, to Whom we say every day, "Lead us not into temptation but deliver us from evil."

Whatever is contrary to the above statements, we clearly consider not to be Catholic.

The canons of the synod of Orange, 529 AD: against Semi-Pelagianism

[There are 25 canons. Here are the most important:]

1. If anyone says that through the offence of Adam's sin the whole of our humanity, body and soul, was not changed for the worse, but rather believes that only the body was subjected to corruption, while the freedom of the soul remained undamaged, he is led astray by the error of Pelagius, and goes against Scripture which says, "the soul that sins shall die" (Ezek.18:20) and "do you not know that if you surrender yourselves to anyone as obedient slaves, you are the slaves

of the one you obey?" (Rom.6:16), and again, "whatever overcomes a man, he is enslaved by it" (2 Pet.2:19).

2   If anyone maintains that the fall damaged Adam alone, and not his descendants, or declares that only physical death (the punishment of sin) but not sin itself (the death of the soul) is passed on to the entire human race by the one man, he ascribes injustice to God[3] and contradicts the apostle's words: "Sin came into the world through one man, and death through sin, and so death spread to all men because all sinned in him" (Rom.5:12).

3. If anyone says that God's grace can be conferred on account of human prayer, and not that grace is the very thing that moves us to pray, he contradicts the prophet Isaiah, or the apostle who says the same thing: "I have been found by those who did not seek me; I have shown Myself to those who did not ask for Me" (Isa.65:1, Rom.10:20).

4. If anyone argues that God waits for our will before cleansing us from sin, but does not confess that even the desire to be cleansed is aroused in us by the infusion and action of the Holy Spirit, he opposes the Holy Spirit Himself speaking through Solomon: "The will is prepared by the Lord" (Prov.8:35, Septuagint), and the apostle's health-giving message, "God is at work within you, both to will and to work for His good pleasure" (Phil.2:13).

5. If anyone says that the increase as well as the beginning of faith, and the very desire for faith, by which we believe in Him Who justifies the sinner and by which we come to the regeneration of holy baptism, proceeds from our own nature and not from a gift of grace, that is, from the inspiration of the Holy Spirit changing our will from unbelief to faith and from ungodliness to godliness, such a person shows himself to be in contradiction with the apostolic doctrine, since Paul writes: "I am persuaded that He Who began a good work in you will bring it to completion on the day of Christ Jesus" (Phil.1:6), and

---

[3] He ascribes injustice to God by saying that *death* is passed on to everyone from Adam, but not *sin*. In that case, God is punishing the human race unjustly when He consigns it to death. The universal inheritance of Adam's sin is the righteous basis for the universal inheritance of Adam's death.

again, "It has been granted to you for Christ's sake that you should not only believe in Him but suffer for His sake" (Phil.1:29); and again, "By grace you have been saved, through faith; and this is not your own doing, it is the gift of God" (Eph.2:8). For those who say that the faith by which we believe in God is natural, declare that all those who are strangers to the Church of Christ are, in some sense, believers.

6. If anyone says that mercy is bestowed on us by God when, without God's grace, we believe, will, desire, strive, labour, pray, keep watch, endeavour, request, seek, and knock, but does not confess that it is through the in-pouring and inspiration of the Holy Spirit that we believe, will, or are able to do all these things that are required; or if anyone subordinates the help of grace to humility or human obedience, and does not acknowledge that it is precisely the gift of grace that makes us obedient and humble, then he contradicts the apostle who says, "What do you have that you did not receive?" (1 Cor.4:7) and also, "By the grace of God I am what I am" (1 Cor.15:10).

7. If anyone asserts that by his natural strength he is able to think as God requires him to think, or choose anything good regarding his eternal salvation, or assent to the saving message of the gospel without the Holy Spirit's illumination and inspiration, Who alone gives freeness and joy in assenting to the truth and believing it, such a person is deceived by a heretical spirit and does not understand what God said in the gospel, "Apart from Me, you can do nothing" (Jn.15:5), nor the apostle's word, "Not that we are sufficient of ourselves to think of anything as coming from ourselves, but our sufficiency is from God" (2 Cor.3:5).

8. If anyone maintains that some people are able to come to the grace of baptism through divine mercy, but others through their own free will — a will that is plainly injured from the first man's transgression in all who are born — he shows that he has departed from the orthodox faith. For he does not confess that free will has been weakened in all human beings by the sin of the first man. Or at least he holds that free will has only been injured to the degree that some are still able to attain to the mystery of eternal salvation by themselves, without divine revelation. Yet the Lord Himself proves

that the opposite is true. For He does not testify that some people can come to Him, but that nobody can, unless a person is drawn by the Father (Jn.6:44). He also says to Peter, "Blessed are you, Simon bar-Jonah, for flesh and blood have not revealed this to you, but my Father in heaven" (Matt.16:17). And the apostle too says, "No-one can say 'Jesus is Lord' except by the Holy Spirit" (1 Cor.12:3) ...

Appendix 2

The writings of Augustine

All the English renderings of Augustine in this book are my own. In the order in which Augustine wrote them, I have quoted from the following. The figure(s) after the title give the date(s) when each work was probably written. Sometimes a particular work was written in stages over a period of time, e.g. *City of God* between 413 and 422.

Expositions of the Psalms (392-420)
On Faith and the Creed (393)
Reply to Faustus the Manichee (397-8)
Confessions (397-401)
On the Nature of Good (399)
On the Catechising of the Uninstructed (399-400)
On the Trinity (399-419)
Harmony of the Gospels (400)
On the Work of Monks (400-401)
On the Merits and Forgiveness of Sins (411-12)
On the Spirit and the Letter (412)
City of God (413-22)
Sermons on John (414-17)
On Nature and Grace (415)
On Human Perfection (415-16)
Sermons on the First Letter of John (415-16)
On the Proceedings of Pelagius (417)
On Patience (417-18)
On the Grace of Christ and Original Sin (418)
On Continence (418 or 420)

On Marriage and Concupiscence (419-21)
On the Soul and its Origin (419-21)
Against Two Letters of the Pelagians (420-21)
Enchiridion (421-3)[1]
On Grace and Free Will (426-7)
On Rebuke and Grace (426-7)
On the Gift of Perseverance (428-9)
On the Predestination of the Saints (428-9)

We also have:
Sermons on the Gospels (a collection of sermons preached at various times)
Letters (throughout Augustine's active Christian life)

For the student who is just beginning to get to grips with Augustine, the following books are recommended:

Augustine's writings

John Baillie, John T.McNeill and Henry P.Van Dusen (editors), *The Library of Christian Classics*, vol.6, *Augustine: Earlier Writings* (translated with introductions by John H.S.Burleigh, London 1953); vol.7, *Augustine: Confessions and Enchiridion* (translated and edited by Albert C.Outler, London 1955); vol.8, *Augustine: Later Works* (translated with introductions by John Burnaby, London 1955). (These are readable modern translations of many of Augustine's most important writings.)

Vernon J.Bourke (editor), *The Essential Augustine* (Indianapolis 1974) (Quotations from Augustine arranged under thematic headings with introductions and comments by Bourke, professor of philosophy at St Louis university from 1946.)

---

[1] *Enchiridion* means manual or handbook.

Henry Chadwick (translator), *Confessions* (Oxford 1991) (The most recent translation, by the great Anglican patristic scholar.)

David Knowles (editor), *City of God* (Harmondsworth 1972) (A good modern translation by patristic scholar Henry Bettenson, introduced by the Roman Catholic Church historian, Knowles.)

P.Schaff (editor), *The Nicene and Post-Nicene Fathers, First Series*, vols.1-8 (Edinburgh 1994) (The most full and accessible set of Augustine's writings in English, although not especially readable. Augustine's anti-Pelagian writings are in vol.5 with a valuable introduction by B.B.Warfield.)

Books about Augustine

Gerald Bonner, *St Augustine of Hippo* (London 1963). (A useful biography marred by a certain lack of sympathy for Augustine's theology of grace.)

Peter Brown, *Augustine of Hippo* (London 1967). (The best biography. A masterpiece.)

Henry Chadwick, *Augustine* (Oxford 1986). (A good short introduction to Augustine's life and thought.)

Mary T.Clark, *Augustine* (London 1994). (In the *Outstanding Christian Thinkers* series published by Chapman.)

Alan D.Fitzgerald (general editor), *Augustine through the Ages* (Grand Rapids 1999). (A very useful dictionary of Augustine's teachings, writings and influence. Large and expensive, but ideal for browsing through on idle intellectual evenings.)

Christopher A.Hall, *Reading Scripture with the Church Fathers* (Downers Grove 1998). (Augustine is covered in chapter 5. The book also deals very helpfully with Athanasius, Basil of Caesarea, Gregory of Nazianzus, John Chrysostom, Ambrose, Jerome and Gregory the Great.)

Trevor Rowe, *St Augustine: Pastoral Theologian* (London 1974). (The Methodist scholar Rowe looks at Augustine on spirituality, preaching, the sacraments, creation, and *City of God.*)

B.B.Warfield, *Studies in Tertullian and Augustine* (vol.4 of Warfield's *Works*, Grand Rapids 1930). (The essay on Augustine and the Pelagian Controversy is the same essay prefaced to vol.5 of Schaff's *The Nicene and Post-Nicene Fathers, First Series.* Warfield also has a general essay on Augustine, one on *Augustine's Doctrine of Knowledge and Authority*, and one on *Augustine and His Confessions*.)

On the internet, it is worth typing **AUGUSTINE OF HIPPO** into a search engine. Many of the sites are Roman Catholic, and do not display any obvious enthusiasm for Augustine's doctrine of grace. They may be more interested in making Augustine into a "Roman" Catholic and a weapon against Protestantism. This is tendentious nonsense. In the present writer's opinion, Augustine was neither a Roman Catholic nor a Protestant. Importing later labels into a historical period when they were unknown is a sin against history. Augustine was what he was, an early Church father of the 4th and 5th centuries. Reformation theology may justly lay claim to Augustine's doctrine of grace, but we do not think it is true merely because Augustine said it — rather because we find that what Augustine says is found in Scripture, which on this topic he expounds masterfully. On other topics there will be other opinions. Still, since the modern Roman Catholic Church is largely characterised by a Semi-Pelagian or even Pelagian view of the natural man's nobility and the possibility of his being saved by his own sincere religious quest, we may rest assured that Augustine would have found nothing in common with it in this most crucial matter.